Research Frontiers on the International Marketing Strategies of Chinese Brands

This book proposes a theoretical framework identifying external and internal factors that influence internationalization strategy of Chinese brands and brand performance. It explores several key strategies – e.g., standardization versus adaptation, price leadership versus branding, OBM export versus OEM export, and incremental versus leap-forward internationalization model. The relationships are examined between various international marketing mix options – e.g., distribution channel and pricing strategies – and brand performance. Through case studies the text also analyzes the internationalization of contract-based firms.

Zuohao Hu, PhD, Kyoto University, is Professor of Marketing at the School of Economics and Management of Tsinghua University. His research interests are marketing strategy, international marketing, channel management, and brand strategy.

Xi Chen, PhD, Tsinghua University, is Associate Professor of Marketing at the Business School of the China University of Political Science and Law. Her expertise is in consumer behavior, international marketing, real estate marketing, and branding strategies.

Zhilin Yang, PhD, New Mexico State University, is Professor of Marketing at City University of Hong Kong. His expertise is on international marketing strategy.

China Perspectives Series

For a full list of titles in this series, please visit www.routledge.com

The *China Perspectives* series focuses on translating and publishing works by leading Chinese scholars, writing about both global topics and China-related themes. It covers Humanities and Social Sciences, Education, Media and Psychology, as well as many interdisciplinary themes.

This is the first time any of these books have been published in English for international readers. The series aims to put forward a Chinese perspective, give insights into cutting-edge academic thinking in China, and inspire researchers globally.

For more information, please visit https://www.routledge.com/series/CPH

Regulating China's Shadow Banks
Qingmin Yan, Jianhua Li

Forthcoming titles:

Internationalization of the RMB: Establishment and Development of RMB Offshore Markets
International Monetary Institute, Renmin University of China

The Road Leading to the Market
Weiying Zhang

Macro-control and Economic Development in China
Jiagui Chen

Economic Development and Reform Deepening in China
Jiagui Chen

Research Frontiers on the International Marketing Strategies of Chinese Brands
Zuohao Hu, Xi Chen, and Zhilin Yang

History of China's Foreign Trade, 2e
Yuqin Sun

Research Frontiers on the International Marketing Strategies of Chinese Brands

Edited by Zuohao Hu, Xi Chen, and Zhilin Yang

LONDON AND NEW YORK

TSINGHUA UNIVERSITY PRESS

First published 2017 by Routledge

2 Park Square, Milton Park, Abingdon, Oxfordshire OX14 4RN

52 Vanderbilt Avenue, New York, NY 10017

Routledge is an imprint of the Taylor & Francis Group, an informa business

First issued in paperback 2020

British Library Cataloguing in Publication Data
A catalogue record for this book is available from the British Library

Library of Congress Cataloging-in-Publication Data
Names: Hu, Zuohao, 1964– author.
Title: Research frontiers on the international marketing strategies of
    Chinese brands / Zuohao Hu, Xi Chen, Zhilin Yang.
Description: London ; New York : Routledge, [2016] | Series: China
    perspectives series
Identifiers: LCCN 2015047844 | ISBN 9781138671836 (hbk) |
    ISBN 9781315616766 (ebk)
Subjects: LCSH: Marketing—China. | Product management—China. |
    Branding (Marketing)—China.
Classification: LCC HF5415.12.C5 H8175 2016 | DDC 658.8/40951—dc23
LC record available at http://lccn.loc.gov/2015047844

ISBN: 978-1-138-67183-6 (hbk)
ISBN: 978-0-367-51666-6 (pbk)

Typeset in Bembo
by Apex CoVantage, LLC

Contents

Foreword

Globalization has been making Chinese firms accelerate their internationalization process. There are three types of comprehensive statistics that evidence the internationalization trend of Chinese firms. First, China's total volume of imports and exports grew from US$509.8 billion in 2001 to US$4,303.3 billion in 2014, with total exports growing from US$266.2 billion to US$2,342.7 billion in the same period. Apart from exports by foreign-invested firms, Chinese firms accounted for nearly 50% of China's total exports. Second, China's foreign direct investment increased from US$2.7 billion in 2002 to US$107.8 billion in 2014. Third, the number of Chinese firms abroad reached 25,000 at the end of 2013, distributed across more than 170 countries and regions worldwide. These statistics reflect the depth and extent of the globalization of Chinese firms. As Chinese firms are entering the international market at a swift pace and in large number, how to "go out, go in, and go up" and improve the international marketing capacities of Chinese firms, particularly the international marketing capacities of Chinese brands, has become not only a major business issue of concern to Chinese businessmen but also a frontier research topic to which China's marketing scholars are paying close attention.

Sponsored by National Natural Science Foundation of China, we have conducted long-term research on the international marketing activities of Chinese firms, and our efforts have led to fruitful results. Our research has focused mainly on the following fields: first, we propose the main research topics and analysis framework of China's international branding strategy and sort out the development process and content of international branding; second, we examine the drivers and relationship mechanisms of the international marketing strategy choice of Chinese brands, e.g., standardization or adaptation, price leadership or branding, OBM (original brand manufacturing) or OEM (original equipment manufacturing), and incremental internationalization or leap-forward internationalization; third, we study the effect of international marketing mix (such as distribution channel and pricing strategies) on brand performance. Some findings of our research have been published in foreign and Chinese academic journals. Our research not only expands the knowledge frontiers in the field of international marketing study on Chinese firms, but it also offers important practical guidance to Chinese firms that are engaged or will be engaged in international marketing activities. It is out of this consideration that we are compiling our findings into this book for our readers. Considering that the internationalization process of Chinese firms is de facto that of Chinese brands, we give this book its title: *Research Frontiers on the International Marketing Strategies of Chinese Brands*.

The book contains 10 chapters, with the main content and viewpoints of each summarized as follows:

In chapter 1, the authors develop an integrated theoretical analysis framework for the key factors influencing the internationalization strategy choice of Chinese brands. The framework identifies how external environment factors and internal organization factors influence international branding strategies and how international branding strategies influence brand performance. Here, external environmental factors include international market, industry and technology, socio-cultural, economy, and country-of-origin effects; internal organizational factors include organizational characteristics, external resources integration capability, international marketing capability, international experience, and product characteristics. International branding strategies mainly include branding strategies and brand positioning in the international market. The authors believe that building an integrated theoretical analysis framework of developing international branding strategies, identifying key factors that effectively affect the international branding strategy choice of Chinese brands, analyzing the extent of their influences, and finding out the relationships between the internationalization strategy choice of Chinese brands and firms' export performance will provide reference for Chinese firms to develop and implement effective international branding strategies in their international marketing activities.

In chapter 2, the authors give a comprehensive review of international branding literature and point out the development of study on international branding. The authors first introduce how to define and measure global brands and discuss issues on the brand positioning and identification in the target international markets and the entry mode choice, in other words, whether a Chinese firm should adopt an OEM or an OBM strategy to enter the target international market. Once inside the international market, international branding would involve the choice of marketing strategy and marketing mix in the context of a whole new market, so the authors go on to examine brand alliance and country-of-origin effects. The authors then discuss how a firm, once it has secured a steady position in the international market, maintains and improves the international influence of its brand(s), and point out means of achieving this such as brand development, brand extension, and strengthening clients' assets. Based on a comprehensive review of existing literature on international branding, the authors point out some future research directions, including consumers' choice and switching of brands in the international market, the measurement of the value of global brands, and brand portfolio.

In chapter 3, the authors analyze and review relevant research papers on global standardization and local adaptation, pointing out that firms that choose a global standardization strategy often aim at utilizing economics of scale and learning effect to achieve cost-effectiveness, develop global unique brand images, and achieve the simplification of organizational structure and the routinization of management control; companies that choose an adaptation strategy tend to look at the global market as being heterogeneous and attach importance to giving play to the activeness and creativity of local subsidiaries, discovering and satisfying the unique demands of local consumers by capturing opportunities in the local market. Which strategy, global standardization or local adaptation, should be adopted in a given situation? The author develops and discusses the assumptions on which each strategy is based and the theories underlying standardization or adaptation; points out that an effective international marketing strategy should be one between pure standardization and pure adaptation, a hybrid of both strategies; and proposes that directions for future research should focus on identifying applicable conditions for each strategy and exploring the standardization/adaptation issues in the marketing process in addition to study on the standardization and adaptation of marketing mix.

In chapter 4, the authors study born-global firms, a type of firm that internationalizes rapidly and that has emerged in considerable quantity in recent years. As the first step of the analysis, the authors review the research literature about born-global firms in the past 10 years. The authors summarize the characteristics and formation mechanism of born-global firms and point out that these born-global firms overturn the conventional Uppsala incremental internationalization model; they internationalize in an accelerated leapfrogging manner, seek target markets actively unrestrained by psychic distance, offer customized high-tech products, and possess learning ability. The authors also explore the formation mechanism of born-global firms, pointing out that the overseas experience, the overseas network resources, and the global vision and risk-seeking traits of founders and managers of these firms propel the firms to accelerate their internationalization process.

In chapter 5, the authors study the effect of the two export marketing strategies (price leadership and branding) on the export performance of Chinese firms with developing country markets and developed country markets based on strategy fitness and market segmentation theory. Analysis shows that not all Chinese companies pursue the same strategy, some adopting the price leadership strategy, taking advantage of low raw material cost, while others embrace the differentiated branding strategy. The empirical findings indicate that when the target market is a developing country, the branding strategy would bring more satisfying export performance than the price leadership strategy, but when the target market is a developed country, neither the price leadership strategy nor the branding strategy has significant influence on export performance.

In chapter 6, the authors study exporters of China's manufacturing industry, develop an analysis framework of factors influencing the OBM/OEM export strategy choice and the relationship between the strategy choice and export performance, and, using empirical methods, examine the antecedents and consequences of Chinese firms' branding strategies in the international market context. The empirical findings reveal the relationship between international marketing capabilities, target market selection, export market characteristics, and industrial characteristics and branding strategy, as well as the relationship between branding strategy and export performance.

In chapter 7, the authors study exporters of China's manufacturing industry and develop a conceptual framework of antecedents and consequences of the strategy choice between distribution adaptation and price adaptation and test research assumptions via data collected by survey of Chinese export firms. The empirical findings indicate that: (1) the adoption of distribution adaptation strategy and price adaptation strategy by Chinese firms is jointly driven by the external and internal factors of the firms, but different internal and external factors have different degrees of influences on the adaptation strategy; (2) the export performance of Chinese firms is directly affected by distribution adaptation and global vision and indirectly by export market environment and learning capabilities. The authors point out that, for Chinese firms, improving their global visions and learning capabilities plays an important role in choosing an effective international marketing strategy and improving their export performance.

In chapter 8, the authors study exporters of China's manufacturing industry, empirically studying the relationship between overseas distribution control and export performance. The study reveals that output control of unilateral governance and flexibility of bilateral governance positively influence export performance. In the meantime, the study also makes clear that innovative organization culture negatively moderates the effect of outcome control on export performance and positively moderates the effect of flexibility on export performance.

In chapter 9, the authors use a multi-case comparative analysis method to study the drivers of entry mode choice between the incremental internationalization mode and the born-global mode on the basis of four typical firms that follow different internationalization processes. The authors develop a two-by-two matrix for identifying and measuring born-global firms in the two dimensions of export speed and export intensity and point out the prominent features in which the two born-global firms are different from the two traditional international firms. Research findings indicate that the congenital learning and experiential learning of entrepreneurs and managers, their global orientations and visions, and the firms' international networks are key factors that drive the firms to adopt accelerated internationalization and become born global.

In chapter 10, the authors use multiple cases of five Chinese contracting and outsourcing firms to study the internationalization modes of China's contract-based international firms. On the basis of summarizing international market entry modes and relevant literatures, the authors propose an analysis framework of factors that drive the internationalization processes of these firms. It is found that the overseas project management experience and global visions of the managers, narrow domestic niche market, and international market opportunities are important determinants in the formation of China's born-global firms in the contracting and outsourcing industry. In the internationalization process of China's contracting and outsourcing firms, their entry modes and processes show no significant relationship with psychic distance when they, either traditional international firms or born-global firms, choose the target market; instead, their entry modes and processes show a significant relationship with the size and potential of the foreign market.

The book has three distinguishing features. The first feature is combining theoretical study with empirical study. The book not only reviews domestic and international frontier research on international marketing of firms from a theoretic perspective, and summarizes international branding theories, standardization and adaptation theories, and new internationalization mode (or born-global) theories, but it also uses a large quantity of empirical studies to shed light on the international marketing practice of Chinese firms and presents readers a scenario of the frontier study of international marketing for Chinese firms. Second is combining qualitative case study method with quantitative method. The book not only incorporates a great number of qualitative cases of Chinese firms' international marketing practices and offers a view of the pattern of indigenous Chinese firms' international operation activities, but it also presents a large amount of quantitative studies. Third is combining western theories with Chinese practices. The book not only comprehensively reviews western leading-edge international marketing theories, but it also indicates the uniqueness of the international marketing of Chinese firms on the basis of using indigenous Chinese firms as study objects.

Chapter 1 was written by Professor Zuohao Hu at Tsinghua University School of Economics and Management (Tsinghua SEM) and Professor Zhilin Yang at Department of Marketing of Hong Kong City University. Chapter 2 was co-written by Assistant Professor Xuenan Ju at School of Business of Central University of Finance and Economics, Professor Zuohao Hu, and Professor Zhilin Yang. Chapter 3 was written by Professor Zuohao Hu, based on the author's paper published in the magazine *Nankai Business Review*. Chapter 4 was co-written by Professor Zuohao Hu and Associate Professor Xi Chen at the Business School of China University of Political Science and Law, based on the authors' paper published in the magazine *China Soft Science*. Chapter 5 was co-written by Associate Professor Xi Chen, Professor Zuohao Hu, and Professor Ping Zhao at Tsinghua SEM, based on the authors' paper published in the *Journal of Marketing Science*. Chapter 6 was co-written by Professor Zhonghe Han at the Business School of Fudan University, Professor Zuohao Hu, and Tsinghua SEM postgraduate student Lichao Zheng, based on the authors' paper published in the magazine *Management World*. Chapter 7 was co-written by Professor Zuohao Hu, Tsinghua SEM postgraduate student Fan Yi, Professor Shunping Han at the Business School of Nanjing University, and Associate Professor Xi Chen, based on the authors' paper published in the *Journal of Industrial Engineering and Engineering Management*. Chapter 8 was co-written by Professor Zuohao Hu, Associate Professor Xi Chen, and Professor Ping Zhao, based on the authors' paper published in the *Journal of Industrial Engineering and Engineering Management*. Chapter 9 was co-written by Associate Professor Xi

Chen, Professor Zuohao Hu, and Professor Ping Zhao, based on the authors' paper published in the magazine *China Soft Science*. Chapter 10 was written based on the dissertation by Tsinghua SEM postgraduate student Qingfei Xue under direction of Professor Zuohao Hu. Here, all the authors of this book give their heartfelt thanks to all the aforementioned publications for their support to academic study and the compilation of this book.

Many thanks to Tsinghua SEM post-doctoral fellow Dr. Min Hou and Dr. Xuenan Ju, who has done a lot of work in polishing the text of some of the chapters in this book. Many thanks to Mr. Zhibin Liu, director of the Economics and Management Section of Tsinghua University Press, and Ms. Lian Sun, Routledge managing editor, who have given great support to the publishing of this book. In addition, the publishing of this book has been supported by National Natural Science Foundation (project approval no.: 71372046 and 71072011). Here we give our heartfelt gratitude to the National Natural Science Foundation.

Dr. Zuohao Hu,
Professor of Marketing
Department of Marketing
School of Economics and Management
Tsinghua University
October 18, 2015

Contributors

Xi Chen, PhD, Tsinghua University, is Associate Professor of Marketing at the Business School of the China University of Political Science and Law. Her expertise is in consumer behavior, international marketing, real estate marketing, and branding strategies.

Shunping Han, PhD, Nanjing University, is Professor of the School of Business, Nanjing University. His research interests include service marketing, service branding, and Internet consumer behavior.

Zhonghe Han, PhD, Keio University, is Associate Professor of the Business School of Fudan University. His research interests are strategy management, international marketing, and brand management.

Zuohao Hu, PhD, Kyoto University, is Professor of Marketing at the School of Economics and Management of Tsinghua University and the Executive Associate Director of the China Business Research Centre. His research interests are marketing strategy, international marketing, channel management, and brand strategy.

Xuenan Ju is the assistant professor at the China Centre for Internet Economy Research (CCIE), Central University of Finance and Economics (CUFE). Her research interests are focused on international marketing strategy and cross-border e-commerce studies.

Qingfei Xue, MA, Tsinghua University, now works as Accessory Business Unit Finance Controller in PC Product Group Finance, Lenovo.

Zhilin Yang is Professor of Marketing at City University of Hong Kong. His expertise is on international marketing strategy.

Fan Yi, MA, Marketing, Tsinghua University, works as a freelancer.

Ping Zhao, PhD, Tsinghua University, is Professor of Marketing at the School of Economics and Management of Tsinghua University. His research focuses on consumer satisfaction, strategic branding, and customer value theory.

Lichao Zheng, MA, Marketing, Tsinghua University, now serves as Assistant Manager in China Life Pension Company Limited.

1 Main topics and research framework of Chinese firms' international branding strategies

Zuohao Hu and Zhilin Yang

1.1 Introduction

In the context of economic globalization, international branding strategy has always been a frontier research topic in the marketing academic research (Hu, 2002a; Schuiling *et al.*, 2004; Wong & Merrilees, 2007; Wu & Deng, 2007a; Keller, 2008; Hu *et al.*, 2009). Meanwhile, as one of the fastest-growing economies in the world, export business constitutes a major driving force of China's economic growth. With the acceleration of Chinese firms' export business and internationalization process, it has become critical for Chinese exporters to learn how to develop effective international branding strategies so as to establish international brands and improve international competitiveness.

International branding strategy choice mainly involves two types of strategic choices. The first type is branding strategic choice, referring to whether or not to establish one's own brands in the international market. In other words, this is the choice between the original brand manufacturing (OBM) strategy or the original equipment manufacturing (OEM) strategy. This is an important choice faced by Chinese exporters now. The second type is brand positioning strategy choice in the international market. In other words, what brand positioning strategy (whether to adopt global brand positioning or local brand positioning) should Chinese firms choose in the international market? This belongs to the brand standardization-adaptation positioning choice. Although internationally some scholars have, from multiple perspectives and dimensions, conducted analyses of key factors influencing international branding strategic choice and its impact on export performance (Onkvisit & Shaw, 1988; Douglas *et al.*, 2001; Zou & Cavusgil, 2002; Morgan *et al.* 2004; Balabanis & Diamantopoulos, 2008; Dimofte *et al.*, 2008), a systematic and integrated theoretical framework, particularly a model that fits the characteristics of Chinese firms, is still missing (Alashban *et al.*, 2002; Wu & Deng, 2007b; Cayla & Arnould, 2008). In addition, there has been little empirical research on the relationship between key determinants of Chinese firms' international branding strategic choice and its consequences on performance. In China, research, either theoretical or empirical, on key determinants of Chinese firms' international branding strategy choice and the strategy-performance relationship still calls for increasing attention

(Chen *et al.*, 2008; Hu *et al.*, 2009). Therefore, it is necessary to construct a comprehensive theoretical model integrating the key determinants of Chinese firms' international branding strategic choice and its relationship with export performance, in order to reveal and illustrate the underlying mechanism. It is also important to identify key factors that significantly influence international branding strategic choice from an empirical perspective, analyze the extent of their influences, and quantify the relationship between Chinese firms' international branding strategy choice and their export performance. The practical aim of this comprehensive approach is to provide implications for Chinese firms to develop and implement effective international branding strategies in their international marketing activities.

1.2 Literature review on Chinese firms' international branding strategies

1.2.1 Research on the selection modes of international branding strategy

1 Research on branding strategic choice

Branding strategy refers to the decision of whether to adopt a branding strategy or a non-branding strategy in the international market. At present, for Chinese firms it is reflected in the strategic choice between OBM and OEM as the export approach. This is an important choice currently facing Chinese exporters (Chen & Hu, 2008; Chen & Luo, 2008).

Although research findings of Chinese and foreign scholars are rather similar regarding the importance of cultivating one's own brand in international marketing and export business, the international marketing practice of emerging economies, including China, shows that they still tend to adopt the OEM method to enter the international market at the initial stage of internationalization (Cheng *et al.*, 2005; Guzmán & Paswan, 2009). Internationally, in order to better integrate global resources and enhance global competitiveness, many firms that own established brands would commission other manufacturing firms to do the processing and manufacturing part. They provide product design and technical/equipment support to the manufacturers so as to meet the requirements for quality and product specifications. Moreover, many global brands outsource part of their businesses sections. They especially like to employ firms from developing countries for OEM production, so as to reduce cost and rationalize their value chains. For emerging-market firms, the OEM approach can help them rapidly enter the international market, reduce marketing cost, and achieve standardized mass production. Over time, some OEM manufacturers can eventually establish their own brands by attaining technological upgrades and innovation through R&D and knowledge learning (Tao & Li, 2008). Nonetheless, some studies also show that the OEM mode has some apparent weaknesses, including low-end products, low technological level, low entry barrier, and low profit margin (Luo, 2007), which are all unfavorable for firms to establish brands and achieve sustainable development in the international market. Therefore, some researchers suggest that, from the perspective of long-term development, the future of Chinese firms' export lies in building their own brands. As a matter of fact, there have always been two different viewpoints regarding firms' export strategy in China's international business research. One stream supports the adoption of cost leadership strategy. This viewpoint suggests that Chinese firms do not possess adequate international marketing experience or sufficient resources like talents, technology, and capital. Consequently, they should adopt the OEM mode to expand the international market based on cost advantages (Jin, 2004). The other viewpoint is for the adoption of one's own brand strategy. This viewpoint suggests that Chinese firms should enhance R&D capabilities, develop high-quality products, and implement differentiated international marketing by virtue of established brands. By this approach, they can gain higher profit in the international market and lay a solid foundation for long-term growth (Nie & Wang, 2006).

In the international marketing academia, the majority of research subjects are multinational corporations and internationally established brands from developed countries. Multinationals from developed countries tend to carry out export and international marketing activities via their own brands. However, there is little research concerning the OEM/OBM strategic choice from emerging-market firms' perspective. Although in recent years Chinese scholars have conducted research regarding the OEM/OBM export strategic choice, such research has been mainly qualitative, rarely quantitative or empirical (Chen & Luo, 2008; Hu *et al.*, 2008).

At the present stage, should Chinese firms adopt the OEM strategy or the OBM strategy when they are choosing an international branding strategy? In other words, under what circumstances should they adopt the OEM or OBM strategy? To answer these questions, we need to construct a comprehensive framework that can identify the key determinants of branding strategic choice and reveal the relationship between the strategy and performance of Chinese firms. Building on this framework, we can conduct empirical research to find out what factors affect Chinese firms' choice between the OEM/OBM strategies, and to what extent. In addition, this framework can reveal how the strategy choice affects the firms' export performance as well. In the meantime, we will study the long-term effect of such strategic choice on export performance from a dynamic perspective.

2 Research on brand positioning strategy choice in the international market

In the international market, brand positioning strategy choice refers to the choice between global and local brand positioning, or the choice between global standardization and local adaptation.

Global brands are defined as brands that use the same marketing strategy and market positioning across all target markets (Schuiling & Kapferer, 2004; Dimofte *et al.*, 2008). Building a global image gives a brand more power and value (Aaker, 1991; Shocker *et al.*, 1994; Keller, 2008). Therefore, many scholars suggest that multinationals should adopt global standardized positioning so as to build global brands. Steenkamp *et al.* (2003) empirically investigate the relationship between consumers' perceived brand globalness and brand value. They find that consumers' perceived brand globalness is positively related to consumers' perceived brand quality and prestige and, through them, to purchase likelihood. Hence the authors suggest that multinational corporations adopt global brand positioning strategy. On the contrary, Schuiling and Kapferer (2004) point out that although building global brands is critical to firms' internationalization process, local brand positioning represents strategic advantages that must be considered. They point out that local brands have six advantages: (1) better response to local needs; (2) flexibility of pricing strategy; (3) possibility of responding to local or international competition; (4) possibility of balancing a portfolio of brands; (5) possibility of responding to needs not covered by international brands; (6) possibility of fast entry into new markets.

The reason for these contradictory conclusions is that these studies fail to relate branding strategy choice to key influential factors. That is, at what level and in what combination would these key factors lead to a specific brand positioning strategy?

The other dimension of brand positioning strategy is the choice between standardization and adaptation. This area of research is an extension of the international marketing standardization-adaptation debate in the field of international branding strategy (Hu, 2002a; Hu *et al.*, 2009). Alashban *et al.* (2002) suggest that a firm's international branding strategic choice is in fact a matter of brand standardization/adaptation choice. The authors explain from two dimensions (brand positioning and brand portfolio) that standardization/adaptation essentially consists of brand positioning strategies (global or local brand positioning) and brand portfolio strategies (single or multiple brands). If a firm uses only one brand and similar positioning across its international markets, then it adopts a complete standardization strategy; on the other hand, if a firm uses multiple brands and different positioning in various international markets, then it adopts a complete adaptation strategy. Other brand portfolio strategies lie in the spectrum between complete standardization and complete adaptation.

Alden *et al.* (1999) suggest that effective international brand positioning strategies will help companies strengthen their brands' equity in the highly competitive international market. Their research identifies three international brand positioning modes: global consumer culture positioning, foreign consumer culture positioning, and local consumer culture positioning. A global consumer culture positioning strategy is defined as one that identifies the brand as a symbol of a given global culture (e.g., Pepsi-Cola targets the global vigorous young people market). Contrasting global consumer culture positioning are foreign consumer culture positioning and local consumer culture positioning. Foreign consumer culture positioning is defined as a strategy that positions the brand as symbolic of a specific foreign consumer culture. That is, brand personality, use occasion, and/or user group are associated with a foreign culture (for example, Gucci in the United States is positioned as a prestigious and fashionable Italian brand). Local consumer culture positioning is defined as a strategy that associates the brand with local cultural meanings. It reflects the local culture's norms and identities, is portrayed as consumed by local people in the national culture, and/or is depicted as locally produced for local people (for example, P&G's introduction of the Olay brand in the Chinese market).

Chinese scholars have also contributed to the academic studies regarding brand positioning strategy choice in the international market. For instance, the book *Chinese Transnational Corporations* written by Wang (2004) involves the development process and brand positioning of some famous Chinese trans-national corporations. Hu and Wang (2009) study the international marketing activities of Chinese consumer electronics manufacturers (Haier, TCL, Bird). They find that these firms generally choose emerging markets as their target markets when exploring the international market. They adopt the same market-ing methods to promote their own brands as they have done in the Chinese market. When entering developed countries, however, they adopt different entry strategies. TCL chooses to acquire local brands, Haier establishes its own sales channels to promote its own brand, and Bird opts for OEM methods. In addi-tion, based on literature review, Hu (2002a) conducts an extensive analysis of the antecedents and consequents of the standardization-adaptation strategic choice of international marketing strategy. Hu *et al.* (2009) construct an integrated con-ceptual model of key determinants of distribution adaptation and price adapta-tion strategy choice and its relationship to export performance and conduct empirical research using China's manufacturing exporters as research subjects. In conclusion, research on brand positioning strategy choice from the Chinese academic perspective is still limited and mainly qualitative. There is currently a lack of empirical research on brand positioning strategy choice (Hu *et al.*, 2009).

1.2.2 Research on key determinants of international branding strategy choice and its relationship to performance

In international marketing research, there have been a great number of exist-ing studies regarding the key determinants of international marketing strategy (also known as global marketing strategy) and its influence on performance (Hu, 2002a; Schuiling *et al.*, 2004; Wong & Merrilees, 2007; Wu & Deng, 2007a; Keller, 2008). Because international branding strategy is an important component of a firm's international marketing strategy (Douglas *et al.*, 2001; Alashban *et al.*, 2002; Cayla & Arnould, 2008), the conceptual framework of the key determi-nants of a firm's international marketing strategy and its relation to performance have also been incorporated into research on international branding strategy.

In the research field of international branding strategy choice and its key deter-minants, there are two major theoretical perspectives regarding the construction of the conceptual framework that influence the mechanism of international branding strategy choice. One is the industrial organization (IO) perspective, which suggests that international branding strategy is an organization's response to external industrial structure (Yip, 1989). Alashban *et al.* (2002) adopt the analysis framework of the industrial organization–based theory to study the antecedents and consequences of international standardization/adaptation strategy choice on brand name. Their empirical findings show that both the standardization and adaptation strategy choices of international brand name are affected by international market structure and environmental factors and that the strategy choice of brand name in turn affects export performance. The second is the resource-based view (RBV), which suggests that a firm's internal organizational factors, or resources, shape the firm's capabilities to design international marketing strategy and to execute the chosen strategy (Barney, 1991). Based on RBV theory, Zou *et al.* (2003) investigate the effect of the marketing capabilities of a firm on its international marketing strategy. They develop a conceptual model that incorporates a firm's product development capability, distribution capability, communication capability, and pricing ability; the firm's international marketing positioning strategy (low-cost positioning and branding positioning); and the firm's performance and conduct empirical analysis.

Cavusgil and Zou (1994) are the first scholars to integrate the viewpoints of the two aforementioned perspectives. They propose a conceptual framework of the relationship between key determinants of international marketing strategy choice and performance. They suggest that international marketing strategy is influenced by internal (firm characteristics and product characteristics) and external factors (industry characteristics and export market characteristics) and that the implementation of international marketing strategy affects corporate performance. Building on the conceptual framework of Cavusgil and Zou (1994), Douglas *et al.* (2001) propose an integrated analysis framework of the key determinants of international branding strategy choice and performance. They suggest that external factors (market dynamics and product-market drivers) and firm-based drivers affect its international branding strategy choice. In this framework, market dynamics include political and economic integration, market infrastructure, and consumer mobility (including the degree of ethnocentrism, etc.); product-market drivers include target market characteristics, cultural embeddedness in products, and industry competitive market structure; firm-based drivers include behavior characteristics (degree of centralization of decision-making, risk attitude, etc.), the importance of corporate identity, and product diversity. They propose that all these factors shape the firm's international branding strategy. Nonetheless, their study is merely conceptual, without having been empirically tested.

In addition, some other important factors that affect international branding strategy choice have also been ignored by scholars, such as a firm's marketing capabilities, country-of-origin effects, and development stage (for instance, Douglas *et al.*, 2001; Alashban *et al.*, 2002; Chen *et al.*, 2008). As a matter of fact, research on the relationship between a firm's marketing capabilities and its international branding strategy finds that a firm's marketing capabilities affect its international branding strategy choice (Zou *et al.*, 2003). Moreover, brand origin is an important factor that affects brand image perception. Country-of-origin effects significantly affect consumers' perceived product quality, brand-related attitude, and purchase intention (Thakor & Lavack, 2003; Balabanis & Diamantopoulos, 2008); a poor country-of-origin image produces a negative effect on consumers' brand attitude and consumers' product evaluation (Han & Terpstra, 1988). Therefore, country-of-origin effects should be taken into account when considering the determinants of international branding strategy. Moreover, research on the relationship between the development stage of a firm's internationalization and its international branding strategy choice indicates that firms at different phases of development should adopt different international marketing strategies (Wind *et al.*, 1973). For instance, for a firm at a polycentric stage that adopts an adaptive international marketing strategy, its brand strategy tends to feature a local positioning strategy that targets the local market. On the other hand, for a firm at the geocentric stage that adopts a global marketing strategy, its brand strategy tends to feature a globally unique positioning strategy. The development stage of a firm's internationalization is an important factor that affects its international branding strategic choice.

Existing literature suggests contradictory empirical findings regarding the relationship between brand strategy choice and export performance. For instance, the study of Brouthers and Xu (2002) finds that cost leadership strategy has a negative influence on export performance, but the study of Zou *et al.* (2003) finds that cost leadership strategy has positive influence on export performance. Samiee and Roth (1992) find that standardized marketing strategy has no salient influence on export performance, while Cavusgil and Zou (1994) indicate standardization has a negative influence on performance, and Kotabe (1990) proposes the very opposite. We suggest that these seemingly contradictory conclusions are caused by the environmental factors of the international market. For instance, the empirical study of Miller (1988) finds that a low-cost strategy is more effective in a steady market environment and a differentiated strategy is more effective in a turbulent market environment. The mixed findings indicate that the effect of international marketing strategy on export performance is moderated by the environmental factor of the international market. Therefore, the effect of international branding strategic choice on export performance, which is an important part of international marketing strategy, has not yet been thoroughly analyzed and examined.

Therefore, it is necessary to construct, based on literature, an integrated theoretical model to reveal the relationships between the international branding strategies of Chinese firms and their key determinants and performance and investigate the moderating effect of market environment factors on the relationship between international branding strategy choice and performance. On this basis, we can conduct empirical analysis based on the practice of Chinese firms.

1.2.3 Case studies of internationally established brands

Internationally established brands are usually global brands owned by well-known multinational corporations. Every internationally established brand has its own growth history and unique branding strategy. Therefore, many scholars adopt the case study method to investigate the branding strategy choice of internationally established brands. For example, P&G and Coca-Cola adopt "power" brand expanding strategies. They have expanded through leveraging their domestic "power" brands in international markets (Douglas *et al.*, 2001). Nestle and Unilever have traditionally adopted country-centered strategies, establishing their international brand structure by building or acquiring a mixture of national and international brands. Taking the brand Pizza Point in India's pizza market as an example, Eckhardt (2005) discusses the management of local brands that are perceived as international products by consumers in emerging markets. Barela (2003) uses the multinational clothing company United Colors of Benetton as an example. The author analyzes the increasing legal and ethical concerns that have been caused by the company's use of social issue–themed pictures to promote its brand from the perspective of management. Using the case study method, Kondo (1995) studies Sony's export marketing activities. He finds that Sony, as a second-mover company, permeated the American market and built its brand image by offering innovative products and establishing its own distribution channels. Keller (2008) studies the successful experience of the Nike brand in the European market. He points out that the main reasons for Nike's success in the European market have been the enhancement of its control capabilities over distribution channels and marketing methods and its great effort to adapt the Nike brand to the European culture. Melewar *et al.* (2006) study Danone's branding strategy in the Chinese market by analyzing Danone's brand structure in China's milk, biscuit, and beverage markets and point out that Danone, on the basis of unifying its globally healthy food definition, strives to adapt its products and brands to the conditions and characteristics of the Chinese market. Meanwhile, in China Danone stresses the French origin of the parent company in the hope of producing desirable country-of-origin effects. Sudhaman (2004) summarizes "late-mover brand" Samsung's experience in building its brand in the international market. He points out that barely a decade ago the company's global reputation was somewhat dubious – a low-end brand that sold shoddy products – but now it has become a global benchmark of product and brand innovation. He suggests that by embracing the mantras of branding, design, and product quality, Samsung has redefined itself as a brand that oozes cool. Into the bargain it has also spearheaded a radical shift in how Korean brands are perceived across the world.

In summary, academic research on international branding strategy has so far mainly focused on brands from developed countries; research on brands from emerging countries (including China) is still limited. Meanwhile, Chinese brands are late movers in the international market, lacking the first-mover advantages that power brands of famous multinationals possess. Therefore, it is necessary to further investigate whether the theoretical frameworks for research based on brands of developed countries' firms and relevant empirical study findings are suitable for the actual conditions of Chinese firms.

According to the latest statistics, in 2011 China's total import and export amounted to US$3.64 trillion (making China the second-largest trading nation in the world), with export accounting for US$1.9 trillion. This is the result of Chinese firms' international marketing activities. As Chinese firms begin to enter the international market at a rapid pace and in great number, the problem of how to develop effective international branding strategies so as to build international established brands and to improve the international competitiveness of the firms has become a subject of common interest for all Chinese business managers. Therefore, the internationalization of Chinese brands is in great need of the guidance of international branding theories that are tailored to Chinese firms. But in China there is a lack of theoretical model research and empirical research on the key determinants of the international branding strategic choice and its relation to performance. Therefore, it is necessary to conduct extensive and systematic research on the key determinants of the international branding strategy choice of Chinese firms and its impact on export performance. It is also necessary to identify key factors that influence the international strategy choice of Chinese firms and the extent of their influences. By this approach we can provide theoretical support to the international branding of Chinese firms and provide implication for Chinese firms to choose and implement their international strategies.

1.3 Theoretical framework of Chinese firms' international branding strategies

Research on the international branding strategy of Chinese firms examines the relationship mechanism between the key determinants of Chinese firms' international branding strategy choice and performance from the following perspectives. Meanwhile, empirical research is conducted based on the practice of Chinese firms.

1.3.1 International branding strategies

International branding strategies are tools that are developed by firms engaged in international marketing activities in accordance with their internal conditions and external environment. They are used to achieve the firms' marketing or brand-building goals (Onkvisit & Shaw, 1988; Schuiling & Kapferer, 2004). For Chinese firms, international branding strategy choice would mainly involve choices in the following two dimensions.

The first dimension is branding strategy choice. Thus, whether or not to adopt the OBM strategy or the OEM strategy in the international market is an important choice facing Chinese exporters at the current stage (Chen & Luo, 2008).

The second dimension is brand positioning strategy choice in the international market. What brand positioning strategies should Chinese firms that are adopting the OBM strategy choose in the international market (i.e., whether to adopt global brand positioning or local brand positioning)? This stream of research is part of the brand standardization/adaptation positioning choice in the international marketing academia (Alden *et al.*, 1999; Hu, 2002a; Steenkamp *et al.*, 2003; Schuiling & Kapferer, 2004; Dimofte *et al.*, 2008).

Implications of international branding strategy choice include the two aspects mentioned here. Therefore, research on the international branding of Chinese firms in this book includes the following two aspects: research on the key determinants of the *international branding strategy choice* of Chinese firms and its impact on export performance; and research on the key determinants of the *international market positioning strategy choice* of Chinese brands and its relationship to export performance.

1.3.2 Relationship between external environmental determinants and international branding strategy choice

Influential factors of international branding strategy choice can be divided into two main categories: external determinants and internal determinants. Together, these factors cause a firm to adopt international branding strategies that mostly suit its circumstance.

Based on existing studies (Cavusgil & Zou, 1994; Douglas *et al.*, 2001; Alashban *et al.*, 2002; Brouthers & Xu, 2002; Hu, 2002a; Zou *et al.*, 2003; Thakor & Lavack, 2003; Wu & Deng, 2007a; Hu & Wang, 2009; Hu *et al.*, 2009), this book focuses on the following five types of external environmental determinants of international branding strategy choice.

1 International market factors

International market conditions affect international branding strategy choice. For instance, in the matter of branding choice, a firm is more likely to adopt the OEM method than the OBM method if it exports to a mature market with high market saturation and intensive competition among existing brands (Brouthers & Xu, 2002). As for international market positioning choice, when a firm targets a homogeneous global market segment, global brands provide an effective approach of establishing a distinctive global identity; on the other hand, adopting an adaptive positioning brand strategy can be an effective choice if the target market is a heterogeneous global market segment (Douglas *et al.*, 2001). Characteristics of the international market include: attributes of the target market, size and potential of the market, local customers' awareness of the product and brand, and market infrastructure, among others. It is necessary to study the relationship between these factors and international branding strategy choice.

2 Industry and technology factors

With different industrial structures and technological levels, international branding strategies can vary greatly. Industrial structure is considered as a critical variable when a firm is deciding its local international marketing strategies (including international branding strategies) (Cavusgil & Zou, 1994). For instance, in the matter of branding choice, industry-leading firms tend to possess powerful R&D capability and market expansion capability. Therefore, they are more likely to adopt the OBM strategy. On the contrary, industry followers often do not have sufficient resources and adequate power on innovation and marketing capabilities, so they are more likely to adopt the OEM strategy. In the matter of international market positioning choice, firms tend to adopt local brand positioning or an adaptive brand positioning strategy when there are powerful local brands and a great number of competitors in the local market (Schuiling & Kapferer, 2004). The study of Sandler and Shani (1992) shows that as transfer of new technologies among countries is speeding up, the technological levels between countries tend to become more homogeneous, which leads more towards the global branding positioning strategy choice. Industrial factors include competition intensity, distribution channel intensity, buyer intensity, and type of industry, among others, and technological factors include degree of technological difference between countries, frequency of technological change, and technological level (high and new technology or established technology), among others. It is necessary to study the relationship between these factors and international branding strategy choice.

3 Socio-cultural factors

The similarity in social, culture, laws, and regulations between home country and host country also significantly affects international branding strategy choice. For instance, if the culture, religion, language, and customs of the foreign target market are similar to those of the home country (i.e., close in cultural distance), a firm may be more likely to adopt the OBM strategy when it comes to branding choice. In the matter of international market positioning choice, a firm tends to adopt global brand positioning in its international branding, but if the cultural difference is salient, it may prefer local brand positioning (Cavusgil & Zou, 1994; Alashban *et al.*, 2002). If the local market exhibits a high degree of ethnocentrism, then a firm may be inclined to adopt local brand localization strategy or adaptive brand positioning strategy. Socio-cultural and legal factors include cultural distance/similarity, similarity of laws and regulations, and so on. In addition, the Chinese government encourages the adoption of a "going global" strategy. Therefore, it is important to consider the effect of the home country's support for a firm entering the international market on its international branding strategy choice. It is also necessary to study the relationship between these factors and international branding strategy choice.

4 Economic factors

Countries at similar economic development levels show similarities in certain aspects. For instance, consumers in developed countries tend to purchase brands of high-quality image, whereas consumers in less developed countries may be more interested in brands of low-price image. Therefore, the economic development level of the host country affects international branding strategy choice (Jain, 1989; Alashban *et al.*, 2002; Hu, 2002b). Economic factors include similarity of economic development between the home country and the host country and openness of the local economy, among others. It is necessary to study the relationship between these factors and international branding strategic choice.

5 Country-of-origin effects

Country-of-origin effect is another important environmental factor that influences firms' international branding choice. Many studies have shown that brand origin is an important factor that affects brand strategic choice. Country-of-origin effects significantly influence consumers' product quality perception, brand attitude, and brand choice behavior (Thakor & Lavack, 2003; Balabanis & Diamantopoulos, 2008). The study of Han and Terpstra (1988) shows that a poor country-of-origin image would produce a negative effect on consumers' brand attitude and product evaluation. When country-of-origin effects are negative, a firm is more likely to consider adopting the OEM strategy when it comes to branding choice and would be more likely to adopt adaptive brand positioning in its international market positioning choice. Therefore, country-of-origin effects affect international branding strategy choice. It is necessary to study the relationship between these factors and international branding strategy choice at home and abroad.

1.3.3 Relationship between internal organizational determinants and international branding strategy choice

A firm may possess many types of resources that affect its international branding strategy choice, but critical resources are those that are hard to imitate, difficult to substitute, and more valuable inside a business unit than outside (Prahalad & Hamel, 1990; Porter, 1991; Stalk *et al.*, 1992). Based on previous research findings (Stalk *et al.*, 1992; Cavusgil & Zou, 1994; Douglas *et al.*, 2001; Hu, 2002a; Zou *et al.*, 2003; Wu & Deng, 2007a; Hu & Wang, 2009; Hu *et al.*, 2009), this book focuses on the following five types of internal determinants of international branding strategy choice.

1 Organizational characteristics

Bartlett and Ghoshal (1989) suggest that the organizational characteristics of a firm have an important influence on its international branding strategy choice. In the matter of branding choice, a firm is more likely to adopt brand export strategy if it has a high level of international market orientation. In the matter of international market positioning choice, a firm that historically has operated on a highly decentralized basis in which country managers have substantial autonomy and control over strategy as well as mundane operations is likely to have a substantial number of local brands. Firms with a centralized organizational structure and global product divisions are more likely to own global brands (Douglas *et al.*, 2001). Organizational attributes of a firm include organizational control, degree of flexibility, degree of risk avoidance, degree of market orientation, size, stage of development of the firm, and so on. It is necessary to study the relationship between these factors and international branding strategy choice.

2 External resources integration capability

A firm's ability to use and integrate external resources affects its international branding strategy choice (Madsen & Servais, 1997; Douglas *et al.*, 2001). For instance, establishing overseas market distribution channel networks through strategic alliance and extensive collaboration with local distributors or dealers are all conducive to a firm's private brand export (Hu *et al.*, 2007). Kondo (1995) studies the role general trading companies played in Japanese household electrical appliance companies' international marketing activities. This research indicates that working with foreign and domestic consulting organizations can help firms explore foreign markets and promote export of brands. Lenovo, in its internationalization process, built its brand by acquiring IBM's PC division. Lenovo then promoted its Lenovo brand by taking advantage of IBM's established market, clients, channel network, and brand foundation. In addition, the studies of Wang (2004) and Hu and Wang (2009) show that it would benefit a firm's OEM export if the firm manages to integrate itself into the global resource systems of internationally established firms (including manufacturing firms and retailing firms). Douglas *et al.* (2001) point out that firms that expand internationally by acquiring local companies often acquire local brands at the same time. If these brands have high local recognition, or a strong customer or distributor franchise, the company will normally retain the brand, thus achieving the localization of brands. Therefore, it is necessary to study the relationship between a firm's capabilities to integrate external resources and its international branding strategy choice.

3 Marketing capabilities

The choice and implementation of a firm's international branding strategy is also affected by the firm's marketing capabilities. In the matter of branding choice, the greater the firm's new product development capability, communication capability, and distribution capability, the more likely it is to adopt its own brand strategy. In the matter of the international market positioning of brands, Zou *et al.* (2003) find that distribution capability and communication capability significantly and positively influence low-cost advantage positioning; new product development capability and distribution capability significantly and positively influence a firm's (international) brand advantage positioning.

A firm's international marketing capabilities and resources include product development capability, pricing capability, communication capability, distribution capability, and so forth (Zou *et al.*, 2003; Wu & Deng, 2007a). These marketing capabilities and resources enable firms to identify business opportunities and develop and execute effective branding strategies in the international market. It is necessary to study the relationship between these elements and a firm's international branding strategy choice.

4 International experience

A firm's international experience affects its international branding strategy choice (Chen *et al.*, 2008). The "three-phase evolution framework" postulated by Douglas and Craig (1989) investigates the influence of international experience on international branding strategy choice. According to the theory of Douglas and Craig (1989), a business evolves in three phases as international experience is accumulated: initial foreign market entry, expansion of national markets, and global rationalization. The authors suggest that in the initial phase, lacking experience or familiarity with overseas markets, a firm will seek to leverage its domestic position towards the international market. Firms most experienced in internationalization, on the other hand, tend to adopt a "geocentric orientation," which is reflected in the tendency to use a globally uniform branding strategy. Therefore, it is necessary to study the relationship between international experience and international branding strategy choice.

5 Characteristics of product and business

The choice and implementation of a firm's international branding strategy is influenced by the characteristics of its products and business. In the matter of branding choice, the intensity of technology of a firm's products affects its branding strategy choice (Madsen & Servais, 1997). Compared to products with low technology content, it is more likely for high-technology products to implement differentiation strategies. The brand features of high-technology products are more prominent, and brand building would be easier. Therefore, firms possessing high-technology content tend to build their own brands. In the matter of international market positioning choice, firms that are involved in closely related product lines or businesses that share a common technology or rely on similar core competencies often adopt standardized brand positioning strategy (Douglas *et al.*, 2001). The characteristics of the product can influence the competitive advantages of brand positioning. Product characteristics that affect international branding strategy choice include culture specificity, degree of product diversity, product complexity, degree of differentiation advantage of product, product life cycle stage, and so on.

Basing on the aforementioned discussion, a basic research framework of this book is proposed, as illustrated in Figure 1.1.

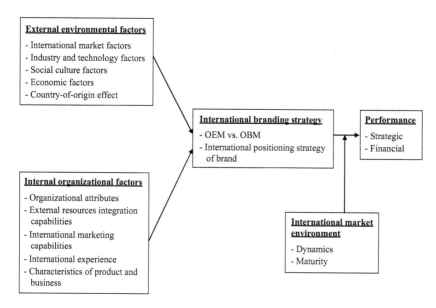

Figure 1.1 Framework of the key determinants of international branding strategy choice and its relationship to export performance

It is worth noticing the relationship between international branding strategy choice and export performance[1] and its moderation effect. Export performance refers to the extent of a firm's achieving its operation goals through the development and implementation of international branding strategy. The purpose of brand building of a firm is to build strong brand equity or brand value (Keller, 2008). Operation goals of firms include financial goals and strategic goals. Financial goals include profit, sales, cost, and so on; strategic goals include market expansion, competition response, increasing global market share and obtaining critical resources, and so forth (Zou & Cavusgil, 2002; Zhang *et al.*, 2008).

1.3.4 Relationship between international branding strategy choice and export performance

The purpose of a firm developing and implementing a specific marketing strategy is to achieve desirable performance. However, literature review suggests contradictory findings regarding the relationship between brand strategy choices and export performance. For instance, the study of Brouthers and Xu (2002) finds that cost leadership strategy has a negative influence on export performance, but the study of Zou *et al.* (2003) finds that cost leadership strategy has a positive influence on export performance. On the other hand, on exploring the choice mechanism of international positioning strategies, conclusions have not yet reached an agreement. While some researchers find that standardization strategy could harm performance (Cavusgil & Zou, 1994), the others do not find significant relationships between them (Samiee & Roth, 1992). We propose that these inconsistent conclusions are caused by the environmental factors of the international market. For instance, Miller (1988) finds that a low-cost strategy is more effective in a steady market environment and that a differentiated strategy is more effective in a turbulent market environment. This mixture of findings indicates that the effect of international marketing strategy on export performance is moderated by the environmental factors of the international market. Therefore, it is necessary to study the moderating effect of international market environment on the relationship between international branding strategy choice and export performance. More specifically, the moderating effect of market environment needs to be examined from two perspectives. The first perspective is the dynamics of the market environment. We need to study the relationship between international branding strategy choice and performance in the context of global market prosperity as well as in the context of global market recession. The other perspective is the maturity of the market environment. We need to study the relationship between international branding strategy choice and performance in developed country markets as well as in developing country markets.

This book constructs a theoretical framework for the international branding strategy choice of Chinese firms and conducts empirical study on this basis. In addition, this book tests the theoretical model of the key determinants of the international branding strategy choice of Chinese firms and its relationship to performance. It also tests some relational hypotheses as well. This book not only enriches the theoretical findings in the research field of brand management and international marketing strategy, but also lays a foundation for future research. In the meantime, practical understanding of the key determinants of the international branding strategy choice of Chinese firms and the relationship between international branding strategy choice and export performance is not only the foundation for Chinese firms to carry out international marketing activities and acquire competitive advantages in the international market, but also the foundation for Chinese firms to choose effective brand strategies in coping with the dynamic changes of the international market environment.

Note

1 For empirical research consideration, performance in this book refers to the export performance of the firm.

2 Development and main contents of international branding research

Xuenan Ju, Zuohao Hu and Zhilin Yang

2.1 Introduction

Increasing transnational transactions are pushing brand internationalization towards center stage. A global brand is normally perceived as one that possesses high popularity in multiple countries. Such brands are also well recognized and accepted by consumers in various local markets. In addition, global brands maintain identical or similar brand positioning, branding personality, and marketing strategies across different international markets.

International brands play various roles in different aspects of transnational business. Economically, an international brand image makes it easier for consumers to accept a higher price. Consumer psychology suggests that such brand creates an international image for its product, leading consumers to evaluate the brand as a symbol of exclusiveness and superior value. As the economic influence of international brands grows, research institutions pay more attention to the conceptualization and identification of international branding. Since the publication of Levitt's (1983) paper on globalization, scholars have started to pay attention to the effect of international branding on firms. On the supply side, international brands can achieve economies of scale in R&D, manufacturing, and resource allocation, as well as marketing. International branding can help a brand enter a foreign market more rapidly by avoiding unnecessary adaptation to a local environment. On the demand side, the relatively steady and consistent brand positioning of international branding enables a firm to benefit from a globally unique brand image. In response to increased similarity across target markets, firms opt for more standardized marketing strategies (Özsomer & Simonin, 2004). But international branding also brings certain challenges. Consumer demand and product usages vary significantly in different countries and regions because of differences of values, culture, and economic development. Consumers in different markets would also respond differently to marketing mix elements. In addition, a product may be at different phases of its life cycle across different international markets. Thus, an international brand may face different market environments worldwide. In different countries and regions, the differences of legal environments and marketing rules also pose challenges to the internationalization of brands.

2.1.1 International branding in practice

AC Nielson and BusinessWeek, both application-oriented research institutions, use objective criteria to define international brands and measure the degree of internationalization. These criteria include the number of international markets the firm has set foot in, the percentage of overseas sales revenue in the firm's total sales revenue, and the minimum revenue from the global market. According to AC Nielsen's 2001 study, at least 5% of sales of an international brand should come from outside the home regions, with total revenue of at least US$1 billion. According to this definition, the study could identify only 43 international brands, concentrating in the following regions: North America, Latin America, Asia-Pacific, Europe, Middle East, and Africa. It is worth noting that the sales volume of each of the top three brands, which are Coca-Cola, Marlboro, and Pepsi, exceeded US$100 billion in 2001, an indication of the powerful economic influence of international brands. When we take the example of the research conducted by Business-Week and Interbrand, we can see the rapid development of international branding. Interbrand focused on the field of brand research as early as 1974 when brand was still synonymous with logo. Later Interbrand began to work with BusinessWeek, publishing *The Top 100 Best Global Brands* every year. According to its 2015 report (see Table 2.1), Interbrand suggests that a truly global brand transcends geographic and cultural differences, has expanded across the established economic centers of the world, and is entering the major markets in the future. In measurable terms, this requires that: (1) At least 30% of revenues must come from outside the home country, and no more than 50% of revenues should come from any one continent alone; (2) It must have a presence on at least three major continents and must have broad geographic coverage in growing and emerging markets; (3) There must be substantial, publicly available data on the brand's financial performance; (4) Economic profit must be positive, showing a return above the operating and financing costs; (5) The brand must have a public profile and awareness above and beyond its own marketplace.

Comparing AC Nielson's 2001 report with BusinessWeek's 2015 report, we can see the increased level of specificity and stringency of measurement criteria, which is a reflection of the development of international branding during those 14 years.

2.1.2 Academics-oriented international branding

There are multiple definitions of international branding in existing international marketing and brand strategy research. In defining the structure of international branding, there exist two distinctively different streams.

The first stream is based on the standardization perspective in international marketing. This stream suggests that the purpose of establishing international brands is to benefit from stronger economies of scale. In this manner,

Table 2.1 Best Global Brands 2015

2015 Rank	Brand	Region/Country	Sector	Brand Value	Change in Brand Value
01		United States	Technology	170,276 $m	+ 43%
02	Google	United States	Technology	120,314 $m	+ 12%
03	Coca-Cola	United States	Beverages	78,423 $m	– 4%
04	Microsoft	United States	Technology	67,670 $m	+ 11%
05	IBM	United States	Business Services	65,095 $m	– 10%
06	TOYOTA	Japan	Automotive	49,048 $m	+ 16%
07	SAMSUNG	South Korea	Technology	45,297 $m	0%
08	GE	United States	Diversified	42,267 $m	– 7%
09		United States	Restaurants	39,809 $m	– 6%
10	amazon	United States	Retail	37,948 $m	+ 29%
11	BMW	Germany	Automotive	37,212 $m	+ 9%
12	Mercedes-Benz	Germany	Automotive	36,711 $m	+ 7%

Source: *2015 Best Global Brands Report* published by Interbrand.[1]

standardized international brands can achieve significant cost reduction/control in international marketing, R&D, resources procurement and allocation, and manufacturing (Buzzell, 1968; Levitt, 1983; Yip, 1995; Craig & Douglas, 2000). In the meantime, some studies also point out that international brands, by creating foreign images that transcend cultural, structural, and regional differences, can benefit from unique brand images in the different markets in which these brands are present. This phenomenon is particularly apparent in certain international market segments, especially among affluent and young consumers (Hassan & Katsanis,1991; Hassan *et al.*, 2003). The standardization perspective defines international branding as brands that adopt similar brand names, positioning strategies, and marketing programs in the majority of their international markets. However, researchers have yet to agree on the definition of standardized international brands. When defining the globalization of brands, Levitt (1983) focuses on the total standardization of branding strategies and market mix elements. Most other studies, however, indicate that total standardization is not realistic in the internationalization of brands. As a matter of fact, different standardization tendencies tend to appear at different degrees of internationalization. Therefore, many scholars suggest that the reason why some brands have higher degrees of internationalization than others is because they can be distinguished and are able to bear diversified extents of standardization (Aaker & Joachimsthaler, 1999; Schuiling & Lambin, 2003; Schuiling & Kapferer, 2004; Johansson & Ronkainen, 2005; Kapferer, 2005). In conclusion, according to the first stream, the defining characteristics of the internationalization level of brands are the marketing strategies they adopt in different international markets and the degree of brand standardization.

In recent years, a different school of thought has emerged. This second stream defines international branding from the perspective of consumers (Steenkamp *et al.*, 2003; Alden *et al.*, 2006). In these studies, a global brand is defined by the extent of globalness it is perceived to have by consumers. Such a brand conducts marketing activities not only in local markets but also in the international market. This stream of definition implies that the brand's activeness and extent of marketing in transnational markets are in proportion to its globalness. In fact, the time has come to recognize the post-global brand – the brand that no longer tries to adhere unreservedly to the model of total globalization, which is no longer perceived as ideal. Today, it is more appropriate to refer to selective globalization (Kapferer, 2005).

The variety of definitions of international branding reflects the disparity of measure criteria, and the lack of a robust measure model causes the inconsistency in definition of international branding. For example, Schuiling and Lambin (2003) conduct exploratory research on the image of global brands as perceived in their country of origin versus other international markets. The results show that global brands are perceived variously in different markets. The diversity of markets a brand is involved in is a criterion for measuring the globalization of the brand (Johansson & Ronkainen, 2005), but the most important factor influencing international branding is the perception coverage of the brand in the international market (Alden *et al.*, 2006). Existing literature dealing with relevant research contents includes: the effect of perceived globalness on brand attitude and preference (Steenkamp *et al.*, 2003); the differences of brand image between local and international brands (Schuiling & Kapferer, 2004); drivers of international branding (Johansson & Ronkainen, 2005); the measurement of brand globalness (Hsieh, 2002); standardization/adaptation of international brands (Rosen *et al.*, 1989; Özsomer & Prussia, 2000; Alashban *et al.*, 2002; Özsomer & Simonin, 2004); international brands competition (Holt *et al.*, 2004); evaluation of country-of-origin effects (Tse & Gorn, 1993; Samiee *et al.*, 2005); positioning strategies of global branding (Alden *et al.*, 1999); and international branding strategies and management in a broader sense (Quelch & Hoff, 1986; Aaker & Joachimsthaler, 1999).

2.2 Identification and positioning of international branding

2.2.1 *Consumers' attitude and preference towards international brands*

In the 1990s, some studies have tested the effect of perceived brand globalness on consumers' brand attitude and purchase likelihood. Research shows that perceived brand globalness could create consumer perceptions of brand supe-riority. Therefore, even if the product is objectively not exceptionally superior, consumers may show preference for it because of its globalness. Undoubtedly, brand affects consumers' preference and perception of firms and products. Research based on social recognition and corporate brand theory finds that consumer recognition has a significant moderating effect on the relationship between corporate brands and product evaluation (Wu *et al.*, 2010). Consumer data from the US and Korea show that perceived brand globalness is positively related to perceived brand quality (Steenkamp *et al.*, 2003). Studies on develop-ing country markets find that the "nonlocalness" of a brand is positively related to consumers' attitudes towards the brand (Batra *et al.*, 2000). The globalness of a brand, however, might not be significantly related to purchase likelihood (Tasoluk, 2006). Following the same logic, Holt *et al.* (2004) conducted a survey of 1,800 consumers from 12 countries, and the result shows that global image explains 12% of the variation in brand preference. Based on consumer cul-ture theory, consumers look to global brands as symbols of cultural ideals and use brands to create an imagined global identity that they share with like-minded people. As for the relationship between brand internationalization and perceived brand quality, research findings indicate that quality is positively related to preference for global brands. For instance, the study of Holt *et al.* (2004) shows that quality signal explains a large part (44%) of variation in brand preference. Also, their findings show that consumers view social responsibility as an important factor when they choose global brands. Consumers expect global brands to shoulder social responsibility as they operate their international busi-nesses. It is noteworthy that consumers consider social responsibility only in the context of global brands and do not pay much attention to social responsibility when it comes to local brands. Consumers' foreign experiences breed consumer social-mindedness and world-mindedness, which increase their positive feelings towards foreign brands (Nijssen & Douglas, 2008). Nijssen and Herk (2009) focus on the exchange relationship between consumers and foreign service providers. They consider and examine common issues of consumer behaviors like consumer loyalty. This study uses a sample of German consumers, because some German consumers frequently cross the national border and seek banking service in the Netherlands. There are rational reasons for such loyalty to foreign financial service, including service satisfaction, mutual trust, value judgments, and consumers' cultural recognition and confidence in industry in international marketing. They suggest that consumer-perceived tax benefits are negatively related to consumers' trust in a foreign service provider located abroad and positively related to economic benefits. In addition, consumer beliefs about the foreign industry have a positive impact on consumers' satisfaction, trust, value judgment, and loyalty to foreign brands. Dimofte *et al.* (2008) discuss American consumers' cognition and affect of foreign brands. The authors find that US consumers hold contradictory notions of what characterizes a global brand beyond its wide recognition, availability, and standardization across markets. In particular, they find that the association of brand globality with higher quality is not as strong as the literature has proposed and that affect directly influences how people perceive global brands. For most American consumers, although brand globality is not considered an important attribute of a brand, it is nonetheless associated with positive affect, and this affect is also reflected among consumers who are explicitly against global brands. In other words, such positive halo effect implies that there exists a certain kind of appeal in international branding that causes global brands to be well received extensively in most marketplaces.

2.2.2 Differences of brand image: International brands versus local brands

Brand image embodies a series of cultural positioning, including the context surrounding the brand, its cultural origin, and its association with the past and the future. Global brands are those that use similar marketing mix strategy across all target markets (Schuiling & Kapferer, 2004; Dimofte *et al.*, 2008). Therefore, building a global image increases brand power and value (Aaker, 1991; Shocker *et al.*, 1994; Keller, 2008). Many scholars suggest that multinational enterprises should adopt global unique positioning so as to build global brands. For instance, Steenkamp *et al.* (2003) investigate the relationship between perceived brand globalness and brand value through an empirical study. They find that consumers' perceived brand globalness is positively related to consumers' perceived brand quality, prestige, and purchase likelihood. Therefore, the authors suggest that global firms adopt global brand positioning strategy. Schuiling and Kapferer (2004), on the other hand, point out that although building international brands is substantial for international firms, local brands also represent strategic advantages that must be considered.

Guzmán and Paswan (2009) study the roles of cultural brands from emerging markets and pay special attention to the comparison of brand images in home and host country. The authors choose two Mexican brands and analyze whether their brands remain consistent in foreign markets as they internationalize. International branding is one of the important challenges facing international firms after they have expanded abroad. These challenges relate to the essence of the brand in terms of brand name and brand visual and sound elements (Whitelock & Fastoso, 2007). The positioning of a brand in a foreign market should be adjusted through its cultural adaptability. Brand image should be closely linked to the international branding process through the reviewing of brand development history (Cayla & Arnould, 2008). Advertising is an important approach for a firm to build its brand image, and consumers' attitudes towards advertising are the basic guidance for consumer behaviors. Lutze (1985) defines consumers' attitudes towards advertising as: the relatively sustained emotional tendency of favor for or aversion to common advertisements. Attitudes towards advertising are closely linked to consumers' attitudes towards a certain marketing method and to consumers' attitudes towards and preference for the brand. There have been numerous studies about advertising. Möller and Eisend (2010), for instance, analyze the effectiveness of banner advertising in a firm's globalization process from cultural and individual perspectives. They find that both national-level cultural and socio-demographic variables have influence on banner advertising effectiveness. The authors collect online survey data from 7,775 respondents from 34 countries, examine consumers' attitudes toward banner advertising and intention to click on banner ads, and conduct analysis combining host-country culture. This study follows Hofstede's cultural dimensions of individualism, uncertainty avoidance, power distance, and masculinity. The findings show that consumers from individualist countries show less acceptance of banner advertising than those from collectivist countries. The acceptance of web banner advertising is related to the consumers' click behavior. The findings suggest that marketers should view banner advertising, although largely standardized when targeting a global audience, as a culture-specific issue. Compared with conventional advertising, however, banner advertising establishes a more effective link between firm and consumer (Manchanda *et al.*, 2006). Therefore, it is important to make use of banner advertising and increase consumers' awareness of this form of advertisement. Survey results show that consumers' attitudes towards banner advertising and click tendency are negatively related to individualism tendency of the culture and positively related to risk avoidance, masculinity, and power distance. Although banner advertising is now an international phenomenon, it is important to view the important role of culture in the implementation of such advertising. After all, it is culture that affects consumers' attention and response to advertisement.

Burgmann *et al.* (2006) suggest that national culture has an important influence on the design and acceptance of a firm's foreign market website. Therefore, it is necessary for multinational firms to possess the capabilities to communicate with and adapt to foreign cultures. Melewar *et al.* (2009) divide the determinants of international advertising program standardization into three categories: macro-environmental determinants, micro-environmental determinants specifically related to the firm and industry in which it operates, and consumer-related determinants. Macro-environmental determinants include governmental regulations, economic development, political environment, infrastructure, culture/language, nationalism, and education; micro-environmental determinants specifically related to firm and industry include competition, organization structure, and marketing institution; consumer-related determinants include consumer tastes and habits, behaviors, and experiences. All these factors jointly influence the standardization of international advertising, as reflected in such aspects as advertising theme, creative expression, and media mix. Among these factors, advertising theme can be most appropriately standardized, whereas creative expression and media mix are most susceptible to adapt to local market environment.

2.2.3 Standardization/adaptation of international branding

In the field of international business research, brand standardization/adaptation is an important part of the international marketing standardization/adaptation debate (Hu, 2002a; Hu *et al.*, 2009). The standardization/adaptation debate is a long-lasting topic in international marketing research. The internationalization process of brands also involves decisions to choose between the two strategies. On the basis of reserving the essence of choice between "unity" and "adapting," standardization and adaptation in the process of international branding are more often reflected in specific problems facing brand building in the internationalization process, such as channel, distribution, marketing mix, multinational market synergy, culture and language, and matters closely related to consumer experience like online advertising. Alashban *et al.* (2002) suggest that the choice of a firm's international branding strategy is in fact a matter of brand standardization/adaptation choice.

Based on literature review, Hu *et al.* (2009) construct an integrated conceptual model of determinants of distribution adaptation and price adaptation strategy choice and its impact on export performance and empirically study China's export manufacturing firms. Based on survey and data model of more than 140 firms, the authors find that: (1) The distribution adaptation strategy and price adaptation strategy that Chinese firms adopt in their international operation are jointly driven by firms' external factors and international factors. However, the extent of influence of each of these factors, external or internal, varies. Export market environment and organizational learning capabilities positively and significantly influence the degree of distribution adaptation; industry and technology attributes, export market environment, and organizational learning capabilities positively and significantly influence the degree of price adaptation, whereas organizational learning capabilities exhibit a greater influence. Therefore, when formulating distribution strategy and pricing strategy, Chinese manufacturing exporters should attach importance to these significant internal and external determinants and pay special attention to improving organizational learning capabilities. (2) Export performance is directly influenced by distribution adaptation strategy and global vision and indirectly influenced by export market environment and organizational learning capabilities. This research suggests that Chinese firms can achieve satisfactory performance only when they formulate international marketing strategies that fit the characteristics of the environment of the international markets and are compatible with their internal conditions. This study also indicates that firms can achieve satisfactory performance by adopting effective strategies (distribution adaptation) and enhancing organizational capabilities (international vision and learning capability). It needs to be stressed here that because distribution adaptation has a significant influence on export performance, Chinese firms should therefore adopt different types of distribution channels in different export markets and adjust their business relationships with local distributors according to changes in local market environment. An effective way for Chinese firms to achieve satisfactory performance at the current stage is to establish competitive distribution channels and maintain good communications with these channels. (3) Empirical findings show that learning capability has the greatest influence on distribution adaptation and price adaptation strategy choices and has an indirect influence on performance through distribution adaptation. In addition, global vision also has a significant direct influence on export performance. Therefore, for Chinese firms, improving their international visions and learning capability (both internal factors) would be beneficial not only for choosing effective marketing strategies but also for improving export performance. A firm would be able to achieve superior export marketing results if its executives possess a global mindset, attach importance to export business, view the international market as their target market, consider it the mission of the firm to explore the international market, embed their global visions into the corporate culture of the firm, and are able to train more employees who possess international visions and perspectives. Meanwhile, empirical results indicate that cultivating a firm's organizational learning capability is a critical issue that no business manager should ignore. As firms' export business expands, they should be able to implement adaptation strategies more successfully if they can keep learning about the international market, improving their export marketing skills, and enhancing the managerial decision-making process.

Currently, much of relevant literature represents the headquarters' viewpoint and broadly assesses antecedents of standardization or adaptation across widely varying markets. Katsikeas (2006) does not evaluate the differences or similarities of the two strategies from a static perspective; instead, the author re-analyzes the issue from the standpoint of strategic fit. He suggests that although strategic fit is an important method to improve corporate performance, previous studies have failed to specify which strategic fit method[2] can improve corporate performance in the international market. Vorhies and Morgan (2003) also point out that marketing practice should focus on the interaction between the firm and exogenous factors (such as environment) and that, in order to improve performance, the firm should actively adjust its strategic development and organization structure so as to adapt to the market environment of the target country. Using strategic fit as the theoretical platform for analysis, Katsikeas and colleagues (2006) investigate international marketing strategy for a specific product or product line within subsidiaries of US, Japanese, and German multinational corporations (MNCs) operating in the UK. Results indicate that degree of strategy standardization is significantly related to similarity between markets with respect to regulatory environments, technological intensity and velocity, customs and traditions, customer characteristics, a product's stage in its life cycle, and competitive intensity. The author uses the aforementioned factors as explanatory variables and corporate performance as the explained variable and conducts regression analysis. The results show that similarity of market environments, technological intensity and velocity, customer characteristics, and competitive intensity are all significantly and positively related to the degree of standardization in the country of origin and the international market. The author continues to put absolute standardization as a variable into the research framework and finds that absolute standardization is negatively related to performance. On the critical question of performance consequences, the findings suggest that superior performance results from strategy standardization only to the extent that there is fit or co-alignment between the MNC's environmental context and its international marketing strategy choice. Birnik and Bowman (2007) discuss market mix standardization. Different from previous research regarding the standardization/adaptation debate, Birnik and Bowman's objective is to extract and synthesize 'best evidence' regarding marketing mix standardization practices in multinational corporations and to identify evidence regarding the performance impact of marketing mix standardization. This study focuses on the practicality of marketing mix, with the purpose of providing useful perspectives and guidance to global firms and policy-makers[3] in the practice of international marketing. The authors use the following factors to evaluate the degree of marketing mix standardization: price, brand and product, packaging, advertising, promotion, customer service, and website. Main factors influencing marketing mix standardization include: type of product or industry, HQ ownership level, entry mode, extent of local production in country, degree of local competitive intensity, size of local market, market similarities, international experience and country of origin of parent company, level of communication between parent and subsidiary, organization structure of parent, and core competence, among others, and all these factors are interconnected. Through case analysis the authors find that industrial products, high-tech products, market similarities, products in the same stage in PLC (product life cycle), and fully owned subsidiaries show stronger evidence of standardization; essential products, luxury products, indirect entry modes, parent and subsidiary having similar competitive positions, high degree of communication between parent and subsidiary, and centralization in decision-making show weaker evidence of standardization. Moreover, Birnik and Bowman (2007) find that consumer products and products that have high local competitive intensity should significantly lower the level of marketing mix standardization; home appliances, culture-bound products, direct entry modes, and customer-based strategy are more suitable for a less standardization strategy. In addition, factors like size of local market, country of origin, and international experience are not significantly related to market mix standardization.

As a matter of fact, most research on standardization is conducted in the context of the marketing mix. However, research on standardization of management processes/characteristics is rare (Shoham *et al.*, 2008). It is especially the case with research regarding the management of distribution channels, and the characteristics of firms' relationships with their foreign representatives are significantly related to corporate performance (Shoham *et al.*, 2008).

Jain (1989) stresses that program standardization and process standardization are two very different aspects of marketing strategy. Program standardization includes various aspects of marketing mix and development and improvement during the process of project implementation. Griffith *et al.* (2000) are the first authors to include international marketing channel management in their study. Results suggest that trust, commitment, conflict, and satisfaction are four important dimensions in the management process. The study of Shoham and Brencic (2008) suggests that the degree of standardization/adaptation of channel management and a firm's relationship with its foreign representatives (coordination, support, control, and communications) are important factors that influence strategic choice and corporate performance. In the study that follows, the authors use 727 Slovene exporters as the sample and conduct quantitative regression analysis on the relationship between the aforementioned factors and performance. The findings show that coordination is significantly and positively related to commitment and the performance of international firms; control of the representatives and foreign representatives' autonomy are significantly and negatively related to commitment and corporate performance; and communication is significantly and positively related to coordination, commitment, and performance. Interviews during the study support the aforementioned findings. The authors suggest that many Slovene exporters suffer from severely constrained resources and that the standardization of channels could be resisted by the representatives, resulting in implementation difficulties. The autonomy mode of foreign representatives is significantly and negatively related to esprit de corps and corporate performance in the standardization mode. Standardized control is associated with higher esprit de corps and cooperation, but not with international performance. This might be due to an imbalanced dyadic power structure, in which the representatives are more powerful. Finally, communication standardization doesn't affect overall performance. Here, interviewed firms suggest that most Slovene exporters are in the early internationalization stages and are still learning how to operate in other markets. Consequently, the impact of high levels of standardization probably masks the impact of high communication levels, rather than how standardized it is.

As a key topic in international marketing, the standardization/adaptation debate has spread to the field of international advertising. Melewar *et al.* (2009) discuss the implementation of advertising standardization of multinational enterprises. The study aims to analyze factors that multinationals consider important in the standardization/adaptation decision in order to develop their international advertising strategies. These factors include competition, culture, education, marketing institution, and consumer-related determinants, all of which should be taken into consideration in the choice of advertising theme, creative expression, and media mix. A standardized advertising strategy possesses unique advantages. Consumers worldwide may share similar needs and consumption motivation. Therefore, advertising promotion should be built on a uniform base. The standardization of marketing is key for the success of multinational enterprises in the international market. Societies and cultures are becoming increasingly homogeneous. By repeating the standardization process, international brands affect the consumption behaviors and habits of local consumers. As consumers become more and more familiar with these brands, they are more likely to accept them. Moreover, national culture has an important influence on the design and acceptance of a firm's foreign market website, so it is necessary for international firms to possess the capabilities to communicate with and adapt to foreign cultures (Burgmann *et al.*, 2006). Existing studies categorize the determinants of advertising standardization as macro-environmental (e.g., governmental regulations, culture/language, nationalism, education, etc.), micro-environmental (e.g., competition, organization structure, and marketing institution), and consumer-related factors (e.g., consumer tastes and habits, behaviors, and experiences). Melewar *et al.* (2009) find that of these, advertising theme is the easiest and can be most appropriately standardized, whereas creative expression and media mix are most susceptible to the local market environment.

Hultman *et al.* (2009) empirically investigate export product strategy fit and performance. This study examines the issue of balancing benefits gained through standardized strategies with those achievable when adapting to local conditions. The study is innovative in that it uses contingency theory as a new research perspective. The authors do not suggest that there is a one-size-fits-all strategy that fits all types of market environments. Using the sample of Swedish exporters, the authors find support for the hypothesis that an array of forces from the macro, micro, and internal environments drives product adaptation, which affects the nature of product strategy fit and its performance outcomes. In terms of the performance relevance of product strategy fit, sociocultural environment, technological environment, marketing infrastructure, stage of product life cycle, and international experience all matter. However, not all elements show significant influence, which cautions against excessive aggregation of environmental variables in conceptualizing environment–product strategy fit to performance links. Cavusgil *et al.* (1993) define product adaptation as the degree to which the physical product differs across national boundaries and point out that macro, micro, and external attributes and characteristics of the firm would all affect product adaptability, but environmental factors or product adaptability itself do not have a direct influence on export performance (Hultman, 2009). Instead, the aforementioned factors affect product adaptability and in turn influence corporate performance. Differences in the economic, regulatory, sociocultural, and technological environment between the home and export markets are positively related to the level of product adaptation. In terms of microenvironment factors, differences in customer characteristics, market characteristics, marketing infrastructure, and competitive intensity between the home and export markets are positively related to the level of product adaptation. In terms of internal factors, a firm's export commitment, scope of exporting experience, and duration of export venture are positively related to the level of product adaptation between the home and export markets. Eventually, strategy fit enhances corporate performance by means of product adaptability and the interaction of the aforementioned factors. Using a questionnaire survey, the study collects data from a sample of 1,016 Swedish exporters. Regression analysis results show that sociocultural environment, technological environment, market characteristics, marketing infrastructure and export commitment, and duration of export venture have a significant positive influence on product adaptability. Regarding export performance, macroenvironment and microenvironment misfits are all significantly and negatively related to export performance. However, internal environment misfit is not significantly related to export performance. The findings broaden our understanding of how exporters develop effective product adaptation strategies. According to contingency theory, no single strategic choice for adaptation is optimal for all firms and circumstances. Product standardization is meant to reduce exporting costs, but highly standardized strategies are unlikely to be inherently beneficial to exporters in general. It is particularly noteworthy that product adaptation, even though not directly linked to performance, is indeed an influential variable.

2.3 International brand marketing strategies

2.3.1 Entry strategies of international brands

When expanding into overseas markets, an international brand faces two critical questions: Where and how? These questions parallel the two aspects of market entry strategy: the choice of target market and the implementation of entry strategies (e.g., OEM [original equipment manufacturing] or OBM [original brand manufacturing]). Regarding the issue of international market choice, Evans *et al.* (2008) propose a conceptual model of the psychic distance–organizational performance relationship that incorporates organizational factors (international experience and centralization of decision-making), entry strategy, and retail strategy implications. The findings suggest that when entering geographically distant markets, retailers should adopt low-cost/low-control entry strategies and adapt their retail strategy to a greater extent than in geographically close markets. Centralization of decision-making is in negative relation to psychic distance and retail strategy, but it provides a driving force for market entry strategies. International experience is positively associated with psychic distance and retail strategy and negatively related to market entry strategy. The authors also find that international experience, psychic distance, entry strategy, and retail strategy adaptation are significant drivers of organizational performance. In terms of financial performance and strategic effectiveness, market entry mode and organizational performance promote one another, and this, in turn, moderates the relationship between psychic distance and organizational performance. From the perspective of distances and market size, Ojala (2009) discusses the market entry mode and first choice of small and medium-sized companies in the software industry. When a smaller firm chooses its international market, it generally considers three factors: geographic distance, psychic distance, and market size. Studies show that about 70% of choice can be explained by geographic distance and market size. When a firm chooses overseas target markets, the optimal model is generally moving from a geographically close country to one that is geographically more distant but with great purchase power. Meanwhile, the size of the software market is the most important factor influencing small and medium-sized companies' choice, but the gross domestic product (GDP) of the target market is not a key determinant of the choice. Cultural distance can only explain the preference of a firm when it chooses a target market, but it is not the ultimate determinant. In terms of development path, restrained by market information, financing, and human resources, a smaller software firm would initially enter markets that are geographically close. In its subsequent expansion, size of the software market would be a dominant factor influencing the firm's choice. Different from Hofstede's (2001) cultural distance theory, the impact of cultural distance is not significant when a smaller software firm is choosing a foreign market. Dow and Larimo's (2009) study reevaluates the impact of psychic distance and international experience on market entry mode choice. They suggest that although international entry mode choice has been extensively studied, conceptualization and measurement of psychic distance and international experience, two key factors that influence market entry mode, have been equivocal. When a refined interpretation of international experience is employed, only experience in similar countries affects entry mode selection. Experience in dissimilar countries seems to have no predictive power (Hofstede, 2001). Although the relationship between the psychic distance of international markets and market entry mode choice has been frequently studied, little research has focused specifically on psychic distance per se. Evans *et al.* (2008) acknowledge the role of distances but also consider distances as exogenous variables between nations. As for international experience, Dow and Larimo (2009) draw a distinction between general international experience and culture-specific international experience. General international experience increases a firm's set of skills in the general process of setting up and managing business activities in a foreign market, whereas culture-specific international experiences refers to experience that enables a firm to solve potential problems in a distant market. In addition, Hofstede (2001) reports that culture-specific experience is a key factor that influences market entry mode choice. The author suggests that the national differences of religions, industrial development, education, and political systems are negatively related to high-control market entry mode. In other words, the greater the differences of religions, industrial development, education, and political system between the markets, the less likely the firm would choose high-control market entry mode. In terms of international experience, general international experience is positively related to high-control market entry mode, but cultural experience is positively related to high-control market entry mode, and the positive relation is more intense when there are significant differences between the target country and the country of origin. This study offers advice to international marketers. When considering market entry mode, international marketers should attach importance to refining the measurement system of psychic distance and international experience so as to make correct judgments.

2.3.2 Brand alliance in the context of globalization

Emerging international companies rely on various resources and forces when exploring the international market. In recent years, the Internet and information have become indispensable in the international market. Alliance is an effective way to avoid risks and share information. Firms that have just started the process of their internationalization are more likely to adopt the alliance strategy, especially in foreign markets that show great uncertainties. Partners play a critical role in the creation of more noteworthy opportunities and are becoming more and more important in helping new ventures reduce the learning costs and accelerate sales revenue growth (Oviatt & McDougall, 2005). There are two types of knowledge that can motivate firms to enter the international market: foreign market knowledge and technological knowledge. Technological knowledge is the application of science and technology-related advantages on high-tech products. Such knowledge helps firms upgrade product quality, increase the smoothness and efficiency of production line operation, and improve their innovation capability. Lord and Ranft (2000) suggest that foreign market experience includes foreign market financial conditions, cultural environment, social customs, political conditions, and differences from the country of origin. Many studies have indicated that international market experience plays an important role in firms' internationalization process. Particularly, firms' international performance is closely related to foreign market knowledge.

The adoption of network theory into the conventional environment-strategy-performance framework can help a foreign firm improve performance. Foreign firms can make use of the network resources and strength of multinational enterprises to stabilize market and technological fluctuations. Firms can also deploy such network resources to adjust strategies. Extant research shows that multinational enterprises often adopt multiple strategies and various resources to cope with different environments. The research finds that different environments cause firms to bear different market responsibilities, resulting in the different roles they play in product innovation and network strength. Although separately marketing strategy and network strength each provide a positive impact on corporate performance, together their influence on performance is mixed. Foreign market knowledge is market knowledge that is obtained in one country and used to provide value and competitive advantages to the market of another country. Because factual discrepancies and inefficiencies often occur during the flow of knowledge within a multinational company (especially so when it flows across different geographic markets), how to use knowledge effectively within the organization has therefore become increasingly critical. Through extensive interview and onsite investigations, the authors find that the relationship between foreign market knowledge that has been accumulated in international marketing practice in the past and the application of such knowledge is rather complex. To a certain extent the abundance of experience in international marketing practice would impede the company's application of foreign market knowledge. On the other hand, the company's capability to rapidly absorb knowledge and adapt to changes would urge it to use foreign market knowledge.

The performance of an international firm is closely related to the degree of its adaptation to the target market. The mode of supervision, either in the form of an explicitly employed supervisor or the autonomy of partners, is an important determinant of the extent of adaptability. Tangible supervision would lead partners in the target market to feel that the cooperation would not bring benefits to them and was not consistent with their own benefit targets, thus weakening the adaptability of the international firm in the target market. On the contrary, a low level of supervision, or none at all, would enable the international firm to better adapt to the environment of the target market. The result is that the partners would repay the trust given them with sincere cooperation, thus improving performance. As the degree of adaptation increases, a selfish partner may change the way it views the international firm from a competitive perspective to a cooperation perspective, achieving win–win results by improving the common interests of both parties.

Choosing the right supervision method is particularly important for the development of international firms. It affects the opportunities, efficiency, value, and performance of the firm in the international market. Although in the US market there is already a significant quantity of research regarding the relationship between supervision and performance, in recent years considering the effect of supervision methods in the international context has gradually become the mainstream. A firm can normally choose from three modes: market mechanism supervision, trust supervision, and formal contract supervision. The active market supervision mode is closely linked to the conventional market mechanism, including tracking the potential providers of product and price, dependence on the choice of suppliers during the bidding process, and the adoption of multiple supply resources. Active market supervision plays an important role in many business transactions. In the international market, however, the buyer would face numerous problems. First, the international market is far less transparent than the domestic market, and unsmooth information communication puts a constraint on the experience of dealing with foreign suppliers. Second, commodities and prices offered by foreign suppliers may not be comparable to those offered domestically, as the level of standardization in the international market, after all, is much lower compared to that in the domestic market. Lastly, building international purchase resource with foreign suppliers requires buyers' time and effort, which would increase buyers' switching costs.

In addition, in transnational exchange relations, customers have a lower level of trust in foreign suppliers than domestic ones. Trust supervision is associated with culture. Establishing trust in transnational transactions involves more problems, and the efficiency of trust as a supervision mode is not ideal in the international market. Compared to the two aforementioned modes, the contract mode provides an effective base for solving potential future disputes between the buyer and the seller, as both parties can explicitly state in a contract the uncertainties of performance and the fluctuation level of the transaction. Setting down obligations and responsibilities on paper and explicitly stipulating punitive measures resulting from performance decline would urge both parties to overcome difficulties and provide solutions on their own initiatives. Because of this, the transaction cost theory has always asserted that a formal contract is the most effective mode to achieve supervision, and such effectiveness is particularly important in the context of globalization. From the perspective of comparative cultural studies, the authors propose that, in a culture with a high level of risk avoidance, the buyer firm would rely on the active supervision mode and is not likely to employ the trust mode. Compared to a culture with a low level of risk avoidance, people are more inclined to sign formal contracts for supervision purposes in a high-risk-avoidance cultural context.

2.3.3 Where are you from? The country-of-origin effects in international branding

A large part of the purpose of brand marketing mix is to enhance and con-solidate brand equity, which, according to the research of Keller (1993), con-sists mainly of brand awareness and brand image. The country of origin is an important factor that affects brand image (Thakor & Lavack, 2003). The country-of-origin effects are complex: the same country could have different country-of-origin effects in different foreign markets, and the country's image can also vary in different product categories (Ahmed et al., 2004). Therefore, a significant amount of relevant literature focuses on the country-of-origin effects in different industries (e.g. Häubl, 1996; Ahmed et al., 2002) and in different countries (e.g. Ettenson,1993; Hulland et al., 1996; Ahmed et al., 2002). Some literature also discusses consumers' perception of brand origin (e.g. Samiee et al., 2005) and ways to weaken/enhance country-of-origin effects (e.g.,Tse & Lee, 1993;Voss & Tansuhaj, 1999).

Many studies have shown that brand origin is an important factor that influences branding strategy choice. Country-of-origin effects significantly influence consumers' perceived product quality, brand attitude, and brand choosing behavior (Thakor & Lavack, 2003; Balabanis & Diamantopoulos, 2008). A poor image of the country of origin produces a negative effect on consumers' brand attitude and product evaluation (Han & Terpstra, 1988). When the country-of-origin effects are negative, a firm may consider adopting the OEM strategy and may opt for adaptation as its brand positioning strategy. Therefore, country-of-origin effects affect international branding strategy choice.

Brand image embodies consumers' knowledge of and trust in various products under the brand, and brand origin is an important determinant of brand image (Thakor & Lavack, 2003). The degree of brand globalization is dependent on the development of global brands that ideally carry the same message and position in different markets (i.e., brand standardization). Con-sistent with this practice, marketing scholars have exhibited much interest in exploring standardized international marketing programs and global market-ing strategies. Country-of-origin effects literature considers product origin a critical product-related factor (Jain, 1989; Samiee & Roth, 1992; Hewett & Bearden, 2001), and its findings have tacitly challenged the implementation of standardized international marketing programs. If brand origin is so important, it would be expected that consumers would possess reasonably accurate abilities to recognize brands' country of origins. In the US, federal labeling laws require that all imported products be clearly marked with their origins, and thus this information is available for consumers. Some international brands have been able to mask their origins. For example, Parker and Kodak are thought to be of local origin in multiple countries. Samiee *et al.* (2005) indicate that lower levels of correct brand origin recognition suggest that either a brand is perceived to be manufactured and available in many countries or brand origin is inconsequential in the choice process. On the other hand, higher levels of correct brand origin recognition demonstrate the saliency of brand origin to consumers, which in turn reinforces the need to develop international marketing and global strategies that are sensitive to and incorporate this information. If this information carries a negative or positive bias, the country-of-origin literature stresses the need to adjust international marketing plans. Eisingerich and Rubera (2010) conduct a cross-national investigation into drivers of brand commitment. The study indicates that firms increasingly employ global brand management strategies for the effective coordination of their global activities. This study examines the influence of culture on four key brand management elements, including brand innovativeness, brand customer orientation, brand self-relevance, and social responsibility. Using responses from 167 UK and 230 Chinese consumers, the authors empirically demonstrate that brand innovativeness and brand self-relevance have a greater effect on brand commitment in cultures that are individualist, short-term oriented, and low on power distance (i.e., the United Kingdom). The findings also reveal that in collectivistic, long-term-oriented, and high-power-distance cultures (i.e., China), the four brand management activities contribute to brand commitment equally.

Some other studies examine the mental mechanism of country-of-origin effects, trying to understand the cause of country-of-origin effects from a consumer psychology perspective, using such tools as modeling, the halo effect model, and the perception explanatory model. These studies, however, build on the same hypothesis that as long as the country-of-origin information is available, consumers would value that information and use it as a key criterion to evaluate product. The findings of Johansson's (1993) survey show that consumers do not desire or value country-of-origin information that much. Similarly, the study of Heslop and Papadopoulos (1993) indicates that although the country of origin is very important, consumers somehow don't like to admit it.

2.4 Improving and maintaining brand power in the internationalization process

2.4.1 *Maintaining brand vitality in international competition: brand research and development*

With the globalization of transaction and production, R&D globalization is also gradually become an important development subject of international firms.

From a network perspective, the innovation and learning capabilities of a firm represent an important development direction. However, few international marketing scholars have studied the possible results and problems international firms may achieve and encounter in cross-national R&D. The innovativeness of firms can and should be evaluated through R&D effort and external R&D cooperation. In specific, firms should know clearly the direction of internal R&D and supplement it through external R&D networks. Kim and Park (2010) discuss the development of international R&D networks and their effect on corporate innovation. They initially examine learning organization theory and focus on the positioning of international firms in the relationship between science and technology content and innovation. The level of science and technology is manifested as the quantity of scientific publication patents a firm possesses. These are an indication of a firm encouraging and valuing the role of science and technology in the firm's development. Research findings show that the level of science and technology application improves innovation environment through the building of effective research facilities; especially when the internal R&D capabilities of a firm are integrated with external network resources, the innovation capability would increase significantly. Effective external networks that are formed during the development of an international firm can ensure efficiency of information collection and dissemination in the R&D process, thus guaranteeing the smoothness and influence of the R&D process. The innovativeness of a firm increases with the rise of the level of the firm's science and technology, in other words, the efforts and inclination to apply scientific knowledge. Meanwhile, effective external networks that the international firm develops in the international market would also promote such increase. When the international firm plays its role as the "gatekeeper" of the country of origin, the R&D of the firm would no longer be confined to its own development. Instead, the advanced knowledge it has absorbed from foreign firms would spread to domestic firms. With that the effect of international networks on innovation would be greatly enhanced. On the other hand, research regarding the relationship between the innovation capability of a firm and its performance from the perspective of dynamic capabilities has attracted more attention. Dynamic capabilities refer to organizational, structural, and technological capabilities that a firm develops in order to gain or maintain competitive advantages. From the perspective of dynamic capabilities research, competitiveness is reflected as the ability to respond to opportunities, quick and flexible strategies, and the managerial ability to carry out external cooperation and internal adjustment. In the international market, dynamic capabilities would work only when management succeeds in adapting to changes by adjusting the resource portfolio. Levinthal and March (1993) define "exploration" as the pursuit of new knowledge, of things that might come to be known, and "exploitation" as use and development of things already known. Yalcinkaya et al. (2007) define "exploration capabilities" as the importer's ability to adopt new processes, products, and services that are unique from those used in the past and "exploitation capabilities" as the importer's ability to improve continuously its existing resources and processes. The authors discuss the relationship between production innovation and market performance from the dynamic capabilities perspective, indicating that marketing and technological resources provide a foundation for the establishment of exploitation and exploration capabilities, respectively, and that these dynamic capabilities influence the degree of product innovation and market performance. The authors use a survey of 111 US importers. The results indicate that marketing resources influence an importer's development of exploitation capabilities, whereas technological resources influence the development of exploration capabilities.

2.4.2 Brand extension in the international market

The extension of international brands is not confined to the domestic market; instead, they expand their competitive scope to all the markets in which they are present and tailor their extension strategies to the different characteristics of each market. Colton *et al.* (2010) use Tesco, the fourth largest retailer in the world, as an example. According to statistics from Tesco, in terms of retail performance the firm has made significant progress both in its home market and in the international market. The retailer monitors and analyzes its competitors' strategies to determine when and how to extend its strategies most effectively. Tesco's efforts to understand customers, competitors, and foreign markets have facilitated effective e-tail strategies in various European and Asian markets. Neilson and Chadha (2008), using the operation of ICICI in Canada as an example, analyze the retail bank's strategic application of brand extension in the international market. As an Indian bank, ICICI has made great progress in both its home country and in the international market by focusing on the retail banking business. The authors suggest that a transnational strategy coupled with an ethnocentric staffing policy allows the parent firm to retain control and that the blend of various variables in the services marketing mix (i.e., price, place, promotion, participants, and process) can help in achieving brand extension and attaining customer satisfaction.

2.4.3 Enhancing international market–based customer brand equity

Existing research also focuses on the exchange relationship between consumers and foreign service providers and examines some common issues of consumer behavior like consumer loyalty (e.g., Nijssen & Herk, 2009). By studying consumers in Germany, the authors find that some German consumers often choose banking service in Dutch. Service satisfaction, mutual trust, value judgments, and consumers' cultural recognition and confidence in industry can explain their cross-border behavior. The authors suggest that consumer-perceived tax benefits share a negative relationship to consumers' trust in a foreign service provider located abroad and are positively related to economic benefits. In addition, consumer beliefs in foreign industry are positively related to satisfaction, trust, value judgment, and loyalty. An appropriate level of standardization and adaptation choice can enhance consumer loyalty and produce a positive impact on promoting the equity of international brands. Birnik (2007) examines the determinants of marking mix from the perspectives of increasing profit and reducing cost, emphasizing that brand personality and preference, larger market share, practical price strategy, and more loyal customers can all enhance performance. In addition, economies of scale and cooperation can also effectively reduce cost.

2.5 Summary and suggestions for future research

This chapter reviews the contents and development of existing literature on international branding research. As a matter of fact, academic research in the field of international branding has also gone through a long period of meaningful exploration. In the initial stage research topics focused mainly on the conceptualization and measurement of international brands. This exploration period synchronized with the formation and development of some international brands, rather authentically reflecting the conditions at that time. When the conceptualization and measurement of international branding took shape, scholars began to shift their focus onto the positioning and identification of international branding, which is about the choice of foreign target markets. This research then leads to the matter of how to develop the optimal mode to enter the international market. Once in the international market, the new challenge is to choose the optimal strategy and marketing mix in the new market, which generally involves the adjustment and restructuring of the marketing system of the brand in the country of origin. In order to implement strategies and marketing mix, firms need to obtain positive feedback so as to develop strategies in the next step. Finally, a successful international brand would not be satisfied merely with sales growth in the international market, but would seek breakthroughs in two aspects: first, from sales internationalization to R&D internationalization; second, acquiring strength from the success of the brand in the international market to enhance brand image and the overall equity of the brand system in the home market.

Even as research on international branding becomes increasingly enriched and refined, there are still areas that have yet to be articulated when compared to conventional brand research. Some of such areas are very important research subjects in the field of brand research, such as brand choice and brand switching. Such research topics, however, tend to concentrate on brand choice and switching among numerous brands in a single market, and not enough attention has been paid to consumers' choice in the context of the international market. Similar issues include value measurement and brand portfolio of international brands. There are various reasons. On the one hand, in the international market, international brands may adopt an adaptation strategy, which would result in different numbers of sub-brands and brand images in each market segment. This causes the loss of some comparability, making comparison and data processing more difficult. On the other hand, as the number of cases adopting strong standardized branding strategies goes down, statistics in this regard become increasing feeble. In addition, international branding research requires extensive cooperation of scholars from different countries. Such cooperation could be restricted by geographical conditions, and the potential for such cooperation can be further tapped. These problems are not unsolvable. Instead, as the cutting edge of frontier topics and points of breakthrough in the field of international branding research, they represent promising directions for future studies.

Notes

1 http://interbrand.com/best-brands/best-global-brands/2015/ranking/#?listFormat=ls
2 The concept of strategic fit was first proposed by Venkatraman in 1998. According to the concept, the key to corporate performance is the fitness of the firm's strategy to its market environment. The concept of "fit" plays a vital role in both strategic management and organizational behavior.
3 In other academic studies, practitioners and policy-makers of multinational firms are rarely studied as a primary factor.

3 Two perspectives of international marketing: standardization versus adaptation

Zuohao Hu

3.1 Introduction

In international marketing research, whether to standardize or to adapt has been a critical question for international marketers since the 1960s (Jain, 1989; Whitelock & Pimblett, 1997). Elinder (1961) proposes the adoption of uniform advertising throughout Europe, which represents the original idea of standardization. Perlmutter (1969) suggests the adoption of world-oriented strategies in international marketing, which are essentially global standardization strategies. Levitt (1983) proposes the hypothesis of world market homogenization and introduces the globalization of markets. Levitt's view reverberated across the academic and the practice field alike, resulting in the emergence of a great number of theoretical and empirical papers either supporting or arguing against global standardization. Research supporting standardization in international marketing suggests that the purpose of standardization strategies is to achieve cost saving through economies of scale and learning effect. Standardized marketing strategies would enable firms to reduce cost in R&D, manufacturing, sales, logistics, and distribution. In addition, standardization helps establish a uniform worldwide image and achieve the simplification of organizational structure and the routinization of management control (Sorenson & Wiechmann, 1975; Levitt, 1983; Porter, 1985). On the contrary, research supporting adaptation in international marketing suggests that the aim of adaptation is to meet the special needs of the local market. Firms that follow the adaptation strategy pay great attention to giving play to the initiative and creativity of local subsidiaries. They capture opportunities in local market, identify unique demands of local consumers, and customize marketing mix to satisfy the needs of local consumers (Buzzell, 1968; Fisher, 1984). The standardization/adaptation debate is very important because the choice has a significant influence on the establishment and enhancement of a firm's international competitiveness (Shoham, 1994).

What is the context of the emergence of international marketing standardization? What does it imply? Upon what assumptions is it based? What is the theoretical background that drives firms to implement standardization strategies? On the other hand, what is the context of the emergence of the international marketing adaptation? What does it imply? On what assumptions is it based?

What is the theoretical background that drives firms to implement adaptation strategies? The answers to these questions would not only be conducive to the understanding of the essence/nature of the standardization/adaptation debate, but would also offer practical guidance for multinational corporations to develop effective international marketing strategies. The aim of this chapter is to explain and answer these questions.

This chapter reviews the existing literature regarding standardization and adaptation, discusses supporting arguments for each view, and explains assumptions and theoretical bases for each view. On this basis, the authors discuss the managerial implication of this chapter and point out the direction for future research.

3.2 The global standardization view

3.2.1 Supporting arguments for international marketing standardization

The view of global standardization first appeared in the field of advertising as an element of marketing mix. At the International Advertising Association (IAA) conference held in Spain in 1961, Elinder, president of a Swiss advertising agency and first vice president of the European branch of IAA, proposed the use of standardized advertising throughout Europe. Later, in the paper *How International Can European Advertising Be* published by Elinder, he expounded on his idea. He pointed out that advertising activity is the reflection of market demand. The popularity of American Magazine *Reader's Digest* in Europe is an indication that Americanism is spreading in the European market. The Americanism trend is resulting in the appearance and increase of "European consumers" (compared to other country-based consumers). Meanwhile, the cross-border transmission of media and personnel mobility within Europe has also promoted the emergence of European consumers in large quantity. The variety of consumer types requires the standardization of advertising campaigns within Europe. Promoting sales to European consumers through standardized advertising campaigns prevents disparity of brand perception and gives ease to people traveling across national borders.

Perlmutter was also among the first scholars to support global standardization. In his 1969 paper Perlmutter proposes the ethnocentrism, polycentrism, and geocentrism analysis framework (EPG framework). He argues that world-oriented multinational corporations should adopt global product strategies (i.e., product standardization) in their international operations. Wind *et al.* (1973) add egocentrism into the EPG framework, expanding it into the EPRG framework. Wind *et al.* suggest that global orientation is the ultimate goal and suggest that multinational corporations adopt global product strategies.

Buzzell (1968) points out the benefits of standardization, including: (1) Substantial cost saving – through standardization economies of scale can be achieved in such aspects as product design, manufacturing, packaging, and advertising, thus reducing cost. (2) Consistency with customers – in Europe's industrial market, for instance, customers in different countries expect that multinational suppliers provide the same products and services. They even demand the same price offering, allowing no discrimination. In addition, the emergence of multimarket audiences makes it necessary for consumer products advertising to maintain the same basic appeals and fundamentally unique brand images. The standardization of brand image, products, and services can meet these demands. (3) Improved planning and control – standardization of marketing planning and marketing policy can facilitate a firm's control over its subsidiaries in other countries. (4) Exploiting good ideas – for instance, a good advertising idea can be shared by subsidiaries in different countries and used in different markets.

The standardization/adaptation debate started from the publication of Levitt's paper *The Globalization of Markets* in 1983. In his paper Levitt writes: "The world is becoming a homogenized market. People everywhere are seeking the same products and lifestyles. Multinational companies should dilute the national and cultural differences but focus on meeting global needs." Levitt suggests that new communication, transportation, and transmission technologies have created a more homogeneous world. People across the world basically want the same things – things that make life more pleasant and give people more free time and greater purchase power. Increasingly homogenous needs and desires create a world market for standardized products. Levitt points out that conventional multinational corporations stress the differences between markets. They adapt to superficial differences and produce supposedly customized products, and they never question whether people can change their differences in terms of preferences and accept standardized products. Customization results in low efficiency and high cost. On the contrary, firms marketing their products worldwide adopt the same marketing methods and sell products that are fundamentally the same to all customers. They value the similarities of the world market and vigorously promote the sales of standardized products and services that suit all parts of the world. These international marketers achieve improved economic benefits through product standardization, distribution, marketing, and management. Consequently, firms can offer more reliable products and transfer the benefits and values generated by standardization to customers. Ohmae (1985) supports Levitt's view, pointing out that consumer demands in North America, Western Europe, and Japan (The Triad) are becoming increasingly homogenized, making it possible to standardize marketing strategies. Ohmae suggests that multinational corporations should attach importance to the commonality of countries and view the world as a single global market. Levitt's viewing of the world as a homogeneous market lays the foundation for the standardization strategy. Many scholars share his view nowadays.

3.2.2 Research scope of global standardization

1 Two dimensions of standardization in international marketing

International marketing standardization research generally includes two dimensions: process standardization and program standardization.

Marketing process standardization refers to the development of uniform marketing management practices for the global market, including the sequencing of tasks, problem-solving processes, decision-making processes, and performance evaluation procedures (Kreutzer, 1988; Jain, 1989). The study of Rafee and Kreutzer (1989) indicates that by building a common company language, creating a corporate culture in the parent company and global subsidiaries through job rotation, and standardized training and education, the firm can contribute to the successful development of a global marketing strategy. Most researchers in this area suggest that it is often more important and possible to standardize global marketing planning and decision-making than it is to standardize the entire marketing program. They are generally skeptical of the viability of complete marketing program standardization.

Program standardization refers to the development of a uniform marketing mix for global markets. It has been the focus of most standardization literature. Marketing mix standardization means the offering of identical product lines at identical prices through identical distribution systems, supported by identical promotional programs, for each country being targeted (Buzzell, 1968; Kreutzer, 1988). Aspects that need to be considered for standardization include product design, branding, packaging, price, advertising, sales promotion, media budget allocation, types and number of intermediates, and logistics, among others.

2   *Relevant research on international marketing mix standardization*

Of the four elements of marketing mix, a large number of studies have focused on promotional standardization, particularly on the standardization of advertising. According to the statistics of Jain (1989), more than half of studies regarding standardization have focused on promotion. Why has promotion standardization been extensively supported and noted? First, with the increasing similarities of consumer lifestyles and the emergence of more standardized products worldwide, the forms and contents of in-person promotion and advertising in different markets have become more and more homogenized, or standardized. Second involves the change of media. For instance, the popularization of commercial TV channels in different countries and the emergence of online media have made it easier for advertising to reach multinational or global audiences, thus requiring advertising to be more standardized (Buzzell et al., 1995).

There have also been many studies concentrating on the standardization of product and brand. Perlmutter (1969) proposes that world-oriented multinational firms should adopt global product strategies (namely product standardization) in their international operations. Levitt (1983) suggests that the advancement of communication technology enabled the rapid transmission of information worldwide and that transportation technology progress has accelerated the movement of personnel and commodities worldwide. Consumers are gradually giving up their unique lifestyle and consumption preferences in pursuing worldwide high-quality and low-cost products and services. This phenomenon is known as globalization, or homogenization, of the world markets. Therefore, for a homogenized global market, firms should employ standardized marketing approaches to offer standardized products to the global market. Takeuti and Porter (1986) indicate that although there are various market segments in a national market, some market segments in different countries possess the same characteristics or overlap one another. Such overlapping market segments constitute a homogenous multinational market, in which standardized products and standardized marketing tools can be used. Whitelock and Pimblett (1997) point out that standardization can be carried out in such aspects as product characteristics, conditions of use, consumption method, packaging, product aesthetics, taste, and labeling. The authors also note that there is an increasingly stronger tendency of the branding standardization of consumer durable goods.

In the matter of channel research, it is generally believed that cultural and traditional elements have a significant influence on the quality and effectiveness of channels. It is very difficult to achieve channel standardization (Douglas & Wind, 1987; Stern & El-Ansary, 1992). Therefore, the general method of developing global marketing channels is to tailor channel strategies to local conditions. Although academicians and practitioners generally concur that marketing channels cannot be standardized (Rosenbloom *et al.*, 1997), the study of Rosenbloom *et al.* (1997) indicates that the decision-making process and the formulation, implementation, and evaluation processes of marketing channels can be standardized.

In the matter of price research, it is generally agreed that the differences of taxation, channel system, competitive intensity, exchange rate, and other elements between countries make it impossible for firms to wield extensive control over price. Therefore, price standardization is very difficult (Buzzell *et al.*, 1995). Sorenson and Wiechmann (1975) point out that due to the differences between countries, price may be the element in the marketing mix that is most difficult to standardize. Because of the existence of price difference among markets in different countries, it is important to avoid transshipments or gray market in international marketing activities. Table 3.1 summarizes the theoretical bases and assumptions of standardization/adaptation topics.

3.2.3 Theoretical bases and assumptions of standardization

Supporters of standardization propose that economies of scale are the main force that drives international marketing standardization (Levitt, 1983; Porter, 1985). Cost and sale price can be reduced if a certain degree of economies of scale can be achieved. This can enhance a firm's competitiveness in global competition and promote customer acceptance worldwide. Levitt (1983) points out that "if a company forces costs and prices down and pushes quality up while maintaining reasonable concern for suitability customers will prefer its world standardized products." The cost savings are not merely confined to production, but also manifested in such aspects as R&D, purchase, distribution, promotion,

Table 3.1 Theoretical bases and assumptions of standardization/adaptation

Item	Standardization	Adaptation
Theoretical bases [drivers]	Economies of scale in low cost; economies of scale in other aspects such as manufacturing, R&D, advertising, promotion, channel, logistics, and accounting, among others	1. Segmentation and positioning • Market segmentation and precise positioning based on differences of each market • Differentiated price based on conditions of each market • Mass customization – customizing products for each individual customer 2. Friction theory • Home-country market vs. host-country market (friction between exporter and local agent) • Internal friction (friction between headquarters and local subsidiaries)
Assumptions	1. Homogeneous world markets (advanced information and communication technologies and convenience of transportation and travel), making cross-national segmentation possible 2. Cost reduction: possibility of low cost and increased sales	1. Heterogeneous international markets (increasing consumer differences in different markets), making internal market segmentation important 2. Price difference sufficient to compensate cost increase
Representative papers	Perlmutter (1969) Sorenson & Wiechmann (1975) Levitt (1983) Ohmae (1985) Kreutzer (1988) Jain (1989) Hill & Kwon (1992)	Buzzell (1968) Fisher (1984) Douglas & Wind (1987) Jain (1989) Samiee & Roth (1992) Shoham & Albaum (1994) Whitelock & Pimblett (1997)

advertising, and logistics (Porter, 1980). In addition, Yip (1989) suggests that standardization can improve planning and control and exploit personnel and ideas, creating economies of scale on the management front. This way, the economies of scale generated by standardization can increase a firm's market share, sales revenue, and profit. The firm can then reinvest in building more efficient plants, organizing new promotion campaigns, and developing better and lower-cost marketable products.

There are two basic assumptions for international marketing standardization strategies. The first is the emergence of a homogeneous world market (Levitt, 1983; Whitelock & Pimblett, 1997). Levitt points out the fundamental assumption for standardization strategies: the homogenization of markets. Levitt suggests that the advancement of communication technology has enabled the rapid transmission of information worldwide and that progress in transportation technology has accelerated the movement of personnel and commodities across the globe. High-quality and low-cost products are gaining more and more popularity worldwide since consumers in various markets are gradually giving up their unique ways of life and consumption preferences. This phenomenon is recognized as the globalization, or homogenization, of the world markets. In addition, a single country market contains multiple segments, and segments in different countries may overlap. These overlapping segments constitute a multinational homogeneous market. The standardization strategy is possible only when such homogeneous markets exist across the world. The second advantage is reduction of cost and improvement of firms' long-term performance. The adoption of a standardization strategy generates economies of scale, thus reducing cost and resulting in cost savings. However, the benefits resulting from standardization should not be offset by the potential losses caused by not adopting adaptation or differentiation. In the meantime, adoption of a standardization strategy can help firms maintain long-term cost leadership advantages and corresponding long-term marginal profits (Porter, 1980; Sheth, 1986; Whitelock & Pimblett, 1997).

In summary, supporters of the standardization strategy in international marketing propose that multinational corporations should choose global standardization strategies so as to achieve cost savings through economies of scale and learning effect because of the homogenization of world markets. Through standardization firms can achieve cost savings or reduction in such aspects as R&D, manufacturing, sales, logistics, and distribution. In addition, global standardization strategies can help firms develop unique images worldwide and achieve the simplification of organizational structure and routinization of management control.

3.3 Local adaptation view

3.3.1 Supporting arguments for international marketing adaptation

When the proposal of advertising standardization appeared in the 1960s it was immediately met with oppositions. Lenormand (1964) indicates that European countries have their own traditions, languages, customs, and cultures that cannot be changed in a short period of time. It would take at least centuries to form a significant population of the "European consumer" as described by Elinder. Roostal (1963) suggests that there are several major obstacles to advertising standardization: incomplete marketing planning, different languages, media, and laws and regulations in different countries, among others. Donnelly and Ryans (1969) conduct a questionnaire survey on more than 70 advertising managers, and the results show that advertising standardization was still not at a dominant position at that time.

Supporters of the local adaptation strategy point out that there are some major flaws in using the assumption of world homogenization and the economies of scale theory to support the standardization view. They suggest that universal standardization is an over-simplistic and once-off solution that would be inapplicable in practice (Killough, 1978; Douglas & Wind, 1987).

Douglas and Wind (1987) summarize the flaws of Levitt's assumptions from four perspectives. First, only a number of products share global market segments with similar or identical needs, and these global market segments are usually not very large in size. Therefore, these homogeneous markets cannot reflect the demands of all sorts of consumers in global markets. In other words, these homogenized market segments cannot represent the global market. Second, Levitt's standardization view stresses the similarities among markets but ignores their differences. Differentiated markets in different countries are generally markets that can generate substantial profits. Therefore, standardization strategy would result in failure to reap the benefits of the large number of differentiated market segments in different countries. Third, Levitt's view implies that consumers would sacrifice preference in certain product features and design for a lower price. As a matter of fact, consumers are often unwilling to trade product features and design for a better price. Fourth, standardization of production systems is not the only way to achieve economies of scale. Recent advancements in manufacturing technologies have made production systems more flexible, enabling multinational corporations to effectively meet differentiated market demands in different countries.

Whitelock and Pimblett (1997) criticize the standardization view from a marketing philosophy perspective. The authors point out that to concentrate on cost and to use this as a justification for standardization indicates a product or production orientation rather than a marketing one. They indicate that standardization is sometimes an excuse firms use to exploit their overcapacities. With overcapacity, a plant might produce more than the market demands in order to gain economies of scale. This would lead to further pushing down prices and eroding margins. Moreover, the authors also criticize the standardization view from the perspectives of competition and consumer behaviors. The authors report that achieving economies of scale through standardization and thus achieving cost savings and reduction would generally cause other firms to respond to the competition by cutting price, which would easily lead to a vicious price war. Moreover, price reduction would only attract price-sensitive consumers. Few manufacturers of global brand products would be willing to sacrifice profit for price competition. Manufacturers of these brands believe that when consumers perceive the value of high quality, they would feel a strong recognition of the brands and be willing to pay a premium for the products of such brands. Therefore, the success of multinational corporations is usually achieved by building up consumer loyalty through differentiated brand and quality, rather than through strategic price difference (Harris, 1985).

The study of Zhao and Mo (2001) indicates that cultural differences require multinational corporations to adopt adaptive marketing strategies. They study customer complaints in China's durables goods industry. Their findings show that due to the cultural differences between the east and the west (easterners have a higher level of collectivism while westerners have a higher level of individualism), westerners like to complain to others about what they have purchased, but easterners like to compliment others on their purchases. Such consumer behavioral differences mandate that firms treat them differently when formulating local marketing strategies.

3.3.2 Relevant research on marketing program and marketing decision-making process adaptation

Supporters of the adaptation view point out that differences of consumer behaviors, conditions of local competition, local market infrastructure, local economic status, political and legal regulations, and firms' internal organizational structure relations and ways of decision-making jointly impel multinational corporations to adopt local adaptation strategies in the matters of international marketing mix and marketing decision-making processes.

1 Relevant research on marketing mix adaptation

Shoham (1994) suggests that only product standardization, not other elements in a marketing mix, is being extensively accepted. In other words, the adaptation of other elements of marketing mix is being widely accepted. There are three reasons why marketing programs are seldom standardized. First, there exist differences in market conditions in different countries. Second, most basic elements that constitute marketing planning vary in different countries. Third, although standardization may bring cost reduction, the benefit of such cost reduction may be insignificant or may not even be perceived in actual operation. The empirical study of Hu *et al.* (2001) on Japanese electrical appliance companies confirms Shoham's research. The findings of Hu *et al.* (2001) indicate that in their global marketing campaigns Japanese electrical appliance firms normally adopt standardized product strategy (at least the standardization of core products), but would adapt to local market conditions in such aspects as price, channels, and promotion.

Buzzell (1968) and Hill and Kwon (1992) find that the differences of conditions of use of products and different regulations on product standardization in different countries spur firms to adopt adaptive product strategies. Kotler's (1986) study further shows that many well-known international brands have blundered due to failure to adopt a product adaptation strategy. Green and Cunningham (1975) and Doherty and Ennew (1995) point out that media type, effectiveness, coverage, and language have an impact on advertising information and promotion policy. Doherty and Ennew (1995) point out that the differences of factors that constitute a country's competitive advantages, including transportation cost, tax rate, income level, transaction habits, and communication methods, among others, make pricing policy dependent on local conditions. Martenson (1987) indicates that the structure and circulation conditions of the distribution systems, the effective number of distributors and retailers, and consumers' preferred shopping locations all vary greatly in different countries. Therefore, it is necessary for multinational corporations to adopt adaptive distribution policies based on local market conditions.

2 Relevant research on marketing process adaptation

Shanks (1985) lists three forces that motivate firms to explore the international market: maturation of the economies of the industrialized nations, emergence of new geographic markets and business arenas, and globalization of financial systems. Levitt (1983) views these factors as drivers of a standardization strategy, but Shanks (1985) suggests that these factors make a firm's coordination and allocation decisions more important and thus require the adoption of an adaptation strategy for marketing processes.

Although Shoham (1994) suggests that the globalization trend means that firms should standardize the decision-making process and adapt contents of marketing mix, Walters (1986) proposes that the standardization of marketing mix and marketing decision-making process simultaneously is impossible. Nonetheless, Hofstede (1993) points out that the contexts of the standardization of the marketing decision-making process are different in different countries, casting doubts on the marketing decision-making process. For instance, the differences of cultures and customs (such as personalities and attitudes towards risks) in different countries significantly influence the marketing decision-making process.

3.3.3 Theoretical bases and assumptions of adaptation

Supporters of adaptation point out that some assumptions used in the economies of scale theory to support standardization are untenable. They propose two theories to support adaptation strategy: the segmentation theory (Samiee & Roth, 1992) and the friction theory (Shoham & Albaum, 1994). The segmentation theory views the world as a homogeneous market. Using a more precise positioning strategy (i.e., local market adaptation strategy) based on the differences of local market segments can produce differentiated advantages and create conditions for quasi-monopolies and price discrimination. On this basis, a high price can be set, thus offsetting cost savings attainable through standardization (Samiee & Roth, 1992). In addition, the emergence of mass customization production technology makes it possible for multinational corporations to design and manufacture products for each market segment (even for each individual customer) and meet individualized demands at low production cost (Pine, 1993). On the contrary, a standardization strategy cannot simultaneously make use of the dual effect of quantity and price to maximize profit in the local market. In addition, the effect of each marketing mix variable varies in different markets. For instance, if the result of a TV commercial is better in a certain country than in another, then the use of a higher percentage of TV advertising in this certain country would be appropriate. The friction theory indicates that although standardization can generate economy of scale, it can also cause frictions between headquarters and subsidiaries (when there are local manufacturing and marketing organizations) and distribution channels (in the case of exporting). Such friction would somewhat impede the implementation of marketing mix strategy, thus increasing operation cost (coordination and allocation). If the cost incurred by such friction exceeds the cost savings attained by the economies of scale of standardization, then an adaptation strategy would be a better choice.

Generally speaking, academicians supporting the standardization view use the economies of scale theory to reduce cost in the profit equation. Academicians supporting adaptation, on the other hand, propose that the friction factor would increase the cost in the profit equation and that precise positioning would increase the price in the profit equation and increase sales revenue.

The adaptation view has two assumptions. First, the global market is heterogeneous. Supporters of the adaptation view suggest that there are significant differences in laws and regulations, natural conditions, traditional culture, economic level, and consumer behaviors, among other factors, in different country markets. Therefore the global market is heterogeneous. Particularly, nowadays a main characteristic of the domestic market is that it is more finely and extensively segmented, and the market itself is becoming more diversified. This is the result of the diversification and individualization of consumers' personal lifestyles. Consumers are becoming pickier and demanding more choices. Moreover, the globalization trend and intensifying of competition spur multinational firms to attach more importance to the needs of local market segments and require these firms to adopt localized marketing strategies. The second assumption is that price difference is sufficient to compensate for the increase in cost. Supporters of the adaptation view suggest that customizing a marketing mix tailored to the local target market can create a quasi-monopoly status that enables firms to set a higher price, thus offsetting the increase of cost incurred by adaptation and maximizing profit.

In conclusion, contrary to standardization, supporters of adaptation in international marketing suggest that the global market is heterogeneous and that multinational corporations should choose appropriate adaptation strategies to meet the unique demands of the local market. Firms that adopt adaptation strategies attach importance to giving play to the initiative and creativity of local subsidiaries, capturing opportunities in the local market, discovering unique demands of local consumers, and customizing marketing mix to satisfy local consumer demands.

3.4 Conclusions and directions for future research

3.4.1 Conclusions

1 The international marketing standardization view suggests that the market a multinational firm serves is a homogeneous (or almost homogeneous) global market. The firm, from the economies of scale perspective, should

adopt a standardized marketing strategy. This way, the firm cannot only attain cost savings in such aspects as R&D, manufacturing, sales, logistics, and distribution, but also can create a unique and uniform image worldwide and achieve the routinization of organizational coordination and control. Especially when the benefits produced by such standardization exceed the potential losses incurred by not adopting differentiation and organizational internal friction, then the adoption of standardization strategies would not only make it possible for firms to offer low-price products and services to global consumers at high quality, but also would enable firms to maintain cost-competitive advantages and make profits.

2   According to the international marketing adaptation view, if the market a multinational corporation serves is a heterogeneous or almost heterogeneous global market, then the firm should adopt an adaptation strategy out of considerations for the differences of segmentation and positioning and for reducing organizational friction cost. In this manner, the firm cannot only obtain differentiated competitive advantage by customizing marketing mix based on local market characteristics, but also can give play to the initiative and creativity of local subsidiaries. Especially when the benefits gained by the higher price that is set based on differentiated advantages and the saving of organization cost exceed the potential losses incurred by not adopting standardization, then the adoption of adaptation strategies would not only enable a firm to meet the unique demands of the local market, but also would help the firm maintain its differentiated competitive advantages and make profits.

3   From the perspective of standardization, there are some flaws in adaptation strategies, such as difficulty to achieve the synergy effect and high operation cost, among others. From the perspective of adaptation, there are also flaws in global standardization, such as restraining the creativity of local subsidiaries, inability to meet different demands of local markets, and susceptibility to missing market opportunities, among others. Therefore, pure standardization and pure adaptation are the two extremes of the international marketing strategy choice continuum. An actual international marketing strategy in practice should be somewhere between complete standardization and complete adaptation (Jain, 1989; Shoham, 1995). It is in fact a matter of a higher degree of standardization or of adaptation.

Five propositions drawn from these three conclusions

Proposition 1: If the international market has a high degree of homogeneity, then the degree of standardization of international marketing would be high.

Proposition 2: If the international market has a high degree of heterogeneity, then the degree of adaptation of international marketing would be high.

Proposition 3: If there is a high possibility that the benefits produced by standardization would be greater than the potential losses incurred by not adopting differentiation and organizational internal friction, then the possibility of a firm adopting standardization strategies would also be high.

Proposition 4: If there is a high possibility that the benefits gained by the higher price that is set based on differentiated advantages and the saving of organization friction cost would be higher than the potential losses incurred by not adopting standardization, than the possibility of a firm adopting adaptation strategies would also be high.

Proposition 5: Generally speaking, pure standardization or adaptation is not possible.

The significance of the study of this topic is twofold: first, in theory it explains the theoretical bases and assumptions of the standardization/adaptation view in international marketing and reveals the essence of the lasting standardization/adaptation debate; second, in practice it offers practical implications for multinational corporations to develop effective international marketing strategies. Hence, the five propositions put forward in this chapter offer viable choices and judgment criteria for firms to customize their international marketing strategies.

3.4.2 Directions for future research

As mentioned prior, neither full standardization nor full adaptation is possible. An effective international marketing strategy should be within these two extremes. It is in fact a matter of a higher degree of standardization or of adaptation. Therefore, future research should focus on the composite study of standardization and adaptation (Kadomatsu *et al.*, 1996). Specifically, what conditions would justify the standardization/adaptation of certain aspects, and to what extent?

In addition, there are two aspects of international marketing standardization/adaptation: marketing process and marking program. To date, a substantial proportion of relevant research has been directed at marketing mix standardization/adaptation. In the matter of marketing process standardization/adaptation, there's been little theoretical research (Kreutzer, 1988) and even less empirical research (Rosenbloom *et al.*, 1997). In addition, although some scholars have pointed out that there is a relation between marketing process and marketing mix, systematic explanation and empirical research have been missing. Therefore, the standardization and adaptation of marketing process and the relationship between marketing process and marketing mix are promising topics for future studies.

4 Characteristics and formation mechanism of born-global firms

Zuohao Hu and Xi Chen

4.1 Introduction

Research on firms' internationalization process has always been a frontier subject in the field of international marketing (Hu, 2002b; Sharma & Blomstermo, 2003; Wu & Yuan, 2003; Xu, 2003). In the 1970s, scholars from the University of Uppsala proposed the "stages" model (Johanson & Vahlne, 1977). According to the stage model, a firm follows a sequence of stages in its international expansion. The firm would initially choose a geographically closer market, and as it gains international experience and foreign market knowledge from its international operation, it would gradually expand into more distant markets. From then the stage model has gained extensive support both theoretically and empirically (Johanson & Vahlne, 1990).

Since the 1990s, an extensive number of studies indicate that an increasing number of small and medium-sized firms make vigorous efforts to explore the international market shortly after their establishment in order to gain competitive advantages. Refusing to be confined to the narrow space of the domestic market, these firms view the global market as a rare opportunity and aim at it from the start. The born-global firms gain a significant proportion of their revenue from overseas markets. Those firms have a rather short time of preparation/accumulation before exporting. Those firms do not follow the conventional stage model in their internationalization processes. Instead they emerge through a completely new pattern of internationalization. These firms are defined as "born globals" academically, and the mode of their internationalization is called the "born-global model" (Knight & Cavusgil, 1996). The born-global phenomenon first appeared in countries with small domestic markets and is now widespread across the world. It is now a topic intensively studied by international marketing researchers.

This chapter reviews relevant academic research on the born-global phenomenon in the past 10 years and attempts to answer two questions. First, what kind of internationalization path do these born-global firms take, and how does the internationalization process of these firms differ from that of traditional firms that follow the stage model? Second, what factors influence these small and medium-sized firms and drive them to take such an innovative approach to internationalization? Following this thought, this chapter first reviews existing literature, then analyzes and summarizes the key attributes of born-global firms and their fundamental differences from traditional Uppsala-model firms, examines the drivers and formation mechanism of born-global firms, and points out the direction for future research.

4.2 The emergence of born-global firms

Before the emergence of born-global research, the academic world had always held the Uppsala model in esteem. The Uppsala model suggests that there are two basic reasons why firms should internationalize gradually in different stages: first, managers' risk avoidance tendency and market uncertainty; second, the lack of foreign market knowledge and experience. Research findings indicate that the stage model is suitable for small and medium-sized firms as well as for large corporations (Johanson & Vahlne, 1990).

Since the 1990s, a substantial number of studies in developed countries indicate the emergence of an important international marketing phenomenon among small and medium-sized exporters and the formation of a new internationalization model thereby (Knight & Cavusgil, 1996; Madsen & Servais, 1997; Chetty & Campbell-Hunt, 2004).

The study of Turnbull (1987a) shows that many small and medium-sized exporters in the UK do not follow the traditional stage model in their internationalization processes. Instead, these firms grow in a leap-forward manner, as manifested in two aspects. First, in terms of target market choice, these firms enter geographically distant markets first instead of close markets. Second, on the export-mode front, these firms don't make progress step by step but skip some intermediate phases and go onto the higher level directly. Rennie's (1983) study of Australian firms finds that the founders of some firms view the whole world as their market from the inception, without giving consideration to the psychic distance of markets. These firms generally compete on quality and value created through innovative technology and product design. They are close to their customers in international niche markets (such as scientific instruments or machine tools), flexible, and capable of adapting their products to quickly changing demands.

Bell (1995) studies small computer software firms and concludes that the conventional stages theory cannot properly explain these firms' internationalization processes. Bell finds that client followership, segmentation targeting, and industry-specific factors, rather than psychic distance from the export destination, strongly influence the processes and manners of the internationalization of these firms. The findings of this research do not support the traditional incremental internationalization model of progressing systematically from exporting to other market entry modes. Bell also discovers that some firms do not even become firmly established in the domestic market before they start exporting (Bell, 1995). Moen and Servais (2002) empirically study a sample of 677 small to medium-sized firms from Norway, France, and Denmark.

The authors examine the influences of three factors – time of establishment, the first time of export, and the interval between establishment and export commencement – on export intensity, distribution, market selection, and global orientation. The results show that born-global firms do exist in great number (one-third of the firms report that the time period between establishment and export commencement is less than two years). On average, these firms outperform other firms in terms of export intensity (or export rate). The results also indicate that the future export involvement of a firm is, to a large extent, influenced by its behavior (export or non-export) shortly after establishment. The results further indicate that the development of resources in support of international market competitiveness may be regarded as the key issue and that the basic resources and competencies of the firm are determined during the establishment phase.

The studies mentioned here show that some small to medium-sized firms aim at the overseas market from the outset of their establishment. These firms vigorously make use of all sorts of resources, and a substantial proportion of their sales revenue is attributed to overseas markets. These small to medium-sized firms, known as "born globals," do not follow the internationalization process of the traditional stage model but adopt a new type of internationalization model.

4.3 Characteristics of born-global firms

Many studies indicate that born-global firms and traditional-global firms differ in several aspects, and these differences illustrate the key attributes of born-global firms.

The most significant trait of born-global firms is that their founders (or managers) possess international visions and ambitions to explore the international market. Oviatt and McDougall (1997) name such managers the core intangible assets of born-global firms and point out that the existence of such managers constitutes the biggest difference between a born-global firm and a traditional-global firm. Chetty and Campbell-Hunt (2004) explain the reasons that cause those differences between born-global and traditional-global firms in their paper. First, managers of born-global firms possess greater prior knowledge and work experience that could reduce the psychic distance to specific markets and minimize risk and uncertainty. Second, the prior international experience of born-global firms' founders (and decision makers) plays an important role in increasing the firms' speed of learning and internationalization. Because born-global firms begin with basic knowledge about internationalization, they are better at accumulating new knowledge about internationalization. Traditional international firms, on the other hand, accumulate their international experience gradually as they grow. Third, managers of born-global firms are better at using up-to-date communication technologies to acquire new knowledge, develop strategies, and maintain relationships to assist them in accelerating their internationalization. Fourth, these managers have developed distinctive entrepreneurial capabilities and the foresight to spot windows of opportunity on a global scale that others overlook.

Chetty and Campbell-Hunt (2004) analyze the differences between traditional-global firms and born-global firms in terms of internationalization speed, prior international experience, and learning capability. First, traditional-global firms follow the stage model in their internationalization; second, traditional-global firms grow at the domestic market first and expand into overseas markets gradually; third, traditional-global firms do not possess prior international experience, and they need to learn and accumulate international knowledge incrementally. Born-global firms, on the other hand, show accelerated internationalization as they have started developing international business since the inception. In addition, in terms of expansion mode, born-global firms launch the domestic market and the international market simultaneously or even launch the international market first. Moreover, the rich prior international experience possessed by born-global firms before establishment allows them to learn fast in their subsequent international operation. The study of Aaby and Slater (1989) indicates that born-global firms' main export considerations include seizing first-mover advantages, seeking overseas target market segments, increasing international market involvement, and attaining international competitive advantages.

Since the entry mode and process of traditional-global firms are functions of psychic distance, they consider psychic distance as an important criterion in the choice of target markets. However, Bell (1995) suggests that client followership, segmentation targeting, and industry trends are truly substantive determinants to global firms' market selection. The choice of foreign market of born-global firms is not significantly related to psychic distance. Traditional-global firms would offer a wide range of products to multiple market segments, but born-global firms tend to offer high-technology and high-quality products to niche markets and provide differentiated and customized products and services, with some products being globally leading. Born-global firms' obsessive attention to quality brings them continuously improving competence and performance (Chetty & Campbell-Hunt, 2004).

Before the establishment of born-global firms, their internationally experienced managers, with their own connections, usually have established international marketing networks that include suppliers, distributors, and dealers. Such networks play an important role in these firms' rapid entry into the international market. From the perspectives of cost and experience, resource-restrained and young born-global firms with limited knowledge of the international market are more inclined to adopt an intermediary mode (agents) or joint-governance mode (joint ventures) and are more dependent on social connections and relationships, so as to make the best use of external resources and enter the international market rapidly (Burgel et al., 2000). Traditional-global firms, on the other hand, tend to build marketing networks step by step and accumulate marketing experience in their internationalization by building their own channels and establishing foreign branches and subsidiaries. Chetty and

Campbell-Hunt (2004) point out that traditional-global firms view networks as an important device and resource in the early stage of internationalization and in the subsequent international expansion process. Born-global firms also share this view and emphasize the importance of networks. The difference is that for born-global firms, the networks must be adequately extensive to enable extensive global reach and created rapidly to support exposure to multiple markets (Chetty & Campbell-Hunt, 2004).

Johanson and Vahlne (1990) explain the differences between traditional-global firms and born-global firms from the perspectives of the two assumptions of the stage model. They suggest that traditional-global firms' adoption of the stage model is based on two basic assumptions: first, firms hope to sustain operation and achieve long-term profit while keeping risk at the lowest level; second, traditional-global firms' lack of international experience and high perception of market risk and uncertainties in the international market lead them to increase their international market involvement incrementally by each stage. Therefore, the accumulation of gaining international experience would be a rather long process. Johanson and Vahlne (1990) point out that although the first assumption may also be suitable for born-global firms, the second one is not. Born-global firms have many entrepreneurs or managers who possess overseas experience. Their perceived risk in the international market is rather low. Their prior work experience and international-oriented ideas, combined with their previous clients and partners on the upstream and downstream of the value chain, can help their firms gain overseas market operation experience and knowledge easier and give them more courage and confidence to explore the international market. Therefore, born-global firms' decision-making process regarding overseas market involvement would be swifter.

Based on the aforementioned review and analysis, the main differences between traditional-global firms (adopting the stage model) and born-global firms (adopting the born-global model) are illustrated in Table 4.1.

4.4 Formation mechanism of born-global firms

The internationalization path of born-global firms differs greatly from that of traditional-global firms. What are the factors that drive them onto such a different path of internationalization? What is the formation mechanism of these firms? Scholars have conducted a great number of empirical studies, from different perspectives, on the formation mechanism of born-global firms. Based on these studies, determinants of the formation of born-global firms can be divided into two major categories. The first category is external environmental factors, which are external conditions necessary for the formation of born-global firms. The second category is firm-level factors, which are internal factors necessary for the formation of these firms. The formation of born-global firms is the result of the comprehensive interaction of these two categories of factors.

Table 4.1 Comparisons of the attributes of traditional-global firms and born-global firms

	Traditional-global firms	Born-global firms
Founders or managers	• International experience accumulated gradually after the establishment of firms and as firms grow	• Entrepreneurs are core intangible assets of born-global firms • Their extensive international activities and living and work experience equip their firms with international experience even before establishment; better at using the latest technologies; global orientation
Internationalization speed and foreign market selection	• Gradual and incremental internationalization • Domestic market developed first; gradual expansion in the domestic market before serial development in new overseas markets • Entry mode and process are functions of psychic distance, which is an importance criterion in the choice of target market	• Actively seek overseas target markets, start international business shortly after establishment, rapid penetration into foreign market segments • Launch the domestic and the international market at the same time or even launch the international market first; foreign market selection determined by factors like business networks and associations • Foreign target market selection shows no significant association with psychic distance
International experience and learning capability	• Lack prior international experience • Need to gradually learn and accumulate international experience • International experience accumulated after the establishment of firms and gradually as the firms grow	• Managers possess extensive international experience before establishment of firms and rapid learning capability in firms' international operation
Product strategy	• Usually offer a wide range of products to numerous market segments simultaneously	• Offer specialized high-tech products and differentiated and customized products and services with high quality to niche markets; such products could be globally leading, contributing to firms' high performance

(*Continued*)

Table 4.1 (Continued)

	Traditional-global firms	Born-global firms
Marketing networks	• Build own distribution networks and gradually accumulate marketing experience	• Adopt intermediary mode or mixed-governance mode instead of building own overseas subsidiaries or branches
Market uncertainty and risk perception	• Lack experience or roadmap in international operation; high risk perception; more inclined to choose safer approaches to foreign market involvement	• Have many entrepreneurs or managers who possess overseas experience and whose perceived risk in the international market is rather small; their prior work experience and international-oriented ideas give firms more courage and confidence to explore the international market, and, therefore, their overseas market involvement decision-making would be swifter

External determinants of the formation of born-global firms include market turbulence, changing consumer behaviors, industrial environment, and technological advances in information and communications technologies, production methods, transportation, and international logistics. These external environmental factors are external conditions that are necessary for the formation of born-global firms.

Changing market conditions are manifested in three aspects: first, the globalization of markets; second, the liberalization of trade; and third, the finer segmentation of markets and increasing appeal of overseas markets. Knight and Cavusgil (2004) point out that globalization plays an important role in the internationalization of firms. Globalization of markets involves countless firms in international sourcing, production, and marketing as well as cross-border alliances for product development and distribution. Globalization is associated with increasing homogenization of buyer preferences around the world, which has made international business easier by simplifying product development and positioning in foreign markets. Therefore, the globalization of markets is conducive to the formation of born-global firms. Second, with new competitive landscape resulting from the liberalization of trade, firms find it easier to export to and explore overseas markets than to compete in the intensively competitive domestic market. Born-global firms seize opportunities in the international market and accelerate their internationalization process. Therefore, the liberalization of trade can promote the emergence of born-global firms. Third, in developed countries, a more specialized, customized, and finer segmented domestic market would cause relevant niche markets at home to lose the economies of scale. As a result, firms would have no choice but to expand their vision, explore the vast space of the international market, and meet the huge demands in the international market with customized products (Madsen & Servais, 1997). Therefore, the finer segmentation of markets and the increasing appeal of foreign markets are also drivers of the formation of born-global firms.

In the matter of changing consumer behaviors, Oviatt and McDougall (1997) stress the importance of the global homogenization of consumer demands in the formation of born-global firms. They point out that technological advances have enabled people worldwide to communicate more frequently and extensively and have caused global consumer demands to become increasingly homogenized. The result is that high-tech products are spreading across the world faster and being accepted worldwide. This generates extensive demands. The trend of the global homogenization of consumer demands and the export traction it generates provide possibilities for firms to export products rapidly to various overseas markets, which facilitates the formation of born-global firms.

In the matter of industrial environment, Jolly *et al.* (1992) indicate that the globalization of industries provides greater possibilities for the emergence of born-global firms. Many industries need global sourcing, and the global sourcing of resources drives firms to internationalize. Similarly, the globalization of clients also impels upstream vendors and service providers to globalize. For instance, the globalization of whole-vehicle carmakers would propel the globalization of many auto parts suppliers.

Technological advances in information and communications technologies, production methods, transportation, and international logistics have also increased the possibilities of the formation of born-global firms. McDougall *et al.* (1994) point out that advances in communication (especially the emergence of the Internet) make it easier for firms to approach overseas customers, overseas distributors, and network partners and suppliers. The development of information and communication technologies enables firms to contact customers more easily and access more information about foreign markets, local distributors, and potential risk investment partners. Madsen and Servais (1997) study factors that contribute to the formation of born-global firms and point out that the development of information technology, the development of new flexible production technologies, the elevated importance of niche markets, and the lowering of trade barriers are all important factors that drive the emergence of a large number of born-global firms. McDougall *et al.* (1994) point out that better transportation and communication technologies reduce firms' fear for the international market. They used to be afraid of going into foreign markets due to concerns about the excessive cost of transportation and their lack of knowledge about those markets. The lowering of the transport cost barrier and the alleviation of overseas market uncertainties give a large number of small and medium-sized firms more chances to participate in the international market. Technological developments in the areas of information networks and communication, production, transportation, and international logistics help small and medium-sized firms seek business partners and acquire needed resources in the international market in exporting and internationalizing activities, which will give impetus to the formation of born-global firms.

Firm-level determinants of the formation of born-global firms include unique advantages of the firms, founders and managers with international experience and vision, organizational innovation capabilities, ability to use external resources, marketing orientation of the firms, technology, and market selection strategies, among others. These are internal conditions that are necessary for the formation of born-global firms.

Born-global firms tend to be small or medium in size. Compared to large firms, smaller firms have unique advantages. For instance, small and medium-sized enterprises (SMEs) enjoy the absence of bureaucratic organization and high information cost that large firms bear. In addition, SMEs are more creative, more customer oriented, more flexible and adaptive, and more sensitive and quicker to use new technologies to satisfy new demands (Covin *et al.*, 1989). These unique characteristics of small and medium-sized firms are necessary conditions for the formation of born-global firms.

Among all the internal factors that affect the formation of born-global firms, founders or management teams with international experience and vision are considered the most important determinants by academics. Madsen and Servais (1997) suggest that it is important to retrospect the history of born-global firms, even beyond their establishment. Such firms are started by genuine entrepreneurs or by very experienced persons, and these persons have extensive international experience (including a personal network) and do not perceive of their native country as the nucleus of their lives. These entrepreneurs don't view entering the international market as an uncertain adventure but as a rare opportunity for growth. They have lofty aspirations, strong internationalization and export motivations, international visions, and great ambitions for international operation. Their international experience and international entrepreneurial orientation give them strong motivation and determination to lead their firms into the international market. The study of Madsen and Servais (1997) indicates that the increase of the number of managers with international background and experience is an important reason for the emergence of born-global firms in large number.

Innovation strategy and organizational innovation capabilities drive the formation of born-global firms. Knight and Cavusgil (2004) use a sample of 203 small to medium-sized exporters in the US and examine the international marketing performance of born-global firms. Empirical research findings show that, for small and medium-sized firms, youth and lack of experience, as well as paucity of financial, human, and tangible resources, are no longer major impediments to the large-scale internationalization and global success of the firm. Moreover, the adoption of innovative international marketing strategies can bring desirable performance. They point out that the achievements of product/technology advantages, effective cooperation with external members, and integrated market decision-making require firms to possess organizational innovation capabilities. Such organizational innovation capabilities are reflected in the following: a firm's rapid response to the international market, a corporate culture of valuing innovation and paying close attention to changes, encouraging employee involvement in management, attaching importance to organizational knowledge learning, and attaching importance to innovating international marketing strategies and operation modes (Knight & Cavusgil, 2004).

The ability to use external resources drives the formation of born-global firms as well. In comparison with other exporting firms, born-global firms more often rely on supplementary competences sourced from other firms, as their internal resources are usually not sufficient to achieve their goals. For instance, Madsen and Servais (1997) point out that in their distribution channels born-global firms more often rely on hybrid structures (direct sales, indirect sales, close relationships, network partners, joint ventures, etc.). Moreover, because of the international background and experience of their founders, they are able to hire and work with people from different backgrounds open-mindedly. This way, they can better exploit the experience and intelligence of external personnel.

Organizational marketing orientation drives the formation of born-global firms. Knight and Cavusgil (2004) find that marketing plays an important role in overseas markets and that organizational marketing orientation[1] is critical to the success of born-global firms. Knight and Cavusgil (2004) suggest that a marketing orientation provides the foundation for firms to interact with diverse foreign markets. Only marketing-oriented firms can rapidly discover and understand the demands of overseas customers, rapidly adopt marketing measures to quickly meet such overseas demands, and conduct a vigorous international operation from inception. In the meantime, firms with a marketing orientation can create specific marketing-related strategies to overcome various challenges and achieve superior performance (Knight & Cavusgil, 2004).

Technology and market selection strategies also affect the formation of born-global firms. Jolly *et al.* (1992) indicate that factors like niche market, industry-specific attributes, and consumer demand customization strongly influence the internationalization processes and behaviors of small and medium-sized firms. They find that compared to traditional exporters born-global firms tend to appear more frequently in the high-tech sector and specialize in specific niche markets. Jolly *et al.* (1992) suggest that high-tech born-global firms tend to conduct sales and marketing activities directly with potential clients, so they need to approach the market rapidly and apply cutting-edge technologies quickly so as to build competitive advantages.

4.5 Conclusions and directions for future research

This chapter analyzes and reviews relevant literature in recent years, reveals the essential differences between born-global firms and traditional-global firms, and examines the formation mechanism and driving forces of born-global firms. The theoretical contribution of this chapter lies in that it extensively and systematically answers two key questions: First, how do born-global firms differ from traditional-global firms, and what kind of internationalization path do they take? Second, what factors drive them onto such an internationalization path, and what is the formation mechanism of these firms? By providing answers to these two questions this chapter enriches the findings of international research on born-global firms and lays a solid foundation for future studies.

Moreover, in terms of practical significance, the research in this chapter provides important reference value for Chinese small and medium-sized firms that are planning to carry out international marketing activities, in three ways. First, this chapter provides a new mode option for Chinese small and medium-sized firms in the choice of internationalization path, helping them make appropriate choices in their internationalization processes. There is a substantial quantity of studies indicating that firm globalization is an incremental process; the Uppsala stage model has been extensively validated both theoretically and practically. Wu and Yuan (2003) also suggest that Chinese firms should follow the rules of the incremental process of the internationalization of multinational corporations, and Hu and Koyo (2006) on Chinese multinational firms (e.g., companies such as Haier and others) also indicates that the internationalization of these multinational firms has basically followed the incremental internationalization pattern. In spite of the previous discussion, the study of this chapter indicates that, besides the incremental stage model, there is another development model, in other words, the born-global model, available for China's large number of small and medium-sized firms that are planning to carry out international marketing activities. This alternative model can help them achieve leap-forward development. Second, this chapter suggests that internationalization should not focus merely on the pursuit of export volume or the number of overseas subsidiaries and branches, but more importantly on the implications of internationalization. In appearance a born-global firm is one that can achieve a substantial part of its total sales revenue from overseas markets, but in essence, such leap-forward growth is the result of the born-global firm's attaching importance to the implications of internationalization. Research suggests that born-global firms have managers who possess international experience and vision, adopt innovative marketing-oriented strategies, and possess organizational capabilities in such aspects as innovation, external resource exploitation, and technology development. All these factors enable born-global firms to achieve accelerated internationalization in a short period of time. This point particularly possesses practical significance to Chinese firms that are carrying out international operations. It requires that Chinese firms make vigorous efforts in the essential aspects of internationalization (e.g., international operation mode, international marketing strategy, organizational innovation and human resources, production and technology development, optimal allocation of resources, etc.), so as to improve the overall internationalization level of Chinese firms. Third, this chapter points out a direction for small and medium-sized firms that are planning to adopt the born-global model. Research shows that before deciding whether to adopt the born-global strategy, a firm needs to have a clear picture of the formation mechanism of born-global firms and vigorously analyze whether it possesses the necessary international and external conditions and whether it is capable of taking measures and using strategies to attain these conditions. This chapter provides these firms with an effective analysis framework, which can help firms that are intending to adopt the born-global model to successfully implement the strategy.

Nonetheless, from the prior review and analysis we can see that there are still limitations to born-global firms research that require further studies. These limitations are reflected to three aspects:

1 Studies concerning born-global firms generally consider that the legitimacy of a born-global firm is the starting time of the firm. However, some scholars believe that when studying a born global, the time perspective should be extended prior to its birth. Probably many of its "genes" have roots back to firms and networks in which its founder(s) and top managers gained industry experience (Madsen & Servais, 1997). Therefore, we need to extend research on born-global firms prior to the time at which they were incorporated and investigate the overseas experience of the founders and the formation of their commercial and business networks.

2 Existing research on born-global firms concentrates basically in the high-tech industry (knowledge-intensive industry) or niche markets, with little discussion on traditional industries (labor-intensive industries) or the service sector (such as the consulting market). Some academicians even go so far as to suggest that born-global firms exist only in the high-tech sector. However, Moen and Servais (2002) conduct empirical research on 677 small and medium-sized firms from Norway, France, and Denmark and find that born-global firms also exist in some traditional industries. Therefore, future research may focus on investigating born-global firms in traditional industries and the service sector.

3 Although this chapter examines the formation mechanism and driving forces of born-global firms, such examination is summarized from various research findings from different perspectives. Therefore, an integrated analysis with empirical tests is still missing. In addition, there have been few empirical studies on the determinants of the formation and performance of born-global firms (Hu & Chen, 2007; Knight & Cavusgil, 2004). Therefore, it is necessary to establish a comprehensive theoretical framework for the formation mechanism of born-global firms and identify and validate key determinants of the formation of born-global firms through empirical research. Finally, it is necessary to investigate what factors drive born-global firms to achieve superior performance and the extent of the influences of such factors.

Note

1 Organizational marketing orientation refers to a firm's capability to create values for overseas customers.

5 Price leadership or branding strategy for Chinese firms

Xi Chen, Zuohao Hu and Ping Zhao

5.1 Introduction

With globalization and the rapid development of China's economy, an increasing number of Chinese firms are carrying out export marketing activities to explore the international market. According to statistics from the Ministry of Commerce of the People's Republic of China, China's export volume amounted to US$969 billion in 2006, with US$405.2 billion contributed by Chinese firms (and the rest US$563.8 billion by foreign-funded firms). This indicates that Chinese firms are conducting international operations mainly through export, which belongs to the early stage of internationalization.[1] Currently, there are two views regarding Chinese firms' export strategies. The first view advocates price leadership strategy (PLS). According to the PLS, many Chinese firms do not possess adequate international marketing experience or sufficient international resources (such as technology and capital). Consequently, these firms should adopt the OEM (original equipment manufacturing) mode to explore the international market based on cost advantages (Jin, 2004). The other view supports the adoption of branding strategy. According to branding strategy, Chinese firms should enhance technology and R&D capabilities and develop high-quality products and implement differentiated international marketing by the virtue of private brands. Only by establishing powerful brands can Chinese exporters gain higher profits in the international market and lay a solid foundation for international operation and long-term growth (Nie & Wang, 2006).

Which strategy, PLS or branding, should Chinese firms adopt in their international marketing processes at the current stage? To answer this question, we need to first study the relationship between export marketing strategies and export performance. As a matter of fact, what export strategies Chinese firms should adopt in order to achieve satisfactory performance in international marketing operation has long been a research topic of interest to China's academics and businesses.

The relationship between international marketing strategy and performance has also long been a frontier research topic in the field of international marketing. Many scholars have conducted empirical research on the relationship between international marketing strategy and performance. However, literature review suggests contradictory empirical research findings in this research area. For instance, while some studies find a negative relationship between low-price strategy (cost leadership) and export performance (Brouthers & Xu, 2002), other studies also find that by adopting a cost-leadership strategy, export performance can be enhanced (Zou *et al.*, 2003) or unaffected (Samiee & Roth, 1992). In addition, some studies find more complicated effects of cost-leadership strategy on export performance. We propose that the different impacts of cost-leadership strategy on export performance are due to the various international markets in which exporting firms are located. Take Miller (1988), for instance; the author finds that low-cost strategy is more effective in a steady market while a differentiation strategy is more appropriate in a turbulent market. This contingent effect indicates that the impact of international marketing strategy on export performance is moderated by international market environmental factors. The marketing segmentation theory tells us that firms should choose corresponding international marketing strategies based on the unique marketing conditions of each country (Kotler, 2003). The strategic adaptation theory tells us that because of the differences of the macro environments between developed countries and developing countries and the differences of industrial competition and consumption demand levels, among other factors, a firm that exports to numerous overseas markets could achieve satisfactory performance only when it chooses an international marketing strategy that fits the specific environments (Venkatraman & Prescott, 1990). Therefore, to study the relationship between international marketing strategies and performance, it is important to research the relationship in the contexts of the different market conditions. Moreover, academic research regarding the relationship between international marketing strategies and performance focuses mainly on firms in developed countries. However, there is insufficient empirical research on the relationship between export marketing strategies and performance in firms located in developing countries (Aulakh *et al.*, 2000). Meanwhile, theoretical and empirical research on the relationship between the international marketing strategic choice and the performance of Chinese exporting firms is still limited. Therefore, it is imperative that Chinese scholars conduct extensive and systematic research to enrich this field (Hu, 2002a).

The purpose of this chapter is to empirically study the relationship between Chinese firms' international marketing strategic choice and performance in the context of different target market conditions applying the strategy adaptation theory and marketing segmentation theory. More specifically, this chapter uses a sample of Chinese manufacturing exporters to examine Chinese exporters' choice between price leadership strategy and branding strategy when facing different target markets (developed countries and developing countries) in order to achieve desirable export performance. This chapter also investigates whether the size and international experience of exporters affect export performance satisfaction.

5.2 Theoretical framework and hypotheses

According to the strategy-environment co-alignment view, if a firm's international marketing strategy is congruent with the overseas market environment, resources will be optimally matched with the environment according to strategic requirements and utilized to the maximum, thus achieving satisfactory performance (Venkatraman & Prescott, 1990). According to the marketing segmentation theory, firms can achieve satisfactory performance only when they choose corresponding marketing strategies based on the specific environment and conditions of respective target country markets (Kotler, 2003). Therefore, the export performance of Chinese manufacturing exporters depends on the exporting strategies they choose for different overseas market environments.

There are great differences between the market environments of developed countries and developing countries. Chinese exporters target both developed countries and developing ones, and we suggest that the influences of price leadership strategy and branding strategy on performance are different in these two types of target markets. Consequently, we propose, on the basis of reviewing relevant theories and literature, to research hypotheses regarding the relationships between the exporting strategies and export performance of Chinese firms under different market conditions.

In terms of market and industry attributes, developed countries have a longer history of market economy, sufficient resources, well-developed markets that are approaching saturation, and greater industrial competition, and multinational corporations from developed countries show greater strengths in such aspects as management experience, capital, and R&D. From the perspective of consumers, consumers demands in developed markets tend to be more diversified and segmented. In order to stimulate and maintain sales, firms need to keep introducing new products into the markets. Therefore, as consumer demands are continuously satisfied consumers' preferences keep changing, too. From the perspective of brand building, developed countries' multinational firms have more resources to cultivate brands (Dominguez & Sequeira, 1993). They have a longer history of brand operation, more experience, many century-old brands (Aaker, 1996), and a great number of loyal customers. Well-established local brands create a brand barrier for market entry. It would require a lot of resources and time for manufacturing exporters located in emerging markets like China to adopt the branding strategy in developed markets, where competition is fierce, consumer demands are segmented, and brand entry barrier is high. The difficulty would be great. Meanwhile, from the perspective of the country-of-origin effects, Han and Terpstra (1988) indicate that a poor country-of-origin image produces a negative influence on consumers' attitudes towards brands and product evaluation. Cordell (1993) and other scholars find that consumers from target developed countries see products and services from developing countries as of low quality and low price. Therefore, when building brands in developed markets, Chinese firms would also be confronted with the challenge of brand barrier. In the matter of

Chinese firms' characteristics, they may be weaker in such aspects as technology and new product development, but they possess great cost-based advantages. Chinese exporters can research, develop, produce, market, and operate well-established products at lower costs, competing in developed markets by means of price strategy. Therefore, we propose that in developed markets with fierce competition from powerful foreign firms it would be difficult for China's manufacturing exporters to achieve satisfactory performance by adopting branding strategy. The price leadership strategy, on the other hand, enables Chinese firms to make the best use of cost advantages. It is consistent with developed country consumers' perception and matches the country-of-origin image of China. PLS, therefore, can help Chinese firms gain competitive advantages and achieve satisfactory export performance. Hence, taking into consideration the characteristics of developed markets and those of Chinese firms, we propose that Chinese firms would achieve better export performance in developed markets by adopting the price leadership strategy than by adopting the branding strategy. Hence, we posit:

H1: The price leadership strategy can bring more satisfactory export performance than the branding strategy when Chinese firms export to developed countries.

In terms of market and industrial attributes in developing markets, there exists a certain degree of protectionism (for instance, restricting the entry of foreign capital) in local markets. In addition, the history of market-oriented economies in developing countries is generally rather short, as their markets are still growing and less mature compared to developed countries. Hence, there is vast growth potential and plenty of opportunities. Local enterprises are still at a stage of experience accumulation and capabilities improvement. They have rather low levels of R&D, brand building, and marketing. Nonetheless, they enjoy some cost-based advantages. From the perspective of consumers, consumer demands in developing countries have not yet reached saturation, and there is great potential to be tapped and vast space for exploration and development (Arnold & Quelch, 1998). Meanwhile, the requirements of consumers in developing countries for product innovation and product quality are not as high as those in developed markets. From the perspective of brand building, emerging enterprises in developing countries tend to be younger, as most home-grown brands are at the early stage of growth and not very mature; there are a limited number of established brands, and brand entry barrier to the local market is rather low. In addition, in terms of country-of-origin effects, Ahmed, d'Astous, and Eljabri (2002) find that although Chinese brands are often associated with low quality in developed markets, they are nonetheless evaluated as high quality in many developing markets. The study of Hulland *et al.* (1996) finds that consumers in developing countries believe that imported products are better than domestically produced products and are willing to pay a premium for them. Considering the characteristics of Chinese firms, it is not easy for them to command apparent cost advantages over local companies. Moreover, the addition of expensive transport costs and tariffs increases the difficulty for Chinese firms to achieve desirable performance by adopting the price leadership strategy to compete with local firms. Nevertheless, Chinese firms can take advantage of local consumers' positive perception of foreign brands and the relatively low brand barrier to the local market; make use of their experience in the R&D, production, and marketing of mature products; and establish differentiated advantages by adopting the branding strategy to avoid head-on price competition with local firms, thus achieving satisfactory performance. Therefore, taking into account the characteristics of developing markets and the characteristics of Chinese firms, we suggest that Chinese firms could achieve more satisfactory performance in developing countries by adopting the branding strategy rather than adopting the price leadership strategy. Thus, we posit:

> H2: The branding strategy can bring more satisfactory export performance than the price leadership strategy when Chinese firms export to developing countries.

5.3 Methodology

5.3.1 Instrument design

The measurements of variables in the questionnaire come from previous literature and have been properly adjusted according to Chinese firms' actual conditions. Building on mature instruments designed by foreign scholars, we interviewed relevant executive managers from 12 Chinese manufacturing exporters regarding the validity and comprehensiveness of the contents of the instrument, asking for their opinions on whether the setting of indicators cover all the main contents of the variables and whether the expression is clear. Based on their suggestions, we modified the item setting and the expression in the instrument to improve the questionnaire and make the instrument more effective. Moreover, we invited three marketing experts to evaluate content effectiveness to ensure its reliability and validity.

Our questionnaire consists of three parts: the first part is the choice of export strategy, investigating a total of six items of the two variables of price leadership strategy and branding strategy; the second part investigates one item of target market selection and five items of firms' export performance; the third part are items measuring the basic attributes of firms such as geographic location, industry, year of establishment, international experience, and firm size. Among these items size and international experience are applied as control variables in the current model. In specific:

1   **Price leadership strategy:** Based on the scale of Cavusgil *et al.* (2003), the measure items are: pricing strategy: a) The sale price of our product is

very low compared to our competitors' in our export market; b) Price is our main approach of competition in the export market; c) We adopt low-price strategy in the export market.

2 **Branding strategy:** Based on the scale of Brouthers and Xu (2002), the measure items are: branding competition strategy: a) Brand building is our main approach of competition in the export market; b) Superior quality is our main competitive advantage; c) Superior technology is our main competitive advantage.

3 **Target market (developed country versus developing country):** Based on the scale of Alashban *et al.* (2002), the measure item is: Please select the most important market of our export business (please select one: North America, South America, Japan, Other Asian Countries, EU, Eastern Europe, Africa, or Hong Kong, Macau & Taiwan).

4 **Firms' satisfaction with export performance:** We use a subjective measure to measure performance in this article, i.e.: whether the interviewee is satisfied with his or her firm's performance. Based on the scale of Bello and Gilliland (1997), the measure items are: a) Whether export performance has met the firm's expected export strategy goal; b) Whether your firm is satisfied with export performance; c) Whether your firm is satisfied with export growth; d) Whether your firm is satisfied with the profitability of export; e) Whether your firm is satisfied with export performance compared to other firms in your industry.

5 **Control variables:** Firm size is measured by using the number of employees, with 1 representing an employee size of 0–200 employees, 2 representing 200–500 employees, 3 representing 500–1,000 employees, 4 representing 1,000 to 5,000 employees, and 5 representing 5,000 or more employees. International experience is measured on five-level Likert scales (from "none" to "plenty").

5.3.2 Sample

This survey investigates China's manufacturing exporters. The time period of the questionnaire survey lasted from May 2005 to January 2006. We sent 1,100 questionnaires to manufacturing exporters listed on industrial yellow pages; of these, 221 questionnaires were returned, and 30 were withdrawn due to incompatibility of firm nature (trading exporter or foreign-funded firms, etc.). A total of 849 questionnaires were delivered successfully. Leaving out those that were either incomplete or apparently erroneous, the final number of valid questionnaires suitable for this study was 147, with a response rate of 17.3%. The questionnaires were completed by relevant personnel (such as overseas market managers) from the export departments of indigenous Chinese manufacturers. Distribution of the final sample is as follows:

Percentage of firms with less than 200 employees: 31.5%; with 200–500 employees: 23.3%; with 500–1,000 employees: 15.8%; with 1,000–5,000 employees: 21.2%; with 5,000 or more employees: 8.2%; one value in this regard is missing. In terms of sales revenue in the previous year, percentage of firms with less than 20 million (RMB): 20%; with 20–50 million (RMB): 16.4%; with 50–100 million (RMB): 17.9%; with 100–500 million (RMB): 24.3%; with 500 million and above (RMB): 21.7%; seven values are missing in this regard. Geographical distribution of the sample is: 23.1% are located in Zhejiang Province, 20.3% are located in Guangdong Province, 14% are located in Jiangsu Province, 12.6% are located in Beijing, 5.6% are located in Hebei Province and Shandong Province, and the remaining 18.8% are located in other places; four values are missing in this regard. Percentage of export in total sales revenue (in the previous year): below 10% for 21.9% of firms, between 10%–30% for 32.9% of firms, between 30%–50% for 19.9% of firms, between 50%–70% for 8.2% of firms, and 70% and above for 17.1% of firms; one value is missing in this regard. Number of years of export business operation: 1–5 years for 55.2% of firms, 6–10 years for 33.6% of firms, 11–20 years for 6.7% of firms, and 20 or more years for 4.5% of firms; 13 values are missing in this regard.

5.3.3 Reliability and validity analysis

In terms of reliability, we use the LISREL software to conduct confirmatory factor analysis (CFA) on the measurement model, and the calculation result is then used to calculate composite reliability (CR). All the construct variables have a CR value of greater than 0.7, consistent with the general acceptance level, indicating that the reliability of construct variables of our sample is appropriate for further analysis.

In terms of convergent validity, we conduct confirmatory factor analysis on the measurement model in this study. Table 5.1 shows the standardized factor loadings. All items are greater than 0.65 and are statistically significant, indicating that all items on the variables that they measure have high convergent validity. Indicators of level of fitting between the measurement model and data are $\chi^2(55) = 84.67$, RMSEA = 0.053, CFI = 0.96, IFI = 0.97, GFI = 0.92, NNFI = 0.95, demonstrating good fit between the measurement model and data. This indicates that the convergent validity of construct variables measures in this questionnaire is good.

In terms of discriminant validity, Table 5.2 shows that the AVE (average variance extracted) value of all construct variables is higher than the critical value of 0.50, and the square root of the AVE of each construct variable is greater than the item-total correlation of the respective construct variable, indicating that the measurement model has good discriminant validity (Fornell & Larcker, 1981).

5.4 Hypothesis tests and discussion

In testing whether there is colinearity between the construct variables, Table 5.2 shows that the correlation coefficient between the two independent variables is

Table 5.1 Path analysis results

Latent variables	Measure items	Number	Factor loadings	CR
Export performance	1 Whether export performance has met the firm's expected export strategy goals	5	0.84	0.91
	2 Whether your firm is satisfied with product export performance		0.92	
	3 Whether your firm is satisfied with export growth		0.89	
	4 Whether your firm is satisfied with the profitability of export		0.71	
	5 Whether your firm is satisfied with export performance compared to other firms in the same trade		0.73	
Price leadership strategy	1 The sale price of the exported product is very low compared to competing products in the export market	3	0.66	0.81
	2 Price is our main means of competition in the export market		0.81	
	3 We adopt low-price strategy in the export market		0.82	
Branding strategy	1 Brand building is our main means of competition in the export market	3	0.64	0.77
	2 Superior quality is our main means of competition		0.80	
	3 Superior technology is our main means of competition		0.72	

$\chi^2(55) = 84.67$ (P = 0.025), RMSEA = 0.053, CFI = 0.96, IFI = 0.97, GFI = 0.92, NNFI = 0.95

Table 5.2 Means, standard deviations, and correlation matrixes

Variables	Means	Variance	Performance	PLS	Branding
Performance	3.23	0.88	0.82		
PLS	2.89	1.03	−0.084	0.77	
Branding	3.53	0.82	0.284★★★	0.083	0.72

Note: The square root of the AVE value of the construct variables is on the diagonal; ★★★ $p < 0.01$

very small. In addition, VIF, the test indicator of multicollinearity, is far smaller than 10, indicating the absence of multicollinearity.

This chapter uses the sub-group analysis method to divide the sample into two sub-groups, constructing a marketing strategy choice model of the relationship between price leadership strategy, branding strategy, and export performance. Moreover, our model investigates the relationship between marketing strategic choice and export performance in the contexts of different market conditions. Multiple regression statistical results are shown in Table 5.3.

Table 5.3 Results of sub-group analyses of different target markets

Sub-group	Sub-group 1 Developed markets	Sub-group 2 Developing markets
Independent variables	β	β
International experience	0.398★★★	0.280★★
Firm size	−0.038	0.018
Price leadership strategy	0.077	−0.179★
Branding strategy	−0.031	0.375★★★
R^2	0.162	0.280
Adjusted R^2	0.106	0.239
F-value	6.855	6.814

Note: In sub-group 1, $n = 68$; in sub-group 2, $n = 79$, ★ $p < 0.10$, ★★ $p < 0.05$, ★★★ $p < 0.01$

Statistical analysis of Table 5.3 shows that in sub-group 1, when the target market is a developed market, the price leadership strategy has a positive influence on export performance (the effect is trivial, $\beta = 0.077$) and the branding strategy has a negative influence on export performance (the effect is trivial, $\beta = -0.031$). This empirical result supports our hypothesis H2. Thus, when the target market is a developed country, adopting the price leadership strategy could bring more satisfactory export performance than adopting the branding strategy. Nevertheless, according to statistical analysis, when the target market is a developed market, neither the influence of the price leadership strategy on export performance nor the influence of the branding strategy on export performance is significant. Thus H1 is not supported. For this outcome we attempt to explain it in the following manner. Because developed markets are approaching saturation, with fierce competition and high brand barriers, many Chinese firms would adopt a price leadership strategy to enter developed markets, hoping to avoid head-on competition against established brands in developed countries, give play to the cost-based advantages of Chinese firms, and improve price attractiveness and competitiveness, with the expectation of achieving satisfactory export performance. However, fierce competition in developed markets keeps driving price down, resulting in increasing difficulty in achieving satisfactory export performance. For example, ChangHong adopted a price-competition strategy to enter the US market, only to end up with great losses. In our interviews with export managers we discovered that the export price of many firms was forced down to a very low level, making it very difficult to achieve desirable profit. Developed markets see the concentrated presence of multinational firms, and competition is fierce. It is difficult for brands of emerging markets to be accepted by local consumers. The cost is high, and the risk is substantial for Chinese firms that are weak in capital and R&D capabilities. Branding strategy could hardly produce satisfactory results. In spite of all those disadvantages, however, some Chinese firms still managed to achieve success in market segments that were ignored by international multinational firms. For instance, Haier Group entered America's mini-refrigerator market using its own brand and developed products that targeted young consumers. Step by step it built up the Haier brand and achieved rather a satisfactory result. Hangzhou Wanxiang Group has also achieved success in establishing its own brand of auto parts in the American market. Based on the prior analysis, we propose that due to the great differences of market environment and consumer conditions, among other factors, between developed countries and China (market environment in developed countries being more dynamic, competition more fierce, and consumer demands more diversified), Chinese firms tend to encounter more difficulties and uncertainties when they are operating in developed markets, and neither price leadership strategy nor branding strategy could guarantee satisfactory performance. There is still no conclusive findings regarding the relationship between export marketing strategy choice and performance.

Statistical analysis of Table 5.3 shows that, in sub-group 2, when the target market is a developing country, the price leadership strategy has a significant negative influence on export performance ($\beta = -0.179$, $p < 0.10$), and the branding strategy has a significant positive influence on export performance ($\beta = 0.375$, $p < 0.01$). Thus, H2 is supported. This finding indicates that when the target market is a developing country, Chinese firms can achieve more satisfactory export performance by adopting the branding strategy than by adopting the price leadership strategy. Our survey of typical firms also supports the finding. For instance, TCL used its own brand to market its products in developing countries like Vietnam and India, and by 2004 it had acquired a 16% share of the color TV market in Vietnam (Hu & Wang, 2005); Bird marketed its products via its own brand in India, Southeast Asia, and other developing countries and also achieved satisfactory performance. We can explain these empirical findings from the following three perspectives: First, we point out in hypothesis that local firms in developing countries possess a certain degree of cost-based advantages and that price competition is fierce in local markets. Therefore, compared to local firms Chinese firms do not possess an apparent advantage in terms of cost, and with additional costs like transport and tariff, it would be very difficult for Chinese firms to achieve satisfactory performance by means of price competition. Second, according to our survey we find that Chinese firms that are conducting export marketing activities tend to be firms that have rich marketing experience in the domestic market or those that possess certain corporate strengths. Very often these firms have more experience and greater capabilities in such aspects as R&D, production, and marketing of mature products than firms in developing markets. Therefore, they are able to achieve satisfactory performance in developing markets by adopting the branding strategy. Third, existing brands in developing countries are not yet mature, and few are recognized as world-class brands. With a low brand-building barrier, it would be much cheaper to build a brand in a developing market. Moreover, consumers in developing markets believe that imported products are better than domestically produced products (Hulland & Lecraw, 1996). Therefore, it would be easier for Chinese firms to succeed in developing countries by adopting the branding strategy.

This chapter introduces two control variables: international experience and firm size. Regression analysis of sub-group 1 and sub-group 2 in Table 5.3 ($\beta = 0.398$, $p < 0.01$; $\beta = 0.280$, $p < 0.01$) shows that the more experience a firm accumulates, the better its export performance. Regression result of the firm size of sub-group 1 and sub-group 2 in Table 5.3 ($\beta = -0.038$, $\beta = 0.018$) is not significant, meaning that the size of the exporting firm has no salient influence on export performance. This indicates that the size of firm, either big or small, is not significantly related to firm performance.

5.5 Conclusions and directions for future research

5.5.1 Contributions

This chapter uses a sample of local Chinese manufacturing exporters to empirically study the relationship between the international marketing strategy choice and performance of these firms and investigates how the choices of price leadership strategy and branding strategy in developed markets and developing markets affect performance satisfaction. The findings of this research have important theoretical and practical value.

The theoretical contribution of our research is reflected in the following three aspects: (1) This chapter uses a sample of local Chinese manufacturing exporters to study the relationship between export marketing strategies (price leadership strategy, branding strategy) and performance under different market conditions. Through empirical study it is found that when the target market is a developed country, neither the price leadership strategy nor the branding strategy is proved to significantly affect Chinese firms' export performance; when the target market is a developing country, the branding strategy could lead to more satisfactory export performance than the price leadership strategy. (2) Empirical research in this chapter finds that the relationship between firms' international marketing strategies and performance is moderated by the target market. A firm can achieve satisfactory performance only when it chooses an international marketing strategy that is tailored to the environment of the target market. Therefore, without taking the environment and conditions of the target market into account, neither a purely price leadership strategy nor a purely branding strategy would be appropriate. (3) Internationally, there is currently not much empirical research on the international marketing strategies and performance of firms from the perspective of emerging markets, and similar research is also scarce in China. Therefore, the empirical research in this chapter enriches research findings in the field of the relationship between international marketing strategies and performance.

Our research is practically instructive in three ways: (1) Empirical findings in this chapter show that when the target market is a developed country, the influence of either the price leadership strategy or the branding strategy on export performance is statistically insignificant. This means that in a developed market the marketing strategy choice of Chinese firms may not necessarily have an impact on performance. There is currently no final conclusion on the relationship between international marketing strategy choice and performance. Therefore, when a Chinese firm is carrying out export marketing activities in a developed market, it should adopt flexible export marketing strategies that are based on the environment and conditions of the target market and tailored to local conditions. (2) Empirical findings in this chapter show that when the target market is a developing country, Chinese firms can achieve more satisfactory performance by adopting the branding strategy than the price leadership strategy. Therefore, when a Chinese firm is exporting to a developing country, it should make the best use of its experience in the R&D, production, and marketing of mature products; differentiate itself from competitors by building brands and offering high-quality products; and avoid head-on price competition against local firms, so as to achieve satisfactory performance. (3) Empirical findings show that international experience, as a control variable, has a significant influence on export performance. This indicates that the earlier a firm starts its exporting activities and the richer international experience it possesses, the better its export performance. In addition, empirical findings show that firm size has no significant influence on export performance. This indicates that performance is not related to firm size. Therefore, firms, big or small, could achieve satisfactory performance as long as they adopt effective international marketing strategies. This chapter provides useful implications not only for Chinese firms but also for firms in other developing countries to choose international marketing strategies for their international operation.

5.5.2 Limitations and directions for future research

There are also some limitations in this chapter. First, besides the target market factor, which is an external contingent, there are also other factors that affect firms' export strategy choice and the strategy-performance relationship. Such other factors include firm-level factors (such as firms' managerial and coordinating capabilities and corporate culture, among others) and other external factors (such as industrial characteristics and geographical conditions, etc.). Future studies could focus on the influences of other factors on the relationship between Chinese firms' international marketing strategies and performance. Second, this research uses cross-section data to analyze how Chinese firms, at their current stage of growth and in given internal and external environments, should choose appropriate export marketing strategies in different target markets. However, firms may need to keep adjusting their original strategy choice in accordance with the dynamic change of the target market and their different growth stages. Therefore, future studies may use longitudinal data to empirically study the dynamic development of the relationship between strategic choice and performance. Third, in the research we find that, when the target market is a developing country, adopting the branding strategy can bring better performance than adopting the price leadership strategy. Nonetheless, many Chinese firms still lack the experience of brand building in the international market, and they are still relying on low-price competition (Jin, 2004). Therefore, future studies may focus on how Chinese firms could evolve from price competition to branding competition.

Note

1 Keegan (1999) divided a firm's international marketing intro three phases: export marketing, multinational marketing, and global marketing. Currently, Chinese firms are mainly at the export marketing phase. In this chapter, international marketing refers specifically to export marketing.

6 Chinese firms' export strategy: OBM or OEM?

Zhonghe Han, Zuohao Hu and Lichao Zheng

6.1 Introduction

As China's international business grows, export performance indicators (such as export volume and profitability) of Chinese firms are attracting the attention of both academic researchers and business practitioners. Particularly after China joined the World Trade Organization (WTO), foreign trade has become increasingly important for China's economy. Meanwhile, competition and pressure facing exporting and importing Chinese firms has also increased. Firms involved with exports are more significantly affected. Therefore, it's imperative to investigate the future of Chinese firms' export development. Chinese firms' export products differ greatly from those of developed countries because a substantial part of Chinese firms export mainly through the OEM (original equipment manufacturing) strategy. This export approach has played and is still playing a dominant role in China. An increasing number of Chinese entrepreneurs and economic management experts realize there are numerous drawbacks to the OEM strategy. Hence, they suggest Chinese firms vigorously promote the OBM (original brand manufacturing) strategy. Therefore, there are two major research topics regarding Chinese exporters, which constitute two central issues in this chapter: (1) How do different export strategies of private and non-private brands affect export performance? (2) What are the influential factors for international marketing strategy choice? Branding strategy in firms' internationalization process has attracted wide attention from both practice and academic perspectives. First, on the practical front, the importance of foreign trade to China's economy is self-apparent. Chinese firms' export business concerns the overall improvement and development of the Chinese economy and is of critical importance in balancing and stabilizing the national economy and improving the overall capabilities and international competitiveness of Chinese firms. The export business of Chinese firms has made huge progress both in scope and in depth over the decades since the implementation of the reform and open policy. It can't be denied that the OEM strategy has played an important role during this process. Even now, the OEM strategy remains Chinese exporters' major approach. Nevertheless, as China's international business grows, an increasing number of entrepreneurs and scholars start to attach importance to exporters' long-term development. Moreover, many public opinions and studies suggest that Chinese exporters should blaze a new trail to cultivate their own brands.

In the field of international marketing, there is a substantial amount of research concentrating on these two topics: the influence of brand on performance and the determinants of branding strategies. Existing literature indicates that properly chosen branding strategies have a positive influence on corporate performance. In addition, in these analysis frameworks, firms' marketing strategies seldom equate to branding strategies, but branding strategies have apparently become an important component of firms' marketing strategies. Extensive research suggests that a firm's branding strategy should be considered part of its international marketing strategy, or even the more critical part (Douglas et al., 2001; Alashban et al., 2002). On the other hand, in terms of export mode and international operation, a large number of Chinese firms adopt the OEM strategy. When branding becomes an alternative to the OEM strategy, it tends to imply branding strategy choice. This feature represents the difference between exporters located in China and exporters located in developed markets, which provides the rationale for this chapter as well. This chapter comprehensively reviews existing Chinese and international literature and empirically analyzes the determinants of Chinese exporters' branding strategic choice and its relationship with firms' export performance.

This chapter considers export branding strategy as part of firms' international marketing strategy and constructs an analysis framework for the determinants of the OBM/OEM choice and its relationship with export performance. In addition, this chapter also empirically examines the influence of Chinese firms' branding strategies on performance in the international market environment and determinants of branding strategy choice. The rest of this chapter is organized as follows. We first review existing literature and propose hypotheses based on the theoretical foundation, then introduce research methodology and test the proposed hypotheses. In the following part, we explain the model results and finally discuss the theoretical contribution and practical implications. Finally, we point out limitations and directions for future research.

6.2 Literature review

6.2.1 Determinants of export performance

There is a substantial amount of research regarding the determinants of firms' export performance (Bilkey & Tesar, 1978; Aaby & Slater, 1989; Madsen, 1989; Chetty & Hamilton, 1993). There are generally two types of research perspectives. The industrial organization–based perspective proposes that cross-national firms should attach importance to identifying the external drivers of corporate strategy and that the performance level of a firm is determined by strategy. In other words, external market and industrial structure determine a firm's strategic choices and, in turn, determine performance (Porter, 1980; Scherer & Ross, 1990); the strategy-environment co-alignment has an important influence on performance (Venkatraman & Prescott, 1990). According to the industrial organization theory, external factors determine what strategy a firm adopts and the influence of that strategy on performance. On the other hand, the resource-based theory suggests that resources are determinants of a firm's strategy and performance (Barney, 1991) and that the differences of firms' strategic resources result in performance disparity (Wernerfelt, 1984; Grant, 1991). Barney (1991) defines firm resources as assets, capabilities, organizational processes, firm attributes, information, knowledge, and so on controlled by a firm that enable the firm to conceive of and implement strategies that improve its efficiency and effectiveness. Therefore, a firm's most important resources should be those that are used preferentially, hard to imitate, and difficult to substitute. Prahalad and Hamel (1990) use the term "core competence" to characterize such internal organizational resources. According to the resource-based theory, the internal resources of a firm are important determinants of its strategy and export performance. In the international marketing analysis framework, organizational capabilities can be reflected by international marketing capabilities, which include the capability to correctly understand international market demands and the capability to use modern marketing tools for differentiation purposes, among others. In summary, the industrial organization–based perspective emphasizes analyzing strategic performance from external markets, whereas the resource-based theory lays emphasis on analyzing a firm's strategic performance from internal resources.

According to Morgan *et al.* (2004), resource-based theory and industrial organization–based theory can be synthesized to analyze a firm's internationalization behaviors. Zou and Cavusgil (2002) combine these two perspectives, analyze the performance outcomes of global marketing strategies, and develop the more systematic global marketing strategy (GMS) analysis model. In the GMS model, determinants of export performance are divided into three categories: internal factors, external factors, and export marketing strategies. The model provides a strong analysis framework for following studies regarding global marketing strategy.

These aforementioned studies consider marketing strategy as an intermediate variable of performance outcome, which is broadly supported by subsequent empirical research. More determinants of export performance have been added, such as the attitudes and characteristics of managers, the characteristics and strengths of firms, the characteristics of industry and foreign and domestic markets (Aaby & Slater, 1989; Rocha & Christensen, 1994), the influence of the level of differentiation of product on performance (Madsen, 1989), the influence of price advantages and branding advantages on performance (Zou *et al.*, 2003), and the influence of branding strategy on performance (Brouthers & Xu, 2002; Gabrielsson, 2005), among others.

6.2.2 The relationship between branding strategy and firm performance

A substantial amount of literature examines the positive influence of successful brands on firm performance. A brand can improve consumers' perceived value (Marquardt *et al.*, 1965). Brand name and brand awareness, among other attributes, can enhance consumers' perception of brand equity and improve their evaluation of products under that brand (Aaker, 1991). The consumer-based brand equity view suggests that high brand awareness can help a brand build high brand loyalty, which would positively affect corporate performance (Aaker, 1991); Brand equity projects a differentiation image for its product and creates a premium, and the differentiation in product and price can bring a firm better performance (Hollis & Farr, 1997). Brand equity plays an important role in enhancing channel members' relationship and the firm-consumer relationship and creating more value for partners. When the branding strategy is consistent with the core competence of the firm, its influence on performance would be more significant. Branding strategies have an important influence on firms' internationalization process. As firms become more internationalized, branding strategy has also been incorporated into the analysis framework of international marketing (Wong & Merrilees, 2007).

6.2.3 Determinants of branding strategies

In the field of international marketing, Zou and Cavusgil (2002) posit a systematic and mature theoretical model, in which determinants of marketing strategies include the characteristics of firms and products and the characteristics of industry and market competition. This analysis approach has also been carried over into the analysis framework in branding-strategy research. Influential factors of firms' branding strategy include firm characteristics and a firm's ability to expand globally, product and market environment characteristics, marketing channel structure, and relationships with partners, among others (Chung, 2002; Luostarinen & Mika, 2004). Gabrielsson (2005) suggests that in the international market environment, factors affecting a firm's branding strategy should also include experience and culture, technological position, environment and competitiveness of the target market, and product technology, among others. Economic, cultural, and political factors in the target market all affect a firm's branding strategy; product technology competiveness would also require a firm to increase brand investment so as to enhance consumers' recognition and awareness of its brand and make purchase decisions. Brand superiority can also protect the firm's competitive position in the international market.

6.2.4 The relationship between OBM and OEM

The views of foreign scholars are rather consistent regarding the positive effect of branding strategy on firms' export performance. Nonetheless, the subjects of study in international marketing research tend to be focused on multinational firms from developed countries or established international brands. The international marketing practice of firms from emerging economies, including China, shows that at the initial stage of their internationalization they still tend to adopt the OEM strategy to enter the international market (Cheng et al., 2005; Luo, 2007). OEM refers to the practice of firms that own advantageous brands commissioning other manufacturing firms to do the processing and manufacturing for them, meeting their requirements for product quality, specifications, and model by providing product design and technical and equipment support to the manufacturers, and then selling products under their own brands. To restructure the businesses of their firms in accordance with the value chain, established international brands would outsource many of their low-value businesses and commission firms, especially those from developing countries, to do the OEM for them. The purpose is to reduce cost and rationalize their value chains, which would be conducive to creating economies of scale for the firms. For startups, the OEM method can help them rapidly enter the international market and reduce marketing costs, achieve technology upgrades and innovation by learning product development knowledge, and eventually build up their own brands (Tao & Li, 2008). Therefore, entering the international market and gaining profit by means of low cost has a positive effect on improving firms' international competitiveness and performance and building firms' own brands. Nonetheless, the OEM mode also has apparent weaknesses. Firms adopting the OEM strategy tend to provide low-end products with low technological level and low entry threshold, as well as low profit (Luo, 2007), all unfavorable for firms to establish superior brands and achieve sustainable development in the international market. Therefore, from the perspective of long-term development, the future of Chinese firms' export lies in building and cultivating their own brands.

In recent years, scholars have also conducted empirical studies on Chinese firms' export strategies, but their studies have yielded different findings, some even contradictory to one another. For instance, some findings indicate that Chinese firms tend to adopt branding strategies in their export market (Zou et al., 2003), while other empirical studies show that more firms are willing to choose the OEM method for export (Chen, 2008). Generally speaking, there is still insufficient empirical research on the determinants of Chinese firms' branding strategic choice and the influence of branding strategy on firms' export performance, and the little literature there is presents different findings. Therefore, topics regarding the determinants and consequences – such as how different branding strategies adopted by Chinese firms would affect their export performances and the main factors that affect firms' branding strategies – would still require further empirical research.

6.3 Hypotheses

6.3.1 *International marketing capability*

In this book, a firm's international marketing capability refers to the firm's ability to understand its target market and conduct overseas marketing. It is an internal factor of the firm. A substantial amount of research indicates that internal factors, particularly the firm's marketing capability, can affect the firm's marketing strategy and have a direct influence on the firm's export performance.

A firm's marketing assets and skills enable it to understand the traits of the target market more accurately. Those assets help exporters effectively develop and implement appropriate marketing strategies as well. The empirical research of Zou *et al.* (2003) finds that distribution capability and communication capability have a significant positive effect on low-cost advantage positioning. A firm's international marketing capability and resources enable it to identify opportunities in the international market, develop effective branding strategies, and effectively implement them. The greater international marketing capability a firm has, the easier it is for the firm to promote its private brand successfully. Hence, the firm would also be more willing to adopt the OBM method for export. Thus, we propose:

> H1a: International marketing capability is positively related to the adoption of branding strategy.

Similarly, a firm that possesses greater international marketing capability can aim at its target market more accurately, develop appropriate marketing strategies, and effectively implement them. Thus, superior international marketing capability leads to greater success in competition and better operation results. The research of Cavusgil and Zou (1994) also indicates that the improvement of managerial experience and international marketing capability would bring better performance. Therefore, we propose:

> H1b: International marketing capability is positively related to export performance satisfaction.

6.3.2 Target market selection

In this book target market selection refers to the proportion of products that are exported to developed countries in total exported products. Existing literature rarely touches upon this variable because relevant research is based on the practice of firms from developed countries. These firms may export to developed countries as well as developing countries, but there is little difference in their branding strategy choice across different target markets. Their brands carry the economic power and technology-leading images that are associated with their developed-country origins. The influence of their brand images is rather consistent across different target markets. However, the actual situation of the export of Chinese firms is different. Due to the brand-origin effects (Aaker, 1991; Leclerc *et al.*, 1994), consumers in the international market may be biased in their choice and evaluation of products simply because of the difference in product origins. These consumers are prone to have the impression that products from developing countries are of lower grade. Therefore, it is difficult for brands from developing markets to be successful in developed countries (Still & Hill, 1984; Chhabra, 1996). Consequently, Chinese firms are more likely to give up their own brands when they are exporting to developed markets. On the other hand, developed markets are mature, with high levels of saturation and fierce competition, increasing entry cost. Meanwhile, there are many established firms and successful brands in developed countries. These firms and brands actively seek cooperation and outsourcing partners all over the world, thus generating a lot of opportunities for OEM export. Consequently, as Chinese firms strive for more OEM export opportunities, the percentage of products under their own brands may decrease. Existing literature points out that branding may not be the best choice for Chinese firms that have a high percentage of export to developed countries (Brouthers & Xu, 2002). The authors suggest that the percentage of Chinese firms' export to developed countries would interact with their branding strategies and, in turn, would affect the firms' export performance. The higher the percentage of export to developed countries, the lower the satisfaction with branding strategy performance. Therefore, we posit:

H2a: The percentage of export to developed countries is negatively related to the adoption of the OBM strategy.

By reviewing literature regarding the effect of the target market's economic development level on firms' export performance we find that some research findings indicate the economic development level of the market has a positive influence on firms' export performance (Kaynak & Kuan, 1993). When analyzing the economic level of a market, Kaynak and Kuan use market entry variables, including: market size, degree of industrialization, policy stability, conditions of foreign exchange management, and packaging, labeling, and marketing standards, among others. The authors point out that market environment factors in developed countries, such as large demands, relatively small market fluctuations, liberal foreign exchange conditions and import control system, market entry requirements, and high employment rate, are favorable for the uninterrupted and steady implementation of firms' export marketing strategies and therefore are positively associated with export performance. Because market maturity has a positive influence on firm's export performance, we therefore posit:

H2b: The percentage of export to developed countries is positively related to firms' export performance.

6.3.3 Characteristics of export market

The characteristics of export market refer to the volatility and competitiveness of the market. Relevant research on the determinants of branding strategies indicates that factors like competition intensity and demand volume in the target market significantly affect firms' branding strategies (McDougall *et al.*, 1994; Chung, 2002). Building and promoting a firm's own brands require huge investments, in such aspects as advertising, R&D, channel relations, and customer relations maintenance, among others. All these expenditures are far more than the cost of the OEM method. As far as the OBM strategy is concerned, the volatility of the target market has a huge influence. Market volatility in this book is manifested in three aspects: uncertainties of the export market; the frequency of change in demands in the export market; and the intensity of competition in the export market. The higher the uncertainties in the target market, the lower the predictability of export performance, and the more likely firms are to adopt conservative strategies. The faster demands change in the target market, the more difficult it would be to estimate the potential market volume and market prospects of the products, and the greater the risks are to pursue the OBM strategy. Therefore, we posit:

> H3: The volatility and competitiveness of the export market are negatively related to firms' branding strategies.

6.3.4 Industrial characteristics

Industrial characteristics include two variables: speed of technological change in the industry and technology intensity. Previous research suggests that faster technical innovation means greater elimination rate in the industry and market competition (Foster, 1986) and that in an environment of intensified competition a firm has more reason to establish strong brand equity so as to improve the competitive advantage of the firm and achieve sustained and stable development (Grant, 1991). Similarly, the international marketing strategies of Chinese firms are also affected by this variable.

In this book, the degree of technology intensity is defined as the technical content of export products. Existing research indicates that the technical content of products would affect firms' branding strategy choice (Madsen & Servais, 1997; Gabrielsson, 2005). Compared to low-tech products, it is easier for high-tech products to pursue a differentiation strategy. The traits of high-tech brands would be more prominent, and brand building would be relatively easy. Therefore, firms possessing high technology tend to build their own brands. We posit:

> H4: The technological characteristics of the industry are positively related to the adoption of branding strategies.

6.3.5 Branding strategies

In this section, a branding strategy refers to the extent to which a firm adopts the OBM strategy. On one hand, branding strategies may be affected by firms' internal and external factors. On the other hand, they may affect firms' performance. Through interviewing typical firms, we find that a huge number of Chinese firms simultaneously adopt both the OBM and the OEM methods for export. The matter is to what extent they adopt each method. Putting the two methods on the opposite extremes would not be appropriate. Therefore, the variable "the percentage of firms' export to developed countries" has been used as an indicator to reflect firms' choice between OBM and OEM.

The design of this variable has rarely been used in previous research because the majority of existing literature is based on the practice of developed countries' firms, which are more likely to adopt the OBM strategy in their international marketing strategies. They might adjust their marketing strategies based on the characteristics of the target market, but they would stick to their own brands all the same. Chinese firms may choose the OBM method as well as the OEM method at the initial stage of their international market. Therefore, the reason we use this indicator is to compare these two strategies. If a firm has a higher percentage of OBM export, then it would indicate that the firm pursues a higher level of branding strategy.

The importance of brand equity is widely recognized in the academic research as well as in business practices. As intangible assets, brands can create added value for firms and bring them higher profit (Aaker, 1996). Brands can provide powerful support to firms' product differentiation strategy. Especially in coping with market competition, brand differentiation can help firms avoid price wars and achieve better financial performance (Hollis & Farr, 1997; Grassl, 1999). A brand attracts its target consumer group with its unique personality and image. Brands can improve perceived quality and thus positively affect consumers' brand attitudes and behaviors (Keller, 1998). Previous empirical research shows that there is a positive relation between branding strategy and performance (Chaudhuri & Holbrook, 2001), and such relation not only exists in the domestic market but also is exhibited in international marketing activities (Zou & Cavusgil, 1996, 2002; Brouthers & Xu, 2002; Zou *et al.*, 2003; Wong & Merrilees, 2007). In conclusion, through product differentiation branding can help firms avoid fierce price and technology competition, improve consumer loyalty, and strengthen channel relations. Branding strategies can help firms achieve better financial and strategic performance. Aspiring firms will make vigorous efforts to pursue branding strategies. Therefore, we posit:

> H5: Firms' branding strategies are positively related to firms' satisfaction with export performance.

6.3.6 Export performance satisfaction

Early research on firms' export performance uses complex indicators (Schlegelmilch & Ross, 1987; Walters & Samiee, 1990; Cavusgil & Zou, 1994), and different researchers adopt different classification methods (Aaby & Slater, 1989; Madsen, 1989). Over time, performance indicators are gradually divided into two major categories: financial and non-financial (Matthyssens & Pauwels, 1996; Zou & Cavusgil, 2002). The performance goals of Chinese firms may be influenced by such factors as the industries to which they belong, firm size, and marketing strategies. In light of this, this book uses firms' self-evaluation to assess their performance achievement, with indicators including: achievement

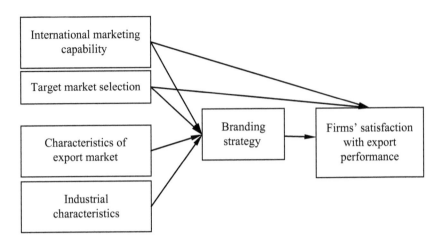

Figure 6.1 Analysis framework of factors influencing the OBM vs. OEM choice and influence on export performance

of strategic goals, overall satisfaction, satisfaction with export growth, and export profitability. Therefore, in this book corporate performance is defined as a firm's satisfaction with its export performance. On the one hand, for exporters this indicator specifically measures their satisfaction with export performance; on the other hand, all the factors we examine boil down to whether firms are satisfied with this result. To a great extent a firm's self-evaluation is congruent with the firm's performance indicator after being compared with industrial status. Existing literature also uses this method (Brouthers & Xu, 2002).

To sum up, a theoretical analysis framework (Figure 6.1) is constructed based on hypotheses H1a–H5.

6.4 Research design

6.4.1 Data collection and sample distribution

Questionnaires were sent to Chinese exporting firms in China's manufacturing industry and completed by division heads (such as overseas market manager) of these firms. A total of 1,572 questionnaires were sent, and 205 were returned, a return rate of 13.1%. Leaving out returned questionnaires that were either incomplete or apparently erroneous (such as those with plenty of omissions or those sent to trading exporter or foreign firms), the final number of qualified questionnaires for this research was 139.

Table 6.1 describes the basic characteristics of sample firms, including indicators like employee size, geographical distribution, export experience, percentage of export to developed countries, and percentage of OBM.

In terms of industry, these firms are mainly from household electrical appliance, textile, machinery, electronics, automobile and parts, chemicals, and food.

Table 6.1 Characteristics of sampled firms

Employee size	Number of firms	Percentage (%)
< 200	51	36.7
200–500	27	19.4
500–1,000	23	16.6
1,000–5,000	20	14.4
> 5,000	13	9.3
Omitted	5	3.6

Export volume (RMB)	Number of firms	Percentage (%)
< 20 million	24	17.3
20–50 million	29	20.9
50–100 million	25	18.0
100–500 million	28	20.1
> 500 million	28	20.1
Omitted	5	3.6

Export experience	Number of firms	Percentage (%)
1–5 years	70	50.3
6–10 years	44	31.7
11–20 years	11	7.9
> 20 years	6	4.3
Omitted	8	5.8

Percentage of export to developed countries	Number of firms	Percentage (%)
< 10%	30	21.6
10%–30%	32	23.0
30%–50%	48	34.5
50%–70%	18	13.0
> 70%	11	7.9

Percentage of OBM	Number of firms	Percentage (%)
< 10%	42	30.2
10%–30%	26	18.7
30%–50%	15	10.8
50%–70%	18	13.0
> 70%	38	27.3

Geographic distribution (Top 5)	Number of firms	Percentage (%)
Zhejiang Province	33	23.7
Jiangsu Province	23	16.6
Guangdong Province	24	17.3
Shanghai	15	10.8
Beijing	11	7.9
Omitted	33	23.7

Geographically, these firms are located in more than 10 provinces across China, relatively concentrated in eastern coastal provinces and cities like Zhejiang, Jiangsu, Guangdong, and Shanghai.

Regarding the variables studied in this chapter, we pay more attention to the dispersion of the distribution of the surveyed sample across these variables. In terms of percentage of export to developed countries, the number of firms with less than 10% is 30, the number of firms with 10%–30% is 32, the number of firms with 30%–50% is 48, 13% of the surveyed firms have 50%–70% of export to developed countries, and the remaining 7.9% have more than 70% of their export to developed countries. In terms of the percentage of OBM export: the number of firms with less than 10% is 42, the number of firms with 10%–30% is 26, the number of firms with 30%–50% is 15, 13% of firms have 50%–70% of OBM export, and another 27.3% of firms have more than 70%. The distribution of firms is rather even in terms of percentage of export to developed countries and percentage of OBM export, without over-concentration in a certain percentage range. Judging from the distribution dispersion of the sample we suppose the sample can well avoid deviation caused by concentration.

6.4.2 Questionnaire design

In order to ensure the validity and reliability of the measurement variables in this research, we use instruments that have been used before in existing literature to the greatest extent possible and make appropriate changes in accordance with the purpose of this research. In specific, measurement items are as follows.

Determinants of branding strategies are divided into four types: (1) International marketing capability: using the instrument of Zou *et al.* (2003), measuring items including: a) Capability to understand international customer demand; b) Advertising and promotion capability; c) Differentiation capability. (2) Whether the target market is a developed country or developing country: based on the measurement of Alashban *et al.* (2002), measuring the item "the most important market for product export (choose one among many)." (3) Characteristics of export market: based on the measurement of Zhang *et al.* (2008), measuring items including: a) Uncertainties of the export market; b) Demand change in the export market; and c) Intensity of competition in the export market. (4) Industrial characteristics: designing two items based on the research of Gabrielsson (2005): a) Speed of technology change in the industry; b) Degree of technological intensity in the industry. The items are measured using a seven-point Likert scale, with 1 representing "strongly disagree" and 7 representing "strongly agree."

Branding strategies are adopted from Brouthers and Xu (2002), measuring items including: branding competition strategies of product export: (1) Brand building is our main competition approach in the export market; (2) Superior quality is our main competition approach; (3) Technology-leading is our main competition advantage. When analyzing the degree of branding, we refer to the research method of Chia *et al.* (2008), which calculates the percentages of three export methods: OEM, ODM (original design manufacturing), and OBM. When a firm's activities in any particular model exceed 50% of the total, it would be classified as operating under that manufacturing model. This chapter builds on this method and examines only the percentages of OBM and OEM: if a certain model exceeds 50%, the firm would be viewed as adopting that strategy. For instance, if the OBM export of a firm exceeds 50%, this firm would be viewed as adopting the branding strategy, and vice versa.

In terms of manufacturers' export performance, in this chapter performance is measured subjectively – thus, by whether a firm is satisfied with its performance. This is based on the instrument of Bello and Gilliland (1997), measuring items including: (1) Whether the firm's export business meets its expected export strategy goals; (2) Whether the firm is satisfied with its overall export performance; (3) Whether the firm is satisfied with its export growth; (4) Whether the firm is satisfied with its export profitability. These items are measured using a seven-point Likert scale. Respondents are asked to answer to what degree their firms are satisfied with performance, with 1 representing "strongly unsatisfied" and 7 representing "extremely satisfied."

6.4.3 Reliability and validity tests

Reliability test

The reliability of the sample is tested using two indicators: Cronbach's alpha and CR (composite reliability). We used the SPSS13.0 software to test Cronbach's alpha of the sample. The results are: international marketing capability 0.79, characteristics of target market 0.75, industrial characteristics 0.74, and export performance 0.91. Construct variables' reliability is between 0.74 and 0.91, all above 0.7. Therefore, our sample has qualified reliability that supports the following analysis. In addition, the CR of latent variables is between 0.77 and 0.96. Specifically, international marketing capability 0.87, characteristics of export market 0.93, industrial characteristics 0.77, and export performance 0.96, all greater than 0.7 (Hair *et al.*, 1998), passing the CR test. The reliability of latent variables in these chapters is desirable, as demonstrated by the results of various tests. Also, the *t* value of all items is greater than 2, meaning all items are significant.

Validity test

Except for the items of the branding strategy instrument that have been significantly modified, all other instruments in the questionnaire have been used by previous researchers. Before finalizing the questionnaire, we interviewed Chinese managers in charge of export businesses. Moreover, we consulted with marketing experts and revised certain methods of questioning and content. Therefore, the content of the questionnaire has rather high validity and should comply with the requirements of construct validity. However, considering the influence of Chinese firms' special factors, this study nonetheless uses confirmatory factor analysis (CFA) to test the construct validity of the instruments, performing confirmatory analysis on the structure of the questionnaire by calculating the fit index (see Table 6.2).

In the CFA method there are various fit indices that can be used to assess the degree of data fitting to the theoretical model, and these goodness-of-fit indices are congruent with the overall goodness-of-fit index of the structural equation model. In the CFA and structural equation model, goodness of fit can indicate whether a model can be accepted on the whole. It is generally accepted that a model with a chi-square smaller than 2 is desirable (Carmines & McIver, 1981); when the RMSEA value is smaller than 0.08, the model has desirable goodness of fit (Hu & Bentler, 1998); if both GFI and AGFI are greater than 0.9, the goodness can be viewed as ideal (Joreskog & Sorbom, 1989; Bentler, 1990). Nonetheless, using GFI of 0.9 and above as a model fitting standard

Table 6.2 Results of confirmatory factor analysis

Research constructs	Measures (observed variables)	Factor loadings	t value	Estimated error variance	CR
International marketing capabilities	Capability to understand international customer demand accurately	0.67	2.35	0.17	0.87
	Capability to advertise and promote effectively	0.50	2.31	0.13	
	Capability to use modern marketing means and methods to perform differentiation marketing	0.56	2.36	0.15	
Target market selection★	Percentage of export to developed countries	1.00			
Characteristics of export market	Overall uncertainties of main export market	0.56	5.77	0.10	0.93
	Change in demand in main export market	0.94	7.90	0.12	
	Competition in main export market	0.51	5.35	0.10	
Industrial characteristics	Speed of technological change in the industry	0.49	2.83	0.15	0.77
	Degree of technological intensity in the industry	0.53	2.78	0.17	
Branding strategy	Percentage of OBM export	1.00			
Firms' satisfaction with export performance	Achievement of strategic goals	0.86	6.28	0.11	0.96
	Overall satisfaction	0.93	6.48	0.11	
	Satisfaction with sales growth	0.88	6.35	0.11	
	Satisfaction with export profitability	0.70	5.73	0.10	

★ Percentage of export to developed countries and percentage of OBM export are single-index latent variables; therefore, their factor loadings are set to 1, unable to estimate their error variance and CR.

Table 6.3 Correlation matrixes and the square root of AVE values

Variables	1	2	3	4	5	6
1 Firm's international marketing capability	0.69					
2 Target market selection	0.020	–				
3 Characteristics of export market	0.088	0.003	0.83			
4 Technological characteristics of the industry	0.387	0.0539	0.019	0.62		
5 Percentage of OBM export	0.143	0.0198	0.004	0.087	–	
6 Firms' satisfaction with export performance	0.500	0.070	0.015	0.306	0.112	0.96

might be a little conservative, 0.8 and above would be sufficient (Bagozzi & Yi, 1988). This chapter uses the AVE (average variance extracted) value to further test the convergent validity and discriminant validity of each factor, so as to understand whether there is homogeneity among the measure items of the factors and whether there is significant differentiation among the factors (Fornell & Larcker, 1981). An AVE value of greater than 0.5 would mean that the questionnaire has a good convergent validity and would indicate that the measure items explain more than 50% of the variance; when the AVE value is greater than the correlation coefficient of all the factors, the discriminant validity of the factor analysis is good (Fornell & Cha, 1994). We used the result of the CFA performed on the SAS system to test the validity of the questionnaire, and the goodness-of-fit indices of the CFA are: chi-square = 99.7/75 = 1.3, RMSEA = 0.049, GFI = 0.91, AGFI = 0.88. See Table 6.3 for the AVE of all factors and their correlation coefficient matrix.

Based on the results in Table 6.3, we can see that all factor loadings in the questionnaire, with the exception of that of the speed of technological change, are greater than 0.5, and the *t* values of all factor loads are greater than 2, indicating that the factor loadings of all items converge well on the factors. All the goodness-of-fit indices accord with the fitting judgment value. We can believe that the measure validity of the questionnaire is acceptable. Moreover, the AVE value of all factors is greater than the judgment standard of 0.5, indicating convergent validity. The AVE of all factors is greater than the respective factor's correlation coefficient with all other factors, indicating good discriminant validity among factors.

6.5 Model results and hypothesis tests

6.5.1 Model results

This chapter uses the CALIS procedure of the SAS system to perform a full model estimate of the structural equation model. The full structure model resulting from the SAS system estimate is shown in Figure 6.2. The goodness-of-fit

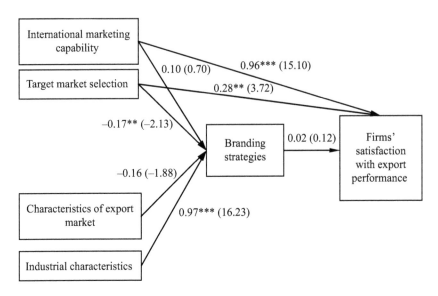

Figure 6.2 Empirical findings of the analysis model

Note: *p < 0.05; **p < 0.025; ***p < 0.001.

indices of the model are: chi-square = 115.8/71 = 1.63, RMSEA = 0.065, GFI = 0.89, AGFI = 0.85, all meeting the judgment value. Moreover, the two indices, chi-square and RMSEA, reach a judgment value that indicates very good model fit. Therefore, we have reason to believe that the overall fit of the structural equation model in this chapter is desirable and that the model can be accepted. In addition, judging from the factor loadings and path coefficient of the variables in the model, only one item, namely the degree of technological intensity in the industry, has a load factor with a *t* value of less than 2 (1.17) and is therefore insignificant; the factor loadings of all others are all significant, indicating that the measure items of the latent variables can well reflect the values of these latent variables.

6.5.2 Hypothesis tests

1   **The effect of international marketing capability on firms' OBM export strategy.** It is posited in this chapter that a firm's international marketing capability is positively associated with its branding strategy (H1a). We find that the path coefficient is 0.10, and the *t* value is 0.70. The path coefficient doesn't show significant impact, indicating that stronger international marketing capability will not motivate the firm to pursue branding strategies. In other words, international marketing capability is not directly, significantly related to choices of branding strategies. Thus, hypothesis H1a is not supported. Nevertheless, the coefficient is positive, indicating that the direction of effect is the same as we have posited. Although a firm's

international marketing capability does not have a significant influence on the percentage of its OBM export, they are nonetheless positively related to certain extent.

2   **The effect of international marketing capability on firms' satisfaction with export performance.** It is posited in this chapter that a firm's international marketing capability is positively related to performance satisfaction (H1b). According to path analysis result, we find that the path coefficient is 0.96, and the t value is 15.10; it is significant on the level of $p < 0.01$, thus providing strong support to H1b. It suggests that in the increasingly homogeneous international market where competition keeps intensifying, firms that possess greater marketing capability would be able to understand demands in the target market more accurately, develop appropriate strategies, and effectively implement them, thus achieving better satisfaction with export performance. In other words, international marketing capability is positively associated with satisfaction with export performance, and hypothesis H1b is supported. Figure 6.2 summarizes the empirical findings.

3   **The influence of target market selection on branding strategies.** It is posited in this chapter that the percentage of export to developed countries is negatively related to OBM export (H2a). According to the path analysis result, we find that the path coefficient is −0.17, and the t value is −2.13; it is significant on the confidence level of $p < 0.025$, thus supporting hypothesis H2a. In other words, the choice of Chinese firms' OBM strategy is significantly affected by the target export market, and target market choice is negatively related to the percentage of OBM export.

4   **The effect of target market selection on firms' export performance.** It is posited in this chapter that the percentage of export to developed countries is positively related to firms' export performance (H2b). According to the path analysis result, we find that the path coefficient is 0.28, and the t value is 3.72, significant on the level of $p < 0.01$. In other words, in a mature market with a large volume of demand and small fluctuation, the predictability of returns on investment would be higher, which would be favorable for the uninterrupted and steady implementation of firms' strategies and therefore can lead firms to achieve better export performance. In other words, the percentage of export to developed countries is positively related to export performance, and hypothesis H2b is supported.

5   **The relationship between the characteristics of export market and branding strategies.** In this chapter it is posited that the volatility and competitiveness of the export market are negatively related to firms' branding strategies (H3). According to empirical results, the path coefficient is −0.16, and the t value is −1.88, indicating that the relationship between the characteristics of the export market and branding strategies is not significant; thus H3 is not supported.

6   **The relationship between the technological characteristics of the industry and branding strategies.** It is posited in this chapter that the

technological characteristics of the industry are positively related to firms' branding strategies. According to analysis result, the path coefficient is 0.97, and the *t* value is 16.23, significant on the level of $p < 0.01$, indicating that industrial firms with higher technology content possess differentiation advantages in pursuing branding strategies. The higher the speed of technology change and the higher the degree of technological intensity in an industry, the more necessary it is for firms to attract consumers by building brand images. In other words, the characteristics of technology are positively related to the percentage of export to developed countries; thus H4 is supported.

7   **The relationship between OBM export and export performance.** It is posited in this chapter that firms' branding strategies are positively related to firms' satisfaction with export performance. According to empirical results, the path coefficient is 0.02, and the *t* value is 0.12, indicating that currently increasing the percentage of OBM export would not significantly affect export performance, at least for Chinese firms. Hence, H5 is not supported.

6.6 Conclusions and directions for future research

6.6.1 Conclusions

On viewing and examining foreign and Chinese literature regarding the relationships between international marketing strategies and firm performance, this chapter constructs a conceptual model of factors that influence Chinese firms' export branding strategies and uses a sample of 139 Chinese manufacturing exporters for empirical testing. As aforementioned in the literature review, there is a scarcity of empirical research on the influence of Chinese firms' branding strategies on export performance, especially empirical research that is based on large-scale firm survey data, and the little amount of existing research presents different conclusions. Therefore, by adjusting the analysis frameworks of existing research, conclusions regarding the influence of international marketing capability on branding strategies and the influence of branding strategies on performance indicate that Chinese firms have their unique characteristics and that strategies should be made in accordance with such characteristics. Meanwhile, empirical findings in this chapter are also reflected in the following aspects: (1) A firm's international marketing capability doesn't directly, significantly affect the firm's branding strategies but has a significant direct influence on the firm's satisfaction with its export performance; (2) The percentage of export to developed countries is negatively related to the firm's degree of OBM export and positively to the firm's export performance; (3) The volatility and competitiveness of the export market is negatively related to firms' branding strategies; (4) Technological characteristics of the industry directly affect the percentage of firms' OBM export; (5) The degree of firms' OBM export does not directly, significantly affect firms' export performance. These empirical findings are also of theoretical importance.

Research findings in this chapter further confirm the sentiment that a firm's international marketing capability and target market selection significantly affect its export performance. A firm that has superior international marketing capability can accurately understand demands in the target market, produce popular products and services, develop and effectively implement appropriate marketing strategies, and obtain more benefits than its competitors from the homogenous international market, and thus the firm will attain greater satisfaction with export performance. As for target market selection, a developed market has large market demands, its consumers have great purchase power, its market fluctuation is small, and return on investment is much more predictable. These are all favorable factors for the uninterrupted and steady implementation of firms' strategies and can help firms attain better satisfaction with export performance. Among the four factors influencing firms' satisfaction with export performance, the influence of OBM export of Chinese firms on actual export performance is not significant. This conversely indicates the influence of the OEM method on Chinese firms. On the one hand, Chinese firms have gained experience and advantages over years of OEM operation. They can achieve market sales growth and performance benefits from this method by taking advantage of the resources of famous international brands. On the other hand, according to the survey data, more than half of the sampled firms have an internationalization experience of only one to five years, lacking experience in international operation and OBM export. Although they have made significant headway in these years, they are still immature compared to established international brands in their judgment of the international market and in the effective implementation of strategies. In this research, although the *t* value of branding strategy is not significant and the value of the coefficient itself is small, the value is nonetheless positive, pointing at the same direction as posited in this chapter, indicating that, although not significant, there is still a certain degree of positive relation between OBM export and firm performance. Chinese firms are becoming more internationalized, accumulating experience and implementing active branding strategies. Improved performance can be expected. In addition, among the four factors influencing firms' satisfaction with export performance, the coefficient of firms' international marketing capability (0.96) is far greater than others. Therefore, in order to improve satisfaction with export performance, firms should actively improve their international marketing capability, focus on grasping market demands and consumption trends in the international market, actively promote technological innovation and product innovation, and improve their marketing communication and promotion capability.

This chapter further confirms that target market selection and industrial characteristics are significantly related to the percentage of OBM export. The choice of Chinese firms' OBM strategy is significantly affected by the target export market. When the target market is a developed country, Chinese firms would indeed reduce the percentage of their OBM export and rely more on established international brands or local brands for market expansion due to such factors as the relatively poor image of the strength of the Chinese economy, relatively low technological status, and country-of-origin effects for certain product categories. In addition, there are more mature international brands, and keener competition, in developed markets, so the cost and risk for Chinese firms to pursue OBM strategy would be higher. On the other hand, established international brands would look for outsourcing due to the influence of cost and competitiveness. This provides opportunities for Chinese firms' OEM products. The study of Chen and Hu (2008) also indicates that Chinese firms would adopt different marketing strategies whether they are entering developed markets or developing markets. They tend to pursue the OEM strategy in developed markets and the OBM strategy in developing markets. Therefore, at the current stage, Chinese firms may adopt flexible and diverse competition strategies in their international operation in accordance with export markets and their own conditions. In addition, this chapter shows that in high-tech industries, it would be easier for firms that possess high-tech products to pursue differentiation and build brands. Therefore, firms should actively promote technology and product innovation, increase the percentage of own-brand products as they gain international competitiveness, and make great efforts to build their own brands.

Findings in this chapter also indicate that firms' international marketing capability is not a significant influence on the adoption of branding strategies. This finding indicates that at the current stage, due to such constraining factors as external conditions, the overall strength of the Chinese economy, and brand-origin image, Chinese firms with strong international marketing capability may not actively pursue branding strategies in their international marketing activities. On the other hand, since the reform and opening up policy of China, a substantial number of Chinese firms have pursued non-branding methods (OEM and other methods) for export. Over the years, these firms have achieved results through these methods and have developed rather mature exporting strategies. Even firms with strong international marketing capability would be reluctant to give up the benefits that can be attained through these non-branding methods and would still maintain a certain proportion of export in this manner. However, international operation is becoming more prevalent. If Chinese firms, especially those with great international marketing capability, don't make active efforts to implement branding strategies, in the long run it will be more difficult for them to build brands in the international market, improve their international competitiveness, and achieve sustainable development. Consequently, as international operation spreads, some external forces may urge Chinese firms to pursue branding strategies. For instance, governments or industrial associations can create conditions and establish mechanisms and platforms, such as foreign exhibitions and trademark registration, for qualified Chinese firms to carry out branding strategies. Firms still need to improve their own competence. They need to pay close attention to technological development trends and increase technology and product innovation efforts. They need to actively explore and seek conditions and opportunities to transform from OEM to OBM, gather strength for future development, and improve international competitiveness. They must work hard for the rise of Chinese brands in the international market.

6.6.2 Limitations and directions for future research

This chapter empirically studied and reached important conclusions regarding the determinants of Chinese exporters' OBM versus OEM choice and influence on export performance, but there are still some limitations: (1) When examining the influence of branding strategies on export performance and the determinants of branding strategies, this chapter fails to note the influence of industries and firm size and firm age. Future studies may explore such traits and investigate the relationships between these traits and branding strategies. (2) Research in this chapter doesn't study the evolution of Chinese firms' export branding strategies in time sequence. Future research may investigate the evolution of Chinese firms' export branding strategies and the change of its influence on export performance. This will be very suggestive for firms at different stages of internationalization to develop appropriate strategies.

7 Antecedents and consequences of distribution adaptation and price adaptation: a study of Chinese firms

Zuohao Hu, Fan Yi, Shunping Han and Xi Chen

7.1 Introduction

The marketing standardization/adaptation debate is a long-lasting topic in the research field of international marketing (Hu, 2002a). Scholars supporting the international marketing standardization view suggest that exporters should adopt a standardized marketing strategy globally to meet the demand of global consumers (Levitt, 1983), but supporters of the adaptation view suggest that exporters should adapt their marketing activities to meet the heterogeneous demand of local market segments in different countries (Fisher, 1984). In the following studies, some scholars propose to investigate the international marketing standardization/adaptation debate from the contingent perspective (Jain, 1989). Scholars who recognize the contingent view suggest that total standardization and total adaptation are two extremes of the international marketing strategy choice continuum. Firms' actual international marketing strategies are more often located in somewhere in between, and it is a matter of a higher degree of standardization or adaptation. The authors also suggest that the degree of marketing-mix adaptation/standardization should be determined by firms' internal and external environmental factors.

Chinese firms are increasingly involved in international markets in the context of a thriving global economy. How does a firm choose an effective international marketing strategy so as to achieve satisfactory performance? This has become a critical issue for Chinese exporters. However, in the current stage Chinese scholars' research on the standardization/adaptation of international marketing is confined to theoretical review and conceptual framework study, lacking systematic and empirical analysis (Hu, 2002a; Wu & Deng, 2007a). Therefore, an empirical study, using Chinese manufacturers as research objects, on the determinants of Chinese firms' international marketing standardization/adaptation choice and influence on export performance will not only enrich theoretical findings in China's international marketing research but also provide important practical value to Chinese firms.

Distribution strategy and pricing strategy are two topics most concerning to Chinese firms that are involved in international businesses. Therefore, this chapter uses a questionnaire survey to empirically study the relationship between

Chinese firms' distribution/price adaptation strategies and export performance and examine key factors that affect distribution adaptation and price adaptation strategies. The purpose is to identify determinants of firms' adaptation export strategy choice and reveal the nature of the relationship between adaptation and performance in the context of Chinese exporters.

7.2 Conceptual model and hypotheses

7.2.1 Theoretical framework

An international marketing strategy is a tool a firm develops in accordance with internal conditions and external factors in order to achieve international marketing goals. In international marketing strategy choice, a key issue is whether a firm should choose an adaptive or a standardized international marketing strategy. Using the standardization-adaptation continuum, this chapter assesses the international marketing strategies of Chinese manufacturing exporters from the perspectives of distribution adaptation and price adaptation. Here, distribution adaptation refers to the extent of using different channel structures in different national markets and adjusting channel structures according to circumstances; price adaptation means the extent of using different prices for the same product in different national markets in accordance with market pressure (Zou & Cavusgil, 2002).

According to the strategic management view, marketing strategies should be viewed as firms' strategic response to the interplay of internal and external factors, and export performance is influenced jointly by firms' international marketing strategies and internal factors. Zou and Cavusgil (1996) integrate the industrial organization (IO) theory and the resource-based view (RBV) to explain the determinants of international marketing strategies and the relationship between strategic performance and firm performance.

The IO theory suggests that external market and industrial structure determine a firm's strategic behaviors, which in turn determine the firm's performance. In other words, the congruence between firm strategy and its environment has a significant, positive influence on performance. In international marketing research, the most important external environment factors are the technological characteristics of the industry and the export market environment (Zou & Cavusgil, 1996).

The RBV theory claims that internal organizational factors are determinants of firms' strategies and performance, proposing that the differences of firms' strategic resources are the ultimate determinants of performance differences (Barney, 1991). Although the RBV indicates that firms' material resources are determinants of performance, it also stresses the importance of intangible resources. In the field of international marketing, a firm's global vision and its learning capability are considered the most important intangible resources (Moen & Servais, 2002).

Based on the aforementioned theoretical framework and research topic of this chapter, we propose the following conceptual framework (see Figure 7.1).

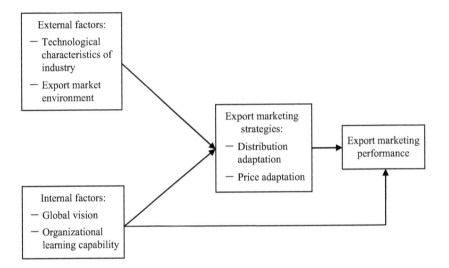

Figure 7.1 Conceptual framework

The conceptual framework in this chapter has three main characteristics: (1) We choose distribution adaptation and price adaptation strategies, which are of the most practical significance to Chinese firms, as firms' exporting strategies and examine their influences on export performance. (2) We divide determinants of export marketing strategies into two categories: internal factors and external factors. External factors include technological characteristics of the industry and export market environment, both of which are the most important factors in the field of international marketing, while internal factors include global vision and learning capability, which are the most important intangible resources for firms' internationalization. (3) Firms' export performance is not only directly affected by international marketing strategies but also directly influenced by firms' internal factors.

7.2.2 *Hypotheses*

Export performance is defined as the extent to which a firm's objectives with respect to international businesses are achieved through the planning and execution of export marketing strategy (Cavusgil & Zou, 1994). Export performance is determined by a firm's export marketing strategy and its capability to execute the established strategy. When an exporter adapts its distribution channel strategy to distribution structure, the effective number of distributors and retailers, and consumers' preferred shopping locations, it would be easier for the exporter to establish cooperation with local distributors and therefore achieve better export performance. Similarly, a price adaptation strategy that is adjusted to conditions of a local market can improve the competitiveness of the firm, enhance consumers' perceived value, expand sales, and thus lead to better export performance (Cavusgil & Zou, 1994).

Based on this analysis, we posit the following hypotheses:

H1a: The degree of distribution adaptation is positively related to a firm's export performance.

H1b: The degree of price adaptation is positively related to a firm's export performance.

In the field of export marketing, technological characteristics of an industry should be considered an important factor that influences export marketing strategy (Jain, 1989). Technological characteristics of an industry include two factors: technology intensity (compared to labor intensity) of the industry and speed of technological change in the industry. In an industry with high technology intensity and fast technological change, products would have greater technological complexity. Therefore, the firm would require foreign distributors to understand the products' technology and possess the skills to sell them and provide relevant services. It would also require foreign distributors to explore the local sales network and sell the products as quickly as possible. Because the structures and operational capabilities of distributors vary greatly in different countries, it is imperative that exporters adopt different distribution channel models in accordance with the structures and attributes of distributors in different markets and adjust the business relationship based on local environmental changes. Therefore, in an industry with higher technology intensity and faster technological change, exporters would be more likely to adopt distribution adaptation strategies. Similarly, with high technology intensity and fast technological change, exporters tend to pursue competitive pricing strategies based on local market conditions so as to recoup investment in technology R&D and accelerate sales volume (in order to reduce stock and valuation loss). Therefore, in an industry with higher technology intensity and faster technological change, firms are more likely to adopt price adaptation strategies.

In export marketing research, export market environment is another important factor influencing strategic choices (Jain, 1989; Zou & Cavusgil, 1996). Expanding into foreign markets would bring exporters opportunities as well as challenges. Export marketing strategies need to align market opportunities with firms' advantages, reducing firms' strategic weaknesses and neutralizing threats. Consequently, export marketing strategies need to be adjusted in accordance with the characteristics of the export market environment. In this chapter, export market environment includes competitive intensity in the export market and customers' demand change. Competitive intensity in the export market requires exporters to construct proper distributional channels and pursue competitive pricing strategies based on the characteristics of the local market. Therefore, it is imperative that firms adopt a higher level of distribution adaptation and price adaptation under severe competition. Meanwhile, customers' demand change in the export market also requires that firms adapt distributional channels and pricing strategies that are able to meet the unique preferences of local consumers. Therefore, higher competitive intensity and faster change in customer demand in the export market would increase the possibility of firms' adopting distribution adaptation and price adaptation strategies.

Based on this analysis, we posit the following hypotheses:

> H2a: Technological intensity and the speed of technological change are positively related to the degree of distribution adaptation strategy.
> H2b: Technological intensity and the speed of technological change are positively related to the degree of price adaptation strategy.
> H3a: Competitive intensity and customers' demand change in the export markets are positively related to the adoption of a distribution adaptation strategy.
> H3b: Competitive intensity and customers' demand change in the export markets are positively related to the adoption of a price adaptation strategy.

In the field of export marketing, a firm's international vision, which is an intangible resource of the firm, is an important internal factor that affects export marketing strategies (Moen & Servais, 2002). A firm's international vision is a firm-wide organizational culture that identifies and responds to international market opportunities. It is a manifestation of the firm's values. Ohmae (1985) suggests that a firm with an international vision tends to pursue world-oriented strategies. Such firms are likely to view different national markets with an equidistant perspective and develop synergetic marketing strategies. Therefore, we propose that firms with global visions are more likely to adopt distribution and pricing strategies with higher degrees of standardization. In other words, their distribution and price strategies are likely to have low degrees of adaptation.

In the field of export marketing, organizational learning capability, which is an intangible resource of the firm, is an important internal factor that affects export marketing strategies (Menon *et al.*, 1999). Organizational learning capability refers to the aggressiveness of an organization and its ability to acquire and share new knowledge and new mindsets. Organizational learning capability has a profound significance on the future development of the firm. A firm with strong learning capability is more sensitive to the change of export market environment and hence can respond faster to market turbulence. Therefore, we propose that a firm with strong organizational learning capability is more likely to pursue distribution adaptation and price adaptation strategies.

Based on this analysis, we posit the following hypotheses:

> H4a: A firm's international vision is negatively related to its distribution adaptation strategy.
> H4b: A firm's international vision is negatively related to its price adaptation strategy.

H5a: A firm's learning capability is positively related to the degree of its distribution adaptation.

H5b: A firm's learning capability is positively related to the degree of its price adaptation.

According to the RBV theory, firm resources not only influence a firm's strategic choice but also its export performance (Zou & Cavusgil, 1996). International vision and organizational learning capability are valuable intangible resources of a firm, and they have a direct impact on a firm's export performance. Firms that have international visions tend to attach more importance, make great organizational commitment, and allocate a substantial amount of resources to their export businesses and thus attain desirable export performance (Zou & Cavusgil, 1996; Moen & Servais, 2002). Similarly, firms with great organizational learning capability may conveniently develop, gather, and share knowledge and resources that can bring them core competitive advantages, help them cope with competition in the international market in a better and timelier manner, and therefore attain better export performance (Menon *et al.*, 1999).

Based on this analysis, we posit the following hypotheses:

H6a: A firm's international vision is positively related to export performance.

H6b: A firm's learning capability is positively related to export performance.

7.3 Methodology

7.3.1 Questionnaire design

All the measure items in the questionnaire come from existing literature and have been adjusted according to the actual conditions of Chinese exporters. We base our questionnaire on the existing instruments that have been developed by foreign scholars including Cavusgil and Zou (1994), Bello and Gilliland (1997), Menon *et al.* (1999), and Moen and Servais (2002). We also interviewed relevant managers from 12 Chinese manufacturing exporters regarding the validity and comprehensiveness of the content. We asked for their opinions on whether the setting of item indicators in the instrument covers all the main contents of the variables and whether the expression is explicit. Meanwhile, we invited three marketing experts to assess the validity of the instrument. Our questionnaire consists of seven parts, measuring respectively: export performance, distribution adaptation, price adaptation, technological characteristics of industry, export market environment, firm's international vision, and firm's learning capability. Variables and items in our model are shown in Table 7.1.

7.3.2 Sample description

This survey studies exporting firms from China's manufacturing industry. We sent 1,100 questionnaires to manufacturing exporters listed on manufacturing

Table 7.1 Results of confirmatory factor analysis

Constructs	Measure items	Standardized factor loadings	t value	Composite reliability
Export performance	Whether export performance has met the firm's expected export strategic goals	0.82	11.79	0.90
	Whether your firm is satisfied with product export performance	0.9	13.59	
	Whether your firm is satisfied with export growth	0.89	13.45	
	Whether your firm is satisfied with export profitability	0.73	10.01	
Distribution adaptation	We adopt different types of distribution channels for different export markets	0.81	8.78	0.76
	We and our distributors would adjust bilateral business relationship in accordance with local market environment	0.75	8.21	
Price adaptation	We adopt different price strategies in different export markets	0.92	8.23	0.81
	The price of the same product differs in different export markets	0.72	7.11	
Industrial characteristics	Technology changes very fast in our industry	0.71	8.35	0.76
	The level of technology intensity is very high in our industry	0.83	9.74	
	The level of labor intensity is very low in our industry	0.62	7.27	
Export market environment	Demand changes very fast in our main export market	0.64	7.64	0.77
	Competition is fierce in our main export market	0.91	10.71	
	There are great uncertainties in our main export market	0.60	7.11	
International vision	We always consider the international market as our target market	0.80	10.54	0.82
	Exploring the international market is the mission of our firm	0.85	11.40	
	Our firm has a culture of actively seeking international market opportunities	0.68	8.59	

(*Continued*)

Table 7.1 (Continued)

Constructs	Measure items	Standardized factor loadings	t value	Composite reliability
Learning capability	Our knowledge of the international market increases and deepens as our export business develops	0.83	11.71	0.86
	Our export marketing and management skills keep improving as our export business develops	0.90	13.16	
	We keep drawing lessons from the past, so as to improve the work experience and efficiency of employees	0.72	9.67	

industry yellow pages; of these questionnaires 221 were returned, and 30 were withdrawn due to incompatibility in firm nature (trading exporter or foreign-funded firms, etc.). A total of 849 questionnaires were delivered successfully. Leaving out those that were either incomplete or apparently erroneous, the final number of valid questionnaires suitable for this study was 148. The questionnaires were completed by relevant personnel (such as overseas market managers) from the export departments of indigenous Chinese manufacturers. Results of confirmatory analysis are presented in Table 7.1.

Geographical distribution of the sample firms: 22.3% in Zhejiang, 19.59% in Guangdong, 15.54% in Jiangsu, 11.49% in Beijing, 6.76% in Shandong, 4.73% in Hebei, and the remaining 19.59% in other regions. Employee size of the surveyed firms: 37.84% with less than 200 employees, 18.92% with 200–500 employees, 14.86% with 500–1,000 employees, 19.59% with 1,000–5,000 employees, and 8.11% with more than 5,000 employees, with 0.68% of missing data. Among the surveyed firms, 50% of them started export business within the past 5 years, 31.08% of them started export business 5–10 years ago, 6.76% of them started export 10–20 years ago, and 2.03% of them started their export 20–50 years ago, with 8.78% of missing data.

7.3.3 Reliability and validity analysis

This research uses the LISREL software to conduct confirmatory factor analysis (CFA). In terms of construct reliability, the factor loadings and errors obtained from model estimation are used to calculate composite reliability (see Table 7.1). Generally speaking, the composite reliability of construct variables should be greater than 0.70. According to our CFA results, the composite reliability of all construct variables are greater than 0.70, indicating desirable reliability.

Anderson and Gerbing (1988) point out that factor loadings of greater than 0.5 would indicate good convergent validity. In this research, the standardized factor loadings of all items on the respective variables that they measure are greater than 0.50 and are statistically significant, indicating that all measuring items have high convergent validity.

In terms of discriminant validity, this research calculates the average variance extracted (AVE) of all construct variables. Generally speaking, AVE of higher than the critical value of 0.50 or greater than the correlation coefficient of that construct variable to all other construct variables would indicate desirable discriminant validity. In our CFA model, the AVE value of all construct variables meets the requirements. Therefore, we propose that the measure model has desirable discriminant validity.

7.4 Hypothesis tests

7.4.1 Testing hypotheses

In this chapter, the structural equation model is used to conduct statistical analysis. The fitting parameters of the model are: chi-square = 178.90, df = 152, chi-square/df = 1.1770; p-value = 0.06711, RMSEA = 0.035; NNFI = 0.96, CFI = 0.97, IFI = 0.97, GFI = 0.89, AGFI = 0.85. All these fitting indices meet the requirement for further analysis, indicating good fit between the structure model and sampled data, and therefore can be used to test our research hypotheses. The standardized path coefficient and degree of significance of all construct variables are shown in Figure 7.2.

7.4.2 Results and analysis

Model results show that distribution adaptation has a significant, positive influence on export performance; thus hypothesis H1a is supported. This indicates

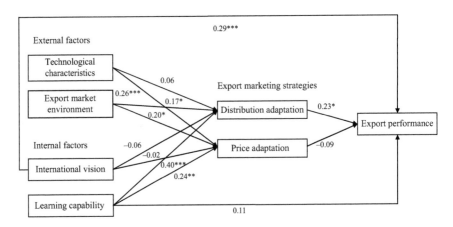

Figure 7.2 Results of Structural Equation Model (SEM) analysis

Note: * p < 0.05; ** p < 0.01; *** p < 0.005.

that adopting distribution channel models that are adapted to the local market environment and enhancing communication with distribution channels can effectively help Chinese exporters understand the local market, avoid operation risks, and improve export performance. Therefore, for Chinese exporters, adopting effective distribution adaptation strategies is a guarantee for successful entry into other markets and desirable performance.

Model results show that price adaptation does not have a significant influence on export performance; hence hypothesis H1b is not supported. This indicates that at the current stage neither adaptation nor standardization on pricing strategy by Chinese firms could guarantee desirable export performance.

In terms of the influence of external environment factors on adaptation strategies, model analysis results show that the technological characteristics of an industry do not have a significant positive influence on distribution adaptation, so hypothesis H2a is not supported; however, technological characteristics have a significant positive influence on price adaptation, and hence hypothesis H2b is supported. This indicates that in an industry with high technology intensity and fast technological change firms would tend to pursue pricing strategies with a higher degree of adaptation, whereas in an industry with low technology intensity and slow technological change firms tend to pursue pricing strategies with a lower degree of adaptation.

Model analysis results show that export market environment, as an external factor, has a significant positive influence on distribution adaptation as well as price adaptation. Therefore, hypotheses H3a and H3b are supported. These empirical findings indicate that when competition is fierce and customer demand changes rapidly in the export market, thus resulting in great uncertainties of market environment, Chinese exporters are more likely to pursue export marketing strategies with a higher degree of distribution adaptation and price adaptation.

In terms of the influence of internal factors on adaptation strategies, statistical results show that although international vision is negatively related to firms' distribution adaptation and price adaptation, in the same direction as we posit in this research, the relationships are not significant. Therefore, hypotheses H4a and H4b are not supported.

Although international vision doesn't have a significant influence on distribution adaptation and price adaptation, statistical analysis results show that it has a significant positive influence on export performance; thus hypothesis H6a is supported. Empirical findings indicate that the greater a firm's international vision, the better its export performance. The reason is that a firm with an international vision tends to attach great importance and make great commitment to its export business, guaranteeing the implementation of its export marketing strategies and the operation of its export business by consolidating resource configuration, thus creating favorable conditions for it to achieve desirable export performance.

Model results show that organizational learning capability has a significant positive influence on distribution adaptation and price adaptation; hence hypotheses H5a and H5b are supported. We find that the path coefficient of the influence of learning capability on distribution adaptation is 0.40, the greatest of all influence coefficients, indicating that the learning capability of Chinese exporters has an important influence on distribution adaptation.

Organizational learning capability does not have a significant direct influence on export performance; hence hypothesis H6b is not supported. However, research shows that learning capability has an indirect influence on export performance, and such influence is passed on to export performance by means of distribution adaptation strategies.

7.5 Conclusions and directions for future research

7.5.1 Conclusions

The main conclusions of this research can be summarized as follows: First, the distribution adaptation and price adaptation strategies adopted by Chinese firms in their international operation are jointly driven by firms' external factors and international factors, but the extents of the influences of these internal and external factors vary. Export market environment and organizational learning capability have significant positive influences on the degree of distribution adaptation, and technological characteristics of industries, export market environment, and organizational learning capability have significant positive influences on the degree of price adaptation, although the influence of learning capability is greater. Therefore, in developing distribution and pricing strategies, Chinese manufacturing exporters should attach importance to significant internal and external driving forces, particularly organizational learning capability. Second, the export performance of Chinese firms is directly affected by distribution adaptation and international vision and indirectly affected by export market environment and learning capability. This indicates that Chinese firms can achieve satisfactory performance only by developing international marketing strategies that are consistent with the characteristics of the market environment they are in and their internal conditions; in addition, it also indicates that firms can achieve satisfactory performance through effective strategic choice (distribution adaptation) and improving organizational capabilities (international vision and learning capability). Third, empirical research shows that the influence of learning capability on distribution adaptation and price adaptation strategies is the greatest (path coefficients 0.4 and 0.24 respectively), and learning capability can also affect performance indirectly by means of distribution adaptation strategies; the direct influence of learning capability on export performance is also considerable (path coefficient 0.29). This indicates that, for Chinese firms, improving their international vision and learning capabilities, both internal factors, will not only help them choose effective marketing strategies but also will help them improve export performance. Meanwhile, empirical findings also show that developing organizational learning capability is a key issue no business manager should ignore. As their export businesses grow, firms that keep reviewing and learning from the conditions of the international market and improving their export marketing skills and management decision-making processes accordingly will find it easier to implement their adaptation strategies.

7.5.2 Limitations and directions for future research

There are also some limitations in this chapter that hint at the directions for future research.

First, adaptation strategies in international marketing involve four aspects: product, pricing, distribution, and promotion. This chapter focuses on key determinants of distribution adaptation and price adaptation strategy choices and their relationships with export performance. Therefore, future studies may investigate key determinants of product adaptation and promotion adaptation strategy choices and their relationships with export performance, so as to comprehensively reveal the characteristics of Chinese firms' international marketing strategy choices.

Second, the research model in this chapter stresses only four internal and external factors, namely technological characteristics of industries, export market environment, international vision, and learning capability. However, internal and external factors involve a much wider scope of factors, such as external factors like social and legal environments of the export market and cultural similarities, and internal factors like firms' international experience and degree of organizational centralization, among others. Therefore, it is necessary to establish a more complicated, integrated model for empirical research in the future.

Lastly, this research surveys a sample of more than 140 Chinese manufacturing exporters and tests the posited relationships of the theoretical model based on the survey. However, as Chinese firms' export businesses grow rapidly, and export market environment and attributes of exporters are constantly changing, future research may focus on the dynamic changes of determinants of Chinese exporters' marketing strategies and their relationships with export performance.

8 The effect of overseas channel control on export performance

Zuohao Hu, Xi Chen and Ping Zhao

8.1 Introduction

Overseas distribution channel control has always been a topic that scholars study and pay close attention to in international marketing research (Keegan, 1995; Hu & Kondo, 2002). As a matter of fact, exporters' overseas distribution channels are imbedded in countries' market environments and marketing systems that differ greatly from one another. Therefore, the overseas channel control strategies become the most challenging part of their export marketing strategies and are closely related to export performance (Cavusgil & Zou, 1994; Bello & Gilliland, 1997). Consequently, how export manufacturers can effectively control their overseas distribution channels and achieve superior export performance has become an important topic in the research field of export marketing that urgently requires a solution.

Currently existing research in the field of channel control has two limitations: (1) The majority of relevant studies have been conducted in the domestic marketing context, and few studies have focused on the relationship between exporters' overseas distribution channel control and export performance (Hewett & Bearden, 2001), and empirical research on Chinese exporters' overseas distribution channel control is rare (Hu, 2002a). (2) In research regarding the types of channel control and its relationship with performance, little academic attention has been paid to the moderation effect of other factors on the relationship between channel control and performance (Bello & Gilliland, 1997).

Considering the aforementioned limitations of current research on channel control and export marketing, this chapter uses a sample of Chinese export manufacturers as research objects and conducts empirical study focusing on the following two questions: (1) In Chinese manufacturers' export marketing activities, how does the overseas distribution control mode (unilateral control or bilateral control) influence export performance, and to what extent? (2) How does innovative corporate culture moderate such relationship?

8.2 Literature review and research hypotheses

In the channel control literature, channel control can be divided into market governance and nonmarket governance (Heide, 1994; Bello & Gilliland, 1997).

Market governance is a kind of sporadic and random exchange initialized by both parties spontaneously (discrete exchange), whereas nonmarket governance is a kind of regular exchange in which a relationship has been established between both parties (relational exchange). Scholars who follow the market and nonmarket typology also divide nonmarket governance into unilateral governance and bilateral governance based on the number of governing bodies (Heide, 1994). Unilateral governance means that one exchange partner has the authority to develop rules, give instructions, and supervise the implementation of established plans. Generally, this authority resides with the manufacturers. They give unilateral instructions to influence the behaviors of distributors so as to coordinate and control channel activities and ensure the fulfillment of manufacturers' anticipated goals. In bilateral governance, however, manufacturers and distributors share common goals. They develop strategies together, make decisions together when facing emergencies, and seek solutions together. Bilateral governance is a mechanism for bilateral cooperation (Nevin, 1995). This chapter focuses on investigating the influence of unilateral governance and bilateral governance on export performance.

8.2.1 Relationships between process control, outcome control, and export performance

Unilateral governance has two forms: process control and outcome control (Jaworski *et al.*, 1993). Process control is export manufacturers' influence and control on the daily operation of overseas distributors, such as influencing the marketing methods, new product introduction, promotion activities, after-sale services, and other marketing activities of distributors. Bello and Gilliland (1997) study American firms' export channels and find that very often manufacturers do not fully understand the complexities of the foreign market. Neither do the exporters completely recognize that domestic selling processes may not transfer to foreign markets. Consequently, manufacturer interventions to influence selling and other marketing activities of the distributor do not improve export performance. Similarly, after interviewing indigenous Chinese exporters, we learn that the marketing approaches of many export products in the domestic market are very different from those in overseas markets. Export manufacturers generally lack sufficient knowledge of overseas markets (for instance, what marketing plans should be made before new product launch in a developed market; which, advertising or discount, would be a more effective promotion method). If they merely transfer their market strategies in the domestic market directly to the overseas markets and intervene in the marketing activities of overseas distributors, it would compromise export performance. In this case, process control would reduce export performance.

Therefore, we posit:

H1: Process control over overseas distributors is negatively related to export performance.

Outcome control is a form of unilateral governance that controls performance outcome. Specifically, in the outcome control mode, the exporter sets operation goals and corresponding performance standards for overseas distributors in advance and conducts regular performance assessment afterward to evaluate the degrees of distributors' achievements of performance goals.

By setting up performance goals that are acceptable to both parties and engaging in regular assessment of overseas distributors' operation performance, export manufacturers that adopt outcome control spur overseas distributors to work hard so as to attain distribution goals they have accepted in advance. Meanwhile, export manufacturers adopting outcome control tend not to intervene in the day-to-day operation of overseas distributors. This way, overseas distributors can allocate resource configuration in accordance with their own ideas and expertise in their daily operation. This approach/mode would provide them with operation autonomy and thus reduce manufacturer-distributor friction. Therefore, adopting outcome control on overseas distribution channels can not only inspire overseas distributors to work hard so as to achieve anticipated export performance goals but also can reduce friction between manufacturers and distributors and therefore improve export performance. The empirical study of Bello and Gilliland (1997) also finds that exporters' outcome control on overseas distribution channels can improve export performance. Therefore, we propose the following hypothesis:

H2: Outcome control over overseas distributors is negatively related to export performance.

8.2.2 Relationship between flexibility and export performance

Bilateral governance is a mutual cooperative mechanism between export manufacturers and overseas distributors. It is a flexible adjustment (flexibility) made by both parties in case of change of environment (Heide, 1994; Bello & Gilliland, 1997). Such bilateral governance is generally reflected in both channel members' willingness to show flexibility in realizing both parties' needs and goals when the market environment changes. It can result in cooperative behaviors (such as formulating plans that both parties agree on) by means of relational processes (such as negotiation and mutual communication), so as to cope with environmental changes. In relational exchange research, such flexible adjustment processes are known as the norm-based mechanism of governance (Nevin, 1995).

Both export manufacturers and overseas distributors cope with environmental changes through flexible adjustments and make coordinated effort to formulate export distribution channel strategies and manage distribution channel activities. By this approach, exporters can improve the efficiency and effectiveness of the entire export distribution channel system, reduce channel cost, and create competitive advantages. In addition, flexibility of bilateral governance can restrain opportunistic behaviors through the socialization of shared value, causing channel members to attach more importance to the long-run benefits of the channel system when making operation decisions. Therefore, the bilateral governance form of flexible adjustment can bring better export performance (Cavusgil & Zou, 1994). Therefore, we posit the following hypothesis:

> H3: Flexibility between export manufacturers and overseas distributors is positively related to export performance.

8.2.3 Moderation effect of organizational innovation culture

Innovation culture is a type of organizational culture that stresses innovation, development of new ideas, communication and participation, and rapid response (Menon & Varadarajan, 1992). An innovative organizational culture can moderate the relationship between the control mode over overseas distributional channel and export performance.

An export manufacturer with an innovation culture can reduce internal organizational friction, increase communication within the organization, and improve operational flexibility by encouraging organizational creativity. An innovative manufacturer would encourage communication and participation, which is conducive to intra-organizational and inter-organizational communication and cooperation. In addition, a manufacturer with an innovative culture tends to respond to environmental changes rapidly and flexibly and develop timely solutions that are beneficial to both sides (Wooldridge & Floyd, 1989). Therefore, under the influence of an innovative culture, the export manufacturer would be able to, thanks to its internal communication and cooperation, offer effective instructions and operation advice to overseas distributors regarding their marketing activities and process control and therefore help them improve export performance. Similarly, under the influence of an innovative culture, the export manufacturer would encourage overseas distributors to increase communication and participate in channel decision-making. The result is that in cases of environmental change both sides can attach more importance to flexible adjustment and work together to develop channel strategies that are beneficial to both sides. This would lead to better export performance. On the other hand, under the influence of an innovative culture, the export manufacturer would pay more attention to changes and innovation. Consequently, when exporters adopt outcome control they might intervene in the operation process of overseas distributors or keep adjusting the goals according to environmental changes. This mode may cause conflict between the two sides and therefore erode export performance. Based on this analysis, we posit the following hypotheses:

> H4a: Innovative culture of export manufacturers moderates the relationship between process control and export performance. Specifically, the stronger a manufacturer's innovative culture, the greater the influence of the manufacturer's process control on export performance.
>
> H4b: Innovative culture of export manufacturers moderates the relationship between outcome control and export performance. Specifically, the

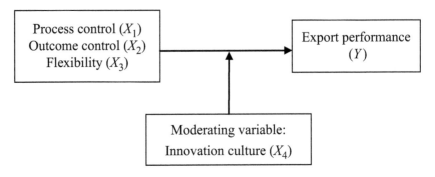

Figure 8.1 The conceptual framework of the influence of overseas distribution channel control modes on export performance

stronger a manufacturer's innovative culture, the weaker the influence of the manufacturer's outcome control on export performance.

H4c: Innovative culture of export manufacturers moderates the relationship between flexibility and export performance. Specifically, the stronger a manufacturer's innovative culture, the greater the influence of flexibility on its export performance.

The conceptual framework in this chapter is shown in Figure 8.1.

8.3 Methodology

8.3.1 Questionnaire design

All measure items of the research variables in the questionnaire are based on existing literature (e.g., Heide & John, 1992; Bello & Gilliland, 1997; Moen & Servais, 2002) and have been appropriately adjusted according to the actual conditions of Chinese firms. The instrument consists of three parts: the first part examines 14 items of the four variables (process control, outcome control, flexibility, and innovative culture); the second part examines five items of firms' export performance; the third part examines basic firm attributes like geographical location, the firm's industry, number of years of establishment, international experience, and firm size, among others. In part three, firm size and international experience are two control variables of the model.

8.3.2 Sample description

This survey investigates China's manufacturing exporters. The time of the questionnaire survey lasted from May 2005 to January 2006. We sent 1,100 questionnaires to manufacturing exporters listed on industrial yellow pages; of these questionnaires 221 were returned, and 30 were withdrawn due to incompatibility of firm nature (trading exporter or foreign-funded firms, etc.). A total of 849 questionnaires were delivered successfully. Leaving out those that were either incomplete or apparently erroneous, the final number of valid questionnaires suitable for this study was 115, with a response rate of 13.5%. The questionnaires were completed by relevant personnel (such as overseas marketing managers) from the export departments of indigenous Chinese manufacturers. Distribution of the final sample is as follows: firms with less than 200 employees: 37.4%; with 200–500 employees: 20%; with 500–1,000 employees: 17.4%; with 1,000–5,000 employees: 14.8%; with 5,000 or more employees: 9.6%; one value in this regard is missing. In terms of export revenue, percentage of firms with less than 20 million (RMB): 14.8%; with 20–50 million: 20.9%; with 50–100 million: 18.3%; with 100–500 million: 20.9%; with 500 and above million: 20.9%; five values are missing in this regard. Geographically, the surveyed firms are located in 24 provinces and cities, the top three locations being Zhejiang Province, Jiangsu Province, and Guangdong Province.

8.3.3 Reliability and validity tests

In terms of reliability, our survey uses LISREL to conduct a confirmatory factor analysis (CFA) on the measurement model, and the calculation result is then used to calculate the composite reliability (CR). All the construct variables have a CR value of greater than 0.7, indicating that the reliability of construct variables in this questionnaire is desirable for the following analysis.

In terms of convergent validity, according to calculation results, the standardized factor loadings of all items, except for the loadings of the first item of innovative culture (which is 0.49), on the respective variables they measure are greater than 0.60 and are statistically significant ($t > 6.50$), indicating that all items on the variables they measure have high convergent validity. Indicators of level of fitting between the measurement model and data are: $\chi^2 = 244.33$ ($df = 125; \chi^2/df = 1.95$), RMSEA = 0.087, CFI = 0.91, GFI = 0.81, IFI = 0.91, indicating good fit between our measurement model and data. CFA results indicate that the convergent validity of construct variables measures in this questionnaire is desirable for the following analysis.

In terms of discriminant validity, this research calculates the AVE (average variance extracted) of every construct variables and finds that every AVE is higher than the critical value of 0.50, thus guaranteeing the capability to explain valid variance and indicating desirable discriminant validity among the construct variables.

8.4 Hypothesis tests and discussion

8.4.1 Model estimation

Based on the conceptual model, we define our regression equation as follows:

$$Y = \beta_1 X_1 + \beta_2 X_2 + \beta_3 X_3 + (\beta_4 X_4 X_1 + \beta_5 X_4 X_2 + \beta_6 X_4 X_3) + \beta_7 X_5 + \beta_8 X_6$$

In this equation,

Y represents export performance,
X_1 represents process control on overseas distributors
X_2 represents outcome control on overseas distributors
X_3 represents the flexibility of export manufacturers' and overseas distributors' response to environmental change
X_4 represents export manufacturers' innovative culture
X_5 represents export manufacturers' international experience
X_6 represents the size of export manufacturers
X_iX_j represents the interaction between X_i and X_j
β represents the standardized regression coefficient of all items

This chapter adopts a multiple linear regression method to estimate the model. To avoid multicollinearity all interaction items have been centered. Multicollinearity test results show that all VIF values are far lower than 5, indicating that a multicollinearity problem doesn't exist. In order to test moderation effect, this chapter uses two models. First, Model I examines three main effects, namely process control, outcome control, and flexibility, and two control variables, namely international experience and firm size, to perform multiple regression. Building on Model I, Model II adds three interactions, namely the interactions between innovative culture and process control, outcome control, and flexibility. In comparison, the significances of both models in terms of control variables and main effects are identical, but the addition of interaction items increases the explanatory power of Model II (R^2 change reaching 0.27). Therefore, based on the results (Table 8.1) of the full model (Model II), we report and analyze the findings of hypotheses test.

8.4.2 Results and discussion

According to model results, although manufacturers' process control on distributors' operation activities has a negative influence ($\beta = -0.124$) on export performance, the influence is not significant. Therefore, H1 is not supported.

H2 is supported ($\beta = 0.495$, $p < 0.01$), indicating that outcome control on overseas distributors has a positive influence on export performance; the β value is 0.495, the greatest of all influence coefficients. This result indicates that Chinese export manufacturers' outcome control on overseas distribution channels indeed has an important influence on the improvement of export performance. We propose that there are two reasons for this result: (1) Outcome control gives overseas distributors autonomy. This enables them to choose appropriate local marketing strategies based on their resource endowments and competitive advantages. Distribution goals help them perform self-control and inspire them to achieve desirable export performance. (2) Most Chinese business managers are used to the management methods of adopting indices and setting quantitative targets and evaluating outcome at the end of the year. Chinese firms' habits of emphasizing outcome control while neglecting process control have given

Table 8.1 Linear regression results

	Standardized regression coefficient (β)	
	Model I	*Model II (full model)*
Main effects		
X_1 process control	−0.094	−0.124
X_2 outcome control	0.476★★★	0.495★★★
X_3 flexibility	0.264★★★	0.323★★★
Control variables		
X_5 international experience	0.214★★★	0.241★★★
X_6 firm size	−0.040	−0.064
Interactions		
X_4 innovative culture × X_1 process control		0.111
X_4 innovative culture × X_2 outcome control		−0.183★
X_4 innovative culture × X_3 flexibility		0.197★★
R^2	0.415	0.456
Adj. R^2	0.387	0.414
ΔR^2		0.027

Note: ★ $p < 0.10$, ★★ $p < 0.05$, ★★★ $p < 0.01$.

them plenty of experience in adopting the outcome control mode (such as how to motivate distributors by setting up effective goals); therefore, such habits are conducive to the formulation of effective outcome control strategies and in turn lead to better export performance.

H3 is supported ($\beta = 0.323, p < 0.01$). Thus, flexibility, as a form of bilateral governance, has a significant positive influence on export performance. Model results show that when external environment changes, export manufacturers and overseas distributors work with each other. They develop new plans and new policies in accordance with the dynamics of the environment and from a win-win operation perspective. They deal with new challenges in a flexible manner and solve new operation problems, thus achieving desirable export performance.

As for the moderation effect of innovative culture, H4a is not supported while H4b and H4c are supported. The fact that H4a is not supported indicates that innovative culture does not have a significant moderation effect on the relationship between process control and export performance. The result of H4b is significant ($\beta = -0.183, p < 0.10$), consistent with the hypothesis that innovative culture negatively moderates the relationship between outcome control and export performance. This indicates that the stronger a firm's innovative culture, the weaker the effect of exporters' outcome control on export performance. H4c is supported ($\beta = 0.197, p < 0.01$). Thus, a firm's innovative culture positively moderates the relationship between flexibility and export performance, which indicates that the stronger a firm's innovative culture, the greater the influence of flexibility on export performance.

Two control variables are introduced to our model: international experience and firm size. The result of regression analysis on international experience ($\beta = 0.241, p < 0.01$) shows that the more international experience a firm has, the better its export performance. Regression results on firm size ($\beta = -0.064$) is not significant. In other words, the size of an exporter doesn't have a significant influence on its export performance. It indicates that the export performance of firms is not significantly related to their sizes.

8.5 Conclusions and directions for future research

8.5.1 Conclusions

This chapter uses a sample of Chinese manufacturing exporters to empirically study the relationship between exporters' mode of control on overseas distribution channels and export performance; organizational innovative culture is introduced as a moderation variable to examine the moderation effect of innovative culture on the relationship between exporters' overseas distribution channel control and export performance. Research findings in this chapter have important theoretical value and practical implication.

The theoretical value of our research is twofold: (1) This chapter investigates the relationship between exporters' overseas channel control mode and export performance. The research finds that outcome control (as a form of unilateral governance) and flexibility (as a form of bilateral governance) have significant positive influences on export performance. However, process control, as a form of unilateral governance, doesn't have a significant negative influence on export performance. (2) This chapter originally introduces innovative culture as a moderation variable in the relationship between distribution channel control mode and export performance. The research finds that organizational innovative culture has a significant negative moderating effect on the relationship between outcome control and export performance and has a significant positive moderating effect on the relationship between flexibility and export performance. These research findings not only fill the gap in the research field of Chinese export manufacturers' control on overseas marketing channels, but also contribute to international theoretical achievements regarding the relationship between exporters' overseas distribution channel control and export performance.

The practical implications of this chapter are reflected in the following aspects: (1) Because outcome control on overseas distribution channels has a significant positive effect on export performance, Chinese export manufacturers need to pursue effective outcome control strategies in their export marketing activities so as to achieve desirable export performance. Specifically, export manufacturers adopting outcome control should set in advance a series of distribution goals and performance standards that are acceptable to both sides and conduct performance assessments ex post so as to evaluate overseas distributors' achievements of these goals. The outcome control mode gives overseas distributors operational autonomy, motivates them to exert more effort on manufac-tures' products, and hence reduces friction and improves export performance. (2) Although empirical research finds that the influence of process control on export performance is not salient, the negative result of the regression coeffi-cient suggests that such a research hypothesis cannot be rejected. This requires that Chinese exporters be cautious about adopting the process control mode on overseas distributors; especially when the exporters are not familiar with the overseas market environment, the process control mode should be used with even greater caution or should not be used at all. (3) Because flexibility, as a form of bilateral governance, has a positive significant influence on export per-formance, export manufacturers should conduct two-way communication with overseas distributors and establish cooperation mechanisms based on shared values, so as to effectively cope with the dynamic change of operational envi-ronment in a timely manner and achieve better export performance. (4) Model results show that innovative culture has a significant positive moderating effect on the relationship between flexibility and export performance. Therefore, for exporters that pursue the bilateral control strategy, an innovative culture that emphasizes innovation, development of new ideas, communication and par-ticipation, and rapid response would significantly improve export performance. Nevertheless, because innovative culture has a significant negative moderation effect on the relationship between outcome control and export performance, Chinese export manufacturers that adopt outcome control strategies, even with an innovation culture, should avoid over-intervention in overseas distributors' autonomous operation, which would demotivate overseas distributors and engender conflicts in the distribution channels. (5) International experience, as a control variable, has a significant influence on export performance. This result indicates that the earlier a firm starts its export marketing activities and the more international experience it has, the better its export performance. Therefore, for Chinese exporters accumulation of international experience is very important for the achievement of desirable export performance.

8.5.2 Limitations and directions for future research

This chapter investigates the relationship between overseas channel control mode and export performance from the perspectives of unilateral governance and bilateral governance. There are three limitations to this research: (1) This chapter studies the influence of flexibility, as a form of bilateral governance, on export performance. Future studies may examine the influences of other forms of bilateral governance besides flexibility on export performance (Heide & John, 1992). (2) The outcome control mode involves setting of numerous indi-ces like sales target, market coverage rate, and so forth, and different indices would produce different control results. Similarly, under the process control mode, control on different items, such as price control, brand value control, and after-sale service control, would affect export performance differently. Therefore, future studies may further examine the influences of specific indices or control items on export performance and the extents of their influences. (3) This chapter uses firm size and international experience as control variables. In fact, many other firm attributes, such as years of establishment, geographical location, and so forth, could also lead to different performance outcomes (Zhao & Zou, 2002). Therefore, in distribution control research it is also necessary to examine the influences of other control variables.

9 Characteristics and driving forces of China's born-global firms: a multi-case study

Xi Chen, Zuohao Hu and Ping Zhao

9.1 Introduction

Research on firms' internationalization process has always been one of the frontier subjects in the field of international marketing. Scholars from Uppsala University initially proposed the stage model in the 1970s (Johanson & Wiedersheim-Paul, 1975; Johanson & Vahlne, 1977), suggesting that firms tend to export to a psychically close market first and then expand to psychically more distant markets.

Since the 1990s, economic globalization has become increasingly prevalent worldwide. A substantial number of studies show that an ever increasing number of small and medium-sized enterprises (SMEs) start to conduct resource integration and configuration on a global scale within a few years of their establishments (Oviatt & McDougall, 1994; Knight & Cavusgil, 1996; McKinsey & Co., 2003; Chetty & Colin, 2004). "Born-global" firms are starting to rise to prominence on the global stage and are attracting more attention in academic research. "Born-global" firms refer to SMEs that begin internationalization rapidly from inception or shortly after their establishments. Within a few years of their founding, born-global firms vigorously use firm resources to explore overseas markets. They seek and acquire competitive advantages, aim at the international market, and achieve a substantial proportion of their total revenue from the international market. The preparation period before export business is very short. Instead of following the conventional stage model during their internationalization processes, born-global firms take a totally new approach to internationalization. Therefore, these firms are defined as "born-global firms" in academic research, and the mode of their internationalization is named the "born-global model" (Knight & Cavusgil, 1996). This phenomenon first appeared in countries with small domestic markets and is now widespread across the world. However, research regarding born-global firms in the context of Chinese exporters is still limited. Therefore, more relevant studies are desirable to fill this gap.

Research questions in this chapter are as follows: (1) What are the differences between the internationalization paths of China's "born-global" firms and traditional-global firms that follow the stage model? (2) What are the driving

forces for born-global firms to take such an innovative approach to internationalization? Answering these questions would enhance Chinese firms' competitive advantages in international markets and help them cope with domestic and
international competition pressure and achieve desirable export performance.

Analyzing the cases of four Chinese SMEs from China's Jiangsu and Zhejiang provinces and adopting the born-global theory and the stage-model theory,
this chapter: (1) investigates whether born-global firms exist in the context of
China's market conditions; (2) reveals whether there is significant difference
between born-global firms and traditional-global firms; and (3) reveals the formation mechanism of born-global firms.

9.2 Literature review

Before the emergence of born-global firms, the Uppsala model was dominant
in international marketing research. In 1980s, research including Reid (1983),
Turnbull (1987a), and Andersen (1993) began to have doubts about the stage
model, proposing that trying to explain the internationalization processes of
all kinds of firms with only one theory might be simplistic (Fina *et al.*, 1996).
Hedlund and Kverneland (1985) and Ganitsky (1989), among others, find that
in practice many firms deviate from the regular path of the stage model by skip-
ping normal internationalization stages.

Since the 1990s, a substantial number of studies in developed countries indicate the emergence of an important international marketing phenomenon
among small and medium-sized exporters and the formation of a new model
of internationalization thereby (Knight & Cavusgil, 1996; Madsen & Servais,
1997; Chetty & Campbell-Hunt, 2004). They find that many SMEs refuse to
be confined to the narrow space of the domestic market. These firms target the
international market from inception. They make use of all resources available
to them and gain a significant proportion of their revenue from overseas markets. Firms with those characteristics are named "born-global" firms, and the
model depicting their internationalization process is the "born-global model"
(Knight & Cavusgil, 1996). Later, numerous scholars began to conduct studies
on born-global firms, but most such studies happened in Northern Europe
(*Madsen et al.*, 2000; Aspelund & Moen, 2001; Rasmussen *et al.*, 2001; Moen &
Servais, 2002).

For instance, Turnbull (1987a) finds that the internationalization processes
of many SMEs in UK do not follow the traditional stage model. Instead, they
grow in a leap-forward manner. Brush (1992) studies the export behaviors of
American SMEs and finds that 13% of the sampled firms start international
activities within the first year of their establishments. Based on the cases of 24
born-global firms, the study of McDougall *et al.* (1994) points out that the
stage model cannot explain why these firms sell their products only to the
international market but not in domestic markets. Rennie (1993) studies Australian firms and finds that the founders of some firms view the whole world as
their market from the outset, without confining themselves to psychic distance.

These firms generally compete on quality and value created through innovative technology and product design. In addition, they have very close relationships with their customers in international niche markets (such as scientific instruments or machine tools), are flexible, and are able to adapt their products to quickly changing demands.

Bell (1995) studies small computer software firms and finds that the conventional stages theory cannot properly explain these firms' internationalization processes. Bell finds that client followership, sectorial targeting, and industry-specific factors, rather than psychic distance, strongly influence the processes and manners of the internationalization of these firms. Bell also discovers that some firms have not even been well established in the domestic market before they start exporting.

Jolly *et al.* (1992) point out that for small high-tech exporters, the potential effectiveness (volume, intensity of competition, etc.) of the market is the key factor affecting the choice of their initial export markets, and psychic distance is largely irrelevant in export market selection. Moen and Servais (2002) empirically study a sample of 677 SMEs from Norway, France, and Denmark. The authors examine the influences of three factors – time of establishment, the first time of export business, and the interval between establishment and export commencement – on export intensity, distribution, market selection, and global orientation. The results show that born-global firms do exist in great number (one-third of the firms report that the time period between establishment and export commencement was less than two years). In terms of export intensity, these firms, on average, outperform other firms. The results also indicate that the future export involvement of a firm is, to a large extent, influenced by its behavior (export or non-export) shortly after establishment, that the development of resources in support of international market competitiveness may be regarded as the key, and that the basic resources and competencies of the firm are determined during the establishment phase.

Chetty and Campbell-Hunt (2004) conduct in-depth case study on four small and medium-sized international firms that follow the traditional stage model and six born-global firms, all from New Zealand. By comparing "born-global firms" with "traditional-global firms," the authors identify 10 unique attributes of born-global firms: domestic market largely irrelevant; founder has extensive experience in relevant international markets; high degree and rapid speed of internationalization; psychic distance is irrelevant; learning occurs more rapidly because of superior internationalization knowledge; realization of competitive advantage requires rapid, full internationalization; target market's scope is focused/niche; active and vigorous use of information and communications technology; rapid development of external networks of business partners; and export business started within a few years of inception.

The aforementioned research suggests that in the era of economic globalization, many so-called "born-global" small and medium-sized firms, instead of following the traditional stage model in the processes of their internationalization, pursue a new approach to internationalization. A substantial amount of research indicates that, compared to traditional-global firms that follow the stage model, born-global firms have some unique features and a different formation mechanism.

9.3 Methodology

9.3.1 Case study method

Many scholars familiar with qualitative research (Glaser & Strauss, 1967; Eisenhardt, 1989; Yin, 1989; Maxwell, 1996; Yin, 1998) and scholars in the field of international marketing (Chetty, 1996) state that multiple-case study is an ideal research method for empirically testing existing theories as well as building new theories based on new phenomena. Different from single-case study, which is more like storytelling, multiple-case study is good for building theoretical constructs (Eisenhardt, 1991). According to existing literature (e.g., Sanders, 1982), the best number of cases for a multiple-case study is between three and six. Following the advice of these scholars and taking into consideration the criteria of case selection, we decided on four research cases. In order to make the selected cases more typical and representative, this chapter chooses four firms that: (1) are from different cities (Wenzhou, Hangzhou, and Suzhou) in the economically developed Jiangsu-Zhejiang region where small and medium-sized firms are highly active; (2) are from different industries (manufacturing and service sector) and of different sizes; (3) are located in different areas (rural and urban); and (4) follow different internationalization paths. We compare and analyze these firms' characteristics from the perspective of born-global theories. Based on the case selection criteria mentioned earlier, we choose the following four companies as objects of our study: an auto-parts manufacturer (Case 1, Company A), a textile company (Case 2, Company B), a network solution provider (Case 3, Company C), and an electronic and electrical equipment accessories manufacturer (Case 4, Company D). We anonymize these companies for the sake of confidentiality and identify these firms as Company A, Company B, Company C, and Company D. At the stage of data collection, in order to obtain data of each company from multiple channels, we develop a preliminary research framework based on existing literature and the research goals in this chapter. The result is a semi-structured interview outline that uses mainly open-ended questions.

In order to attain satisfactory construct validity, we made use of various company information sources, including in-depth interview with company founders and management teams, company websites, internal documents provided by these companies, questionnaires completed by interviewees, product and company brochures, and other second-hand information. The average length of an interview with each company founder or manager was 60–90 minutes; one person from our team conducted the interview while another recorded the minutes. The entire interview was tape-recorded. After each interview we compiled a detailed case report based on the interview outline and recorded material; we discussed and analyzed the audio record and reached conclusive answers, so as to guarantee the reliability and validity of the information organization and analysis process. At the stage of case establishment, in order to attain desirable construct validity, we asked every company executive whether they had any new opinions to be incorporated into the cases. We used the identical research processes and methods for each case to ensure comparability and reliability. Finally, we established a comprehensive library of multiple-case study.

9.3.2 Descriptive information about cases

1 Company A

Company A is a manufacturing firm that produces industrial forging machinery and auto parts. In 1990 the company was transformed into a privately operated forge. In 1994, the company acquired a hardware plant. In 1997, it adopted the share-holding system and was officially incorporated. In 2004, the company started to seek overseas clients and established business relationships with clients from Japan, America, Europe, and Australia. The company started its international business at the eighth year of its establishment. In 2007, the sales revenue of the company was 70 million (RMB), 15% of which came from overseas markets.

The international market of Company A consists four clients from Germany, America, Australia, and Japan respectively. In the process of its internationalization the company established connection with clients mainly through word of mouth (upstream and downstream), recommendation by other foreign clients, and trade fairs. Part of the company's mission is to develop the international market, so the company would take orders from overseas clients as long as price and quality were acceptable. It would then make efforts to consolidate business relationship with these clients. Step by step the international market is becoming a beneficial supplement to its domestic market.

2 Company B

Company B is a modern company. Its main business is textiles, but it also operates diversified businesses like weaving, fiber, and trading. The company was established in 1990 and began its export business 12 years later in 2002. In 2007, 70% of its textile products were exported (directly or through foreign trading companies), and 30% were sold in the domestic market. The company established relationships with its foreign clients mainly through domestic trade fairs first and then through overseas trade fairs. It also received some of its orders from other trading companies. Later the company established its own foreign trading branch and approached clients directly. Now, the three methods of export mentioned earlier coexist in Company B.

The European Union is Company B's preferred target market. The purpose of its overseas expansion is to support and sustain the domestic market so as to improve the operation of its domestic business. In consequence, the proportions of its domestic sales and international sales are adjusted dynamically. In 2008 changes in the conditions of the macro economy (including the depreciation of RMB) caused the company to adjust the proportion of its domestic sales to 70%.

3 Company C

Company C has been brought into existent by venture capital. It was founded by a returnee to China who had studied abroad. The company provides communication outsourcing services. Its offerings include novel products like multi-service company gateways and remote management. The company is located in a high-tech park, together with many multinational companies that are actively engaged in international business as well. Company C's main target clients are small companies. The company's operation model is to first sell equipment (hardware) to SMEs and then provide outsourcing services based on equipment. Its products feature high technology, are complicated, and are heavily reliant on technology, occupying a leading position in the industry.

The company was founded in August 2006. It has 80 employees and three senior executives, the founder himself and two partners (one partner is Chinese and the other is American). The company adopts a flat management structure. It is a technology-intensive, capital-intensive, and talent-intensive R&D company. Due to the long R&D cycle of its products, the company didn't start its selling operation until March 2008, which also marked the launch of its international activity. United States is Company C's primary market, accounting for 30% of its total sales. The reason why the company chose America as its first international market was that the management team had extensive learning, work, and living experience in US and were familiar with American market. In the following step, the company plans to enter Southeast Asian countries, because those markets are similar to China's. In addition, they have some local partners in the region, which would make it much easier for operation.

4 Company D

Company D was founded in 2001. It is a Mainland–Hong Kong joint venture. In 2002, the second year of its establishment, the company commenced internationalization. Now export accounts for 40% of its total sales. Company D's main business is the manufacturing of electronic and electrical equipment components. It spans two industries: electronics (gas appliance, electronic impulse igniter, etc.) and electrical equipment (components for automatic washing machines, etc.); 60% of Company D's products are technology-intensive and knowledge-intensive, and the other 40% are labor-intensive products. Its products are in a leading position both at home and abroad.

Initially the company decided to explore the international market because of the small size and limited potential of the domestic market. The company's chairman of the board and general manager used to be the director of an electronics research institution in Zhejiang Province. The chairman has rich professional experience, understands the development trends of the industry, and commands a lot of important resources. When Company D explored the international market, the company followed the global strategy by entering foreign markets sequentially. The sequence of its target market entry has been Japan, Southeast Asia, Europe, and the US. Japan's electronics industry and electrical equipment industry are highly developed. Company D is now a supplier to two world-class Japanese electronic and electrical equipment companies. The Southeast Asian market is similar to the Chinese market and shows some unique conveniences. The European and American markets contain plenty of opportunities, and the company is now a supplier to several famous European and American brands. Company D keeps growing and learning as it supplies to established international brands. The company's next target market is Italy. During the interview, the company's chairman mentioned that Italian cookers were exemplary and that entry into the Italian market would mark a higher degree of the company's globalization.

The prior section provides the basic information about these four cases. Table 9.1 shows more details of these companies.

9.4 Case analysis

9.4.1 Defining born-global firms

Regarding the specific indices and criteria of born-global firms, scholars have proposed different measurement standards due to differences of research purposes and research contexts. There are mainly two dimensions: first, the length of time between company establishment and the first time of export; second, the percentage of overseas sales in total sales. In terms of the length of time from establishment to export commencement, scholars' opinions vary from two years (McKinsey & Co., 2003), to six years (Zahra *et al.*, 2000), and eight years (Reid, 1983). As for the percentage of export, Knight and Cavusgil (1996) suggest that born-global firms should achieve 25% of sales from export shortly after establishment, whereas McKinsey & Co. (1993) suggest the proportion should be 75%.

This chapter adopts the most widely used criteria to identify born-global firms. In specific, the conceptualization of born-global firms follows Knight and Cavusgil (1996) and Madsen *et al.* (2000) and defines born-global firms as: (1) starting to sell products to the international market within three years of establishment; and (2) at least 25% of sales coming from overseas markets. Firms meeting both criteria are defined as born-global firms.

9.4.2 Firms' classification: A two-by-two attribute matrix

We present a two-by-two matrix conceptual model (see Figure 9.1) to distinguish born-global firms from traditional-global firms by comparing the

Table 9.1 Attributes of the four companies

Company attributes	Company A (Auto-parts manufacturer)	Company B (Textile Company)	Company C (Network solution provider)	Company D (Electronic components)
Year of establishment/ Year of launch of export business	1997/2004	1990/2002	2006/2008	2001/2002
Main businesses	Manufacturing all sorts of forged auto parts; basically a labor-intensive company	Producing clothing fabrics; basically a labor-intensive manufacturing company; currently attempting to transform into a capital-intensive and technology-intensive company and increase its technology content	Offering communication hardware and software services; products include multi-service company gateway, remote management, and solutions; it is a knowledge-intensive, capital-intensive, and talent-intensive high-tech company	Producing electronic products and electrical equipment products; mostly knowledge-intensive products, with a small proportion of labor-intensive products
Geographical location	One subsidiary in an urban area with another subsidiary in a rural area	In a rural area	In a high-tech park in an urban area	In an industrial technology park in an urban area
Shareholders or partners	A family business, run by the father in the first years, now managed by the son who is a university graduate	A family business transformed from a collectively owned company	Three founding partners, in charge of overall operation, finance, and sales respectively	Joint control by Hong Kong capital and Chinese capital; current general manager/ chairman of the board in charge of management and business
Employee size	About 300	About 1,300	80	260

(Continued)

Table 9.1 (Continued)

Company attributes	Company A (Auto-parts manufacturer)	Company B (Textile Company)	Company C (Network solution provider)	Company D (Electronic components)
Sales (in RMB)	70 million; the majority of sales come from the domestic market, including orders from domestic manufacturers and domestic companies that operate export business	80 million	Sales in the last three quarters of 2008 estimated to be RMB 30 million (starting production in March)	60 million
Percentage of export	Export accounting for 15% of total sales	Export accounting for 70% of total sales	Export accounting for 3% of total sales	Export accounting for 40% of total sales
Source of clients	Getting to know clients in trade fairs; regular clients recommending the company to new clients	Meeting clients in trade affairs, mostly from EU countries	Business partners that the company's managers got to know when they were studying and living abroad; mostly American clients; currently planning to enter Southeast Asia	Mainly through word of mouth; mostly from Japan, Southeast Asia, the US, and Canada

attributes and industrial distribution of these two firm types. The horizontal axis represents export speed, which is characterized as either "fast" or "slow" using the benchmark of whether the firm has started export within three years of its establishment; the vertical axis represents export intensity, which is characterized as either "strong" or "weak" judged by whether the percentage of export in total sales exceeds 25%.

In Figure 9.1 we can see that both Company C and Company D are in the fourth quadrant. On the dimension of "export speed," both Company C and Company D start export within three years of their establishments, and

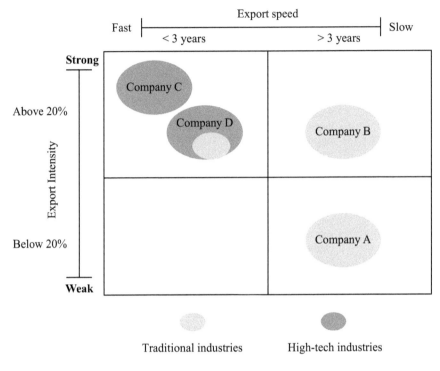

Figure 9.1 A two-by-two attribute matrix of born-global firms

the length of time from establishment to first export is two years and one year respectively. They aim at the international market from inception, and the period of preparation before export is rather short. They do not follow the traditional stage model but take a totally new approach to internationalization. In terms of "export intensity," Company C reaches 30% and Company D 40%, achieving a substantial proportion of their total sales from the international market. Therefore, both Company C and Company D are placed in the fourth quadrant and classified as born-global firms.

Company B falls on the first quadrant. Its export intensity is 70%, meeting one of the criteria for born-global firms, but it fails to meet the export speed criteria. Therefore, it can't be identified as a born-global firm. Company A belongs to the second quadrant. It fails to meet the criteria of a born global either in terms of export speed or in terms of export intensity. It enters the international market eight years after its establishment. Its involvement in the international market follows the gradually incremental pattern, and it is therefore defined as a traditional-global firm.

In terms of industrial distribution, Company C and Company D are high-tech companies, as highlighted in light gray. Company D has a small portion of traditional business, but the major part of it belongs to the high-tech industry (as indicated by the concentric circles). Both Company B and Company A, high-lighted in dark gray, belong to traditional industries. From this matrix we can see that both Company C and Company D differ from Company A and Company B in all three aspects of export speed, export intensity, and industry type. In the following step, we analyze and explain the distribution of the cases in the matrix.

Firstly, in terms of export speed and export intensity, Chetty and Campbell-Hunt (2004) state that traditional-global firms follow the stage model, interna-tionalize gradually, develop the domestic market first, and then serially develop overseas markets. Their export activities are motivated by lack of domestic demand and market anemia. They internationalize so as to explore the vastness of the international market. On the contrary, founders and managers of born-global firms possess extensive international experience. They perceive less risk in overseas markets. Their prior work experience, their global orientation, and their existing clients and business partners across the value chain all make it easier for them to acquire overseas markets operation experience and knowl-edge, which gives them courage and confidence to explore the international market. Aaby and Slater (1989) suggest that born-global firms' motivation to export is to seize "first-mover" advantages and acquire international competi-tive advantages. For them exporting is self-motivated. They would actively seek the overseas target market segment and increase their involvements in overseas markets. Managers' personal networks and experience provide a ready model for them to follow. Therefore, the process of born-global firms' overseas market involvement tends to be swift, showing a pattern of accelerated internationali-zation. In terms of expansion, born-global firms would develop the domestic market and overseas markets simultaneously or may even start first in overseas markets. The selection of overseas markets is determined by business networks and connections. In many cases, these firms explore several overseas markets at the same time.

Among these cases, Company A and Company B start their international businesses 8 and 12 years respectively after inception. The pace of their export-ing is slow, and export accounts for a relatively small proportion of their total sales volumes. Company A only has 15% of its total sales from export. In con-trast, Company C and Company D are more active in exploring the interna-tional market and internationalize quickly. Shortly after its inception, Company C launched its American company and Chinese company at the same time and started international business rapidly. Its founder has study and work experi-ence in America and is more familiar with the American market than with the Chinese market. Overseas sales account for 30% of the total sales volume. Com-pany D was established in April 2001, and initially it operated only in domestic market. The manager of Company D has plenty of prior knowledge about foreign markets. The company's goal to explore the international market and build a global brand drives the company's rapid internationalization. Moreover, with unfair competition and unscrupulous behaviors like tardy payment in the domestic market, the company decided to start exporting in 2002, the second year of its inception. Its internationalization is rapid and proactive.

Second, in terms of industrial distribution, traditional-global firms offer a wide range of products to numerous market segments. However, born-global firms tend to offer high-tech and high-quality products to niche markets and provide differentiated and customized products and services, with some products being globally leading. Born-global firms' obsessive attention to quality brings them continuously improving competence and performance (Chetty & Campbell-Hunt, 2004).

Among these cases, Company A is an auto-parts company and Company B is a traditional textile company. Both Company A and Company B belong to traditional labor-intensive industries, and their product policies are different from those of Company C and Company D. Company A is in the forging industry, which has a rather low entry barrier. Although experienced forging workers are high-tech professionals, the industry is still largely a labor-intensive traditional industry. Currently, the company has two types of products. The first type is non-standard parts and non-interchangeable parts that other companies are unable to produce and require delicate and complicated techniques and processes. Such products possess high added value, but the proportion of this type of product is rather small. The other type is low-tech products that can be easily made; sales could be satisfactory as long as cost is well controlled and an upper level of quality standard is maintained. The proportion of the second type of products is much larger than the first.

Besides traditional textile products Company B makes vigorous efforts to provide differentiated textile products (such as the addition of functional fiber, anti-bacterial function, and UV deodorization). Although it keeps making innovations, its products are largely standardized for the sake of volume production, and its production techniques are relatively simple. Company C belongs to the service sector. It provides customized network services by means of hardware. It is an emerging industry. It offers high-tech products that are extremely complicated and heavily reliant on technology. Its employees possess high levels of technological skills and education. So, Company C is a talent-intensive, capital-intensive, and technology-intensive company. Moreover, Company C shows strong customization capability, as is reflected in its follow-up service and continuous tracking after providing hardware to customers. General Manager Ma, founder of Company C, is very proud of the company's products, as they are all supplied to global leading downstream manufacturers. Similarly, a small proportion of Company D's products are labor intensive, but the substantial part of its involvement in the electrical equipment industry and the electronics industry requires large and expensive production equipment, high technical skills, and intensive knowledge. Its products possess high entry barriers and are difficult to copy. These attributes represent the company's most important intangible assets. During interviews, both Company C and Company D mentioned that they were in the process of applying for relevant product patents.

What factors drive Company C and Company D to exhibit unique traits in export speed and export intensity and make them born-global firms? What are the background causes of such a distribution of the firms in the matrix? We will discuss these issues in the next section.

9.4.3 Driving forces for the formation of born-global firms

Existing studies indicate that there are differences between born-global firms and traditional-global firms in numerous key aspects, and these differences illustrate the key attributes of born-global firms. Hu and Chen (2007) propose a conceptual framework of the differences between born-global firms and traditional-global firms. These differences are shown in Table 9.2, which points out the driving forces of the formation of born-global firms.

Prior to inception, managers of born-global firms generally have extensive experience that enables their firms to enter the international market at an early stage and acquire international competitive advantages. Chetty and Campbell-Hunt (2004) discuss possible explanations. First, managers of born-global firms possess plenty of prior knowledge and work experience that could reduce the psychic distance to specific markets and minimize risk and uncertainty. Second, the prior international experience of born-global firms' founders and decision makers plays an important role in increasing the firms' speed of learning and internationalization. Because born-global firms begin with basic knowledge about internationalization, they are better at accumulating new knowledge about internationalization. Traditional international firms, on the other hand, accumulate their international experience in a gradual and incremental manner. Third, managers of born-global firms are better at using communications technologies to help their firms acquire knowledge, develop strategies, and maintain relationships to assist them in accelerating their internationalization. Fourth is managers' globalization orientation. These managers have developed distinctive entrepreneurial capabilities and the foresight to spot windows of opportunity on a global scale that others overlook. Consequently, managers' international experience and knowledge significantly distinguish born-global firms from traditional-global firms. For born-global firms, these capabilities are brought by managers pari passu the establishment of the firms; for traditional-global firms, on the other hand, international experience can't be gained ex ante and has to be accumulated as they grow and internationalize. According to the organizational learning theory, there are five stages of knowledge acquisition – namely, congenital learning, experimental learning, vicarious learning, grafting and search learning, and notice (Huber, 1996; Palmer & Hardy, 2000). From the organization-based perspective, scholars point out that the founder of a firm has a huge influence on the firm's subsequent development because of the congenital learning of the founder. Congenital knowledge refers to knowledge about overseas markets that founders of the firm or other important figures associated with the founding of the firm possess prior to the inception of the firm. It plays an important role in determining whether the firm will become a born global or not.

Table 9.2 Differences between born-global firms and traditional-global firms

Comparison items		Traditional-global firms	Born-global firms
Founders or managers	Congenital learning and experimental learning	• Lack prior international experience and congenital experience • Foreign knowledge learning speed depends on learning capability; needs to be accumulated gradually • International experience gradually accumulated after inception and as firms grow	• Firms' managers already had plenty of international experience and congenital experience before inception • Strong learning capability in the field of internationalization; better at using latest technology
	International orientation and vision	• View the international market and the domestic market as separable • Weak international orientation and vision	• Strong global orientation; view the international market and the domestic market as an inseparable whole • Strongly motivated and firmly determined to perform international operation
Operation networks		• Networks play a role in the early stage of the firms' internationalization and subsequent international expansion	• Networks are important tools and resources for firms' initial internalization and subsequent international expansion • Networks provide firms with access to rich knowledge and experience and compensate firms' resource scarcity
Target market selection		• Gradual and incremental internationalization • Domestic market developed first; gradual expansion in the domestic market before serial development in new overseas markets • Entry mode and process are functions of psychic distance, which is an importance criterion in the choice of target market	• Actively seek overseas target markets, start international business shortly after establishment, rapid penetration into foreign market segments • Launch the domestic and the international market at the same time, or even launch the international market first; foreign market selection determined by factors like business networks and associations • Foreign target market selection showing no significant association with psychic distance

In addition, experimental learning means different things to born-global firms and traditional-global firms. Chetty and Campbell-Hunt (2004) mention that born-global firms are better at accumulating new knowledge about internationalization because they begin with basic knowledge about internationalization. Traditional-global firms, on the other hand, accumulate experience gradually as they grow. Therefore, the experimental learning capability of born-global firms is stronger than traditional-global firms.

Based on the prior discussion, we present Proposition 1: Compared to traditional-global firms, born-global firms possess more international experience and knowledge and stronger congenital and experimental learning capabilities, are better at using the latest technology, and can effectively reduce risk in international operation. Therefore, born-global firms are able to start international business operation shortly after inception and grow to be born-global firms.

Among internal factors that affect the formation of born-global firms, founders or management teams with global experience and vision are widely considered the most important driving factor. Madsen and Servais (2000), among others, suggest it is important to explore the history of born-global firms, even beyond their birth. Such firms are started by genuine entrepreneurs or by very experienced persons, and these persons have extensive international experience (including a personal network) and do not perceive their native country as the nucleus of their lives. They don't view entering the international market as an uncertain adventure, but rather as a rare opportunity for growth. They have lofty aspirations, strong internationalization and export motivations, international visions, and great ambitions for international operation.

Based on the aforementioned discussion, we present Proposition 2: Born-global firms have strong international orientation and international visions, view the international market and the domestic market as inseparable, can discern opportunities in the global market, and are strongly motivated and determined to enter the international market. Because of these they are able to start international business operation shortly after inception and grow to be born-global firms.

The study of Madsen and Servais (1997) indicates that due to inherent scarcity of resources, born-global firms need to seek and maintain partnership with a large number of external network organizations. The study of Vida (2000) finds networking plays a vital part in obtaining knowledge and experience in SMEs' internationalization. The research of Rundh (2003) finds that networks can help firms enter countries that are geographically far away from the home market and that differ greatly from the home market in terms of market characteristics. Bell (1995) suggests that firms with international relation networks have access to more information and knowledge brought by international customers and the international market. Therefore, it would be easier for them to develop "learning advantages" and to enter the international market than firms that have networks only in the domestic market. Rialp et al. (2005) propose that born-global firms often rely on resources provided by other international firms and establish effective international networks (key distribution channels, clients, suppliers, partners, etc.) by means of effective international operation.

Therefore, we present Proposition 3: International network resources compensate Chinese firms' resource scarcity, provide experience and knowledge for the rapid internationalization of Chinese firms, and help them enter the international market quickly, thus promoting the formation of born-global firms.

Traditional internationalization theory suggests that firms internationalize by gradually increasing involvement in the international market (Andersen, 1993). The traditional view suggests that after their inception, firms begin to internationalize slowly and gradually after a rather long time in the domestic market. Because the entry mode and process of traditional-global firms are functions of psychic distance, traditional firms consider psychic distance an important criterion in the choice of target markets. When expanding into overseas markets, they tend to choose a psychically close market first and then gradually choose psychically more distant markets so as to avoid major risks and uncertainties.

So we present Proposition 4: Contrary to traditional-global firms' target market selection, psychic distance is not an important selection criterion for born-global firms, and their entry mode and process are not significantly related to psychic distance.

Based on these propositions regarding the characteristics and driving forces of traditional-global firms and born-global firms, we present the differences of the two types of firms in Table 9.2.

9.4.4 Case studies on the driving forces for the formation of born-global firms

A most notable trait of born-global firms is that their founders or managers possess international visions and ambitions to explore the international market. Oviatt and McDougall (1997) describe such managers as the core intangible assets of born-global firms and point out that the existence of such managers constitutes the biggest difference between a born-global firm and a traditional-global firm. In these four cases, we see the important influences of managers' congenital learning, experimental learning, international vision, and global orientation on the formation of born-global firms.

1 Managers' congenital learning and experimental learning

The founders of Company C and Company D had plenty of industrial experience before the founding of their companies. They had congenital knowledge that the founders of Company A and Company B did not possess. This is a key factor that promotes their firms to become born-global firms. The founders and managers of Company C and Company D all have a strong international background. In the case of Company C, all its three founders have living and work experience in the US. Two of them got their doctorates in the US, and the general manager of the company had years of work experience at Bell Laboratory. They all have rich international experience. When interviewed they all said that their overseas experience helped them accumulate plenty of foreign market knowledge and that it was the domestic market they were not very familiar with and therefore needed to learn more about. The founder of Company D used to be the director of a scientific research institute. During his term in that office he had plenty of opportunities to go on investigation trips abroad. He has visited many advanced foreign electronics and electrical equipment companies and has a lot of international knowledge. His has gained a lot of congenital experience from working with numerous prestigious Japanese electrical equipment electronics companies. In the case of Company A, the general manager got his bachelor's degree in China before he joined the management of the company. He didn't have study, living, or work experience abroad. Upon graduation he joined the company that his father founded. He didn't have congenital experience. The general manager of Company B founded the company with his uncle. They too lacked congenital experience when they started the business.

2 International vision and orientation of managers

Many scholars point out that the management teams of born-global firms view the global market as an integrated market. They don't confine their firm to a single market or view the international market as a supplement to the local market (Sharma & Blomstermo, 2003). Knight and Cavusgil (2004) find that such firms are started by genuine entrepreneurs or by very experienced persons, and these persons have extensive international experience and do not perceive their native country as the nucleus of their lives. They view entering the international market as an opportunity for growth. Their international experience and international entrepreneurial orientation give them strong motivation and determination to push their firms into the international market. They have developed distinctive entrepreneurial capabilities and the foresight to spot windows of opportunity on a global scale that others overlook (Chetty & Campbell-Hunt, 2004). Johanson and Vahlne (1990) suggest that born-global firms have many entrepreneurs or managers who possess overseas experience. Their perceived risk in the international market is rather small. Their prior work experience and international-oriented ideas, combined with their previous clients and partners on the upstream and downstream of the value chain, can help their firms gain overseas market operation experience and knowledge relatively easily and give them more courage and confidence to explore the international market. Hence, their overseas market involvement decision-making would be swifter.

In the case of Company C, its three senior executives all have living and work experience in the US, and two of them obtained their doctorates in the US. They view the world as a whole, without a strong sense of national boundaries or national differences. They take a trip to Europe every one or two months. For them traveling to a foreign country is like someone from China traveling to a different province in China. The general manager has traveled to more than 30 countries around the world, is familiar with foreign countries, does not have a strong sense of exoticness, and can readily accept new ideas worldwide. All these make it possible for the firm to carry out business activities across the world within a short period of time. When interviewed, the general manager also says that they don't see entering the international market as a precarious venture, but as a rare growth opportunity. The purpose of the firm's involvement in the international market is not to support the domestic market but rather the firm's strategic goal because they don't separate the Chinese market from the international market. They believe the global market represents a unified market opportunity. Strong international exporting motivations and foresight and international vision are all drivers of the firm's accelerated internationalization.

In the case of Company D, its manager and founder, the former director of an electronics research institute in Zhejiang province, possesses profound technical and market experience. Plenty of investigation and business trips abroad and learning opportunities have given the founder a wide international vision. When he was running the company it used to supply to a number of renowned Chinese companies, but the lack of standards in the financial policies of upstream companies in China, incomplete systems, and serious speculation activities all went against Company D's standardized management style. Therefore, the company decided to give up the domestic market gradually and seek growth in overseas markets. With a global vision and big ambitions, the manager has led the company to become a leader in the industry, becoming the exclusive supplier of certain parts to some of the worlds' top electrical equipment and electronics companies. From the perspective of Company D's manager, the international market is the company's big growth engine and the most spectacular arena. The manager's strong international orientation drives the company continuously towards the top level of the industry globally. The company has decided on a target market entry sequence: Japan, Southeast Asia, Europe and the US, and eventually Italy, where the kitchenware industry represents the cutting-edge of electrical equipment design.

On the contrary, Company A and Company B view the international market as a supplement to their domestic market. The domestic background of their managers also causes them to rely more heavily on the domestic market and seek steady growth. The purpose of internationalization is to support and supplement the domestic market. Provided that there are no significant risks of exchange rates and raw materials, the companies would do international business when there is demand. They realize that the international market is a desirable complement when they receive unexpected orders in domestic trade fairs. Company A is a family business. Neither the current general manager nor his father have overseas experience. They don't have a strong global orientation. After 12 years of rather conservative operation in the domestic market the company started to slowly get involved in the international market. This year, the textile industry, which Company B is in, has seen big impacts. The rise of raw material price and the negative influence of exchange rates have forced

Company B to adjust the proportion of its export, from 70% export and 30% domestic sales previously to 30% export and 70% domestic sales now. Hence, Company B still prioritizes the domestic market and considers the international market as a contingent operation choice that needs to be adjusted at times.

3 Network resource

The importance of networks for the formation and development of born-global firms is manifest in these four cases. The manager of Company C got to know many business partners and cooperative partners upstream and downstream the value chain during his stay in the US. That laid a foundation for the company's entry into the American market and is the reason why the company chose the US as its first overseas market. In the next step the company plans to enter the Southeast Asian market, mainly because they have developed association networks in this region and can find cooperative partners (such as agents) to help them motivate the market. Before the founding of Company D, its manager cultivated a relationship network in the industry during his learning and business trips abroad. After inception, the company came into contact with more clients by means of word of mouth and developed many cooperative partners upstream and downstream the value chain.

Both Company A and Company B started building their network resources only after they entered the international market. They have neither ready-made networks at their disposal nor market information and knowledge that could be obtained from established association networks.

4 Pace of internationalization and target market selection

Entry mode and process are functions of psychic distance in target market selection. Traditional-global firms consider psychic distance an important criterion when selecting a target market. However, Bell (1995) suggest that the synergy of such factors as client followership, segmental targeting, and industry-specific factors significantly influence born-global firms' target market selection.

Among these cases, eight years after its founding Company A began to take small export orders and started to internationalize by means of export and licensing. It adopted a cautious and steady internationalization process. In the selection of target markets, Company A doesn't have a specific internationalization path in mind, and it is irrelevant to psychic distance. When internationalizing, Company A acquires its clients in a relatively random manner, mainly through word of mouth (upstream and downstream), recommendation by other overseas clients, and trade fairs. It doesn't intentionally seek a target market that it is already familiar with or that is psychically close. The sequence of its target market entry is not planned. The case of Company B is similar. Before 2001, Company B's textile production capacity greatly exceeded the demand volume of the domestic market. Hence, the company started to consider the feasibility of expansion into overseas markets. With the government's policy guidance and support for foreign trade, the company began to enter the international market. Its internationalization is passive in nature. As for market entry sequence, it has no plan regarding which market to enter first and which later. It meets its clients mainly in trade fairs.

During the interview, the founder and manager of Company C mentions that the company has a detailed strategic plan for overseas market entry and that there is a sequence of their target market selection. At present, the American market still accounts for 100% of its international business. The company is planning to enter the Southeast Asian market in the next step. The reason for this plan is that the Southeast Asian market is close to China and the manager has acquired partners and association networks in the region that could facilitate cooperation. Therefore, the company has prior plans and considerations for the development path of its international business.

In the case of Company D, its target market selection is based mainly on the "product level" standard. According to the company's chairperson, as a supplier of electronic and electrical equipment parts, the company's downstream buyers are all world-renowned brands in the electronics and electrical equipment industries; working with high-standard partners can help the firm quickly approach an international leading level. The company entered Japan first, a market with an advanced electronics industry, and then the Southeast Asian market. The company's next target is the Italian market, which is the undisputed leader in the field of design, aiming at improving the company's product standard and becoming a global leader. Therefore, the company has considerations for the sequence of its international market selection.

Hence, in the matter of target market selection, the selection modes of traditional-global firms and born-global firms are contrary to conclusions in the existing literature. Traditional-global firms do not choose their target markets in sequence as suggested by literature; instead, their choices are rather random. On the contrary, Chinese born-global firms follow strategic plans in their

Table 9.3 Results of research propositions testing

		Traditional-global firms		Born-global firms	
		Company A	Company B	Company C	Company D
Founders/ managers	Congenital learning and experimental learning	Supported	Supported	Supported	Supported
	International orientation and vision	Supported	Supported	Supported	Supported
Marketing network		Supported	Supported	Supported	Supported
Target market selection		Not supported	Not supported	Not supported	Not supported

choices of target markets, and their choices show a regular pattern regarding the psychic distance of the target markets. Contrary to the proposition, psychic distance is not irrelevant.

This discussion explains why Company C and Company D belong on the upper left of the matrix and why they exhibit traits in terms of export speed and export intensity. We find that there are indeed a series of driving forces, in such aspects as founders/entrepreneurs and networks, that distinguish born-global firms from traditional-global firms and enable born-global firms to explore the international market shortly after establishment and acquire competitive advantages. These analyses also empirically validate most of the conclusions in the conceptual framework proposed by Hu and Chen (2007). Nonetheless, due to the unique characteristics of Chinese firms, the conclusions regarding "target market selection" of Chinese born-global firms are different from those in previous research frameworks, marking the new findings of this research.

Based on these propositions and case study conclusions, a table is drawn to show whether the propositions are supported in this study (see Table 9.3).

9.5 Conclusions and directions for future research

9.5.1 Conclusions

This chapter presents the following findings:

First, this research proves the existence of born-global firms in the context of China's market environment. A two-by-two matrix of company characteristics is constructed using the multiple-case study method, showing the characteristics of traditional-global firms and born-global firms on three dimensions: export speed, export intensity, and the firm's industry. The research finds that Company C and Company D belong to born-global firms. They fall on the upper left of the two-by-two matrix; their "export speed" and "export intensity" traits are exhibited shortly after inception as companies disregard market risk and actively explore the international market. Most of these companies come from high-tech industries, producing high-tech products. In addition, a part of Company C's international business comes from the traditional electrical equipment industry, indicating that in the context of China's market conditions companies that operate traditional industrial business may also become born-global firms.

Second, this chapter analyzes the determinants of the aforementioned differences between traditional-global firms and born-global firms and explains why Company C and Company D are positioned on the upper left of the matrix, in four aspects: founders/managers' congenital learning and experimental learning, network resources, and target market selection. This chapter also explains the driving forces for born-global firms' capabilities to rapidly get involved in the international market shortly after inception and expand international business.

142 Xi Chen et al.

Compared to traditional-global firms, founders/managers of born-global firms possess rich international experience and knowledge that enhance their congenital learning and experimental learning capabilities, enabling them to rapidly develop the international market shortly after inception and grow to be born-global firms. Born-global firms also have a strong international orientation and wide international vision. They don't see the overseas market as a different, separable market, but as an integrated whole. They have a vague idea of national boundaries, they have extraordinary international foresight and vision, and they explore international development opportunities proactively. Networks also play a very important role in the formation of born-global firms, as they provide firms with overseas market knowledge and experience, reduce uncertainties and risks in the target market, and facilitate firms' entry into overseas markets. Finally, this research finds that contrary to foreign literature, Chinese born-global firms enter target markets in a specific sequence and following strategic plans, which is different from relevant foreign research where target market selection relies on psychic distance or other related resources, such as local distributor resources, network partner resources, and so on. In addition, Chinese traditional-global firms do not follow the entry sequence of going from psychically close markets to psychically more distant markets, as indicated by relevant foreign literature. Instead, they enter overseas markets in a random manner, seizing opportunities and taking orders as they happen.

Third, in terms of industrial distribution, almost all born-global firms studied in this chapter come from the high-tech sector. Although a small part of Company C's business belongs to traditional industries, the company still relies heavily on intellectual property rights, inventions, and innovations. Its products are both knowledge intensive and capital intensive. The two traditional-global firms are both from traditional industries and are labor-intensive companies. Therefore, there is a significant relation between born-global firms and type of industry in the context of Chinese exporters. Generally speaking, born-global firms are more likely to be found in high-tech and knowledge-intensive companies.

Fourth, with few exceptions (Knight *et al.*, 2003), most western literature regarding "born-global firms" suggests that such firms tend to be found in knowledge-intensive firms, but the research in this chapter finds that Chinese born-global firms can also be found in traditional industries (such as the electrical equipment industry).

Fifth, the majority of research on born-global firms comes from Europe, especially Northern Europe, which is the origin of research on such types of firms. European nations have small territories and the volumes of their domestic markets are limited, so it is easy for firms to develop outward-expansion visions. Nonetheless, findings in this chapter prove that such firms exist even in a vast market like China. Therefore, the judgment that born-global firms come from countries with small domestic market volumes, as posited in western literature, is not valid in China.

9.5.2 Limitations and directions for future research

There are also limitations to this research. First, this chapter adopts a case-based scientific qualitative research method, and the qualitative case study method has its inherent flaws. For instance, the understanding of the interviewer may not be congruent with what the interviewee intends to express and therefore may lead to different conclusions. In addition, the sample of the case study method may not be sufficiently representative, and the universality and accuracy of the conclusions may need to be further tested. Moreover, the companies studied in this chapter are from the economically developed Jiangsu–Zhejiang region. Are born-global firms also widely distributed in other economic regions? If so, do they share the same characteristics with firms studied in this chapter? What are the characteristics of their regional distribution? This chapter can't provide answers to these questions. Third, due to limited space, this chapter only explains the resource-based determinants of the formation of born-global firms. Many other external environmental factors, such as macro environment, market environment, consumer characteristics, and science and technology development, also significantly influence the formation of born-global firms. Future study may focus on these factors. Finally, this chapter may have proposed a series of determinants, but we can only judge the direction of their influences. The accurate extents of their influences require further research.

This chapter is practically instructive. Currently, China is in the middle of rapid internationalization. Small and medium-sized Chinese firms are faced with both opportunities and challenges. The increase of market opportunities and the improvement of managers' capabilities have caused the formation of firms that venture into the international market right from inception. However, as we have mentioned, such firms are also confronted with severe global challenges. This chapter hopes to shed some light on the following questions: What are the unique attributes of born-global firms that distinguish them from traditional-global firms? As born-global firms, how do they see and understand these unique attributes? What are the key determinants of the formation of these firms? How do firms understand these determinants? How do firms make use of resources and advantages so as to keep a foothold in fierce international competitions?

10 The internationalization of China's contracting and outsourcing firms: a multi-case study

Qingfei Xue

10.1 Introduction

There are three major modes of firm internationalization: exchange-based, contract-based, and investment-based internationalization. The exchange-based mode is a basic choice for firm internationalization, including direct export and indirect export. The contract-based mode is an intermediate choice, including licensing agreement, franchising, management contract, and turnkey contract. Among these, there is a new form of management contract: outsourcing, which has two common forms – original equipment manufacturing (OEM) and original design manufacturing (ODM). The investment-based mode refers mainly to foreign direct investment (FDI), which includes wholly foreign–owned operation, joint venture, transnational acquisition, and equity internationalization. The internationalization of China's private enterprises is still at an early stage. Their entry modes are simple: 90% of them choose the exchange-based mode to enter the international market, with the rather simplistic purpose of seeking market opportunities. Firms that are inclined to adopt the contract-based mode and the investment-based mode to enter the international market include technology startups, state-owned enterprises that have a tradition of international operation, and some specialized foreign-trade companies.

To date, research on international market entry modes focuses mainly on exchange-based internationalization and investment-based internationalization. However, little academic attention, at home or abroad, has been paid to the emerging contract-based internationalization. In China, the emerging contract-based internationalization mode is adopted not only by firms that follow the incremental internationalization model but also by more firms that show born–global characteristics. Their formation is either driven by the congenital experience and resources of their founders/managers or determined by advantages in cost and labor.

The contract operation entry mode can be defined as a contract arrangement in which the "licensor" company provides a usable asset to the "licensee" company in return for patent royalty, license fee, or other forms of compensation. The licensed asset could be a patent, a business secret, or a company name. The merits of this mode include low operation risk, export promotion, circumventing the host country's restrictions on export or FDI, and low cost. Its flaws include weak control and cultivation of potential competitors.

Our research questions in this chapter are as follows: (1) Why do Chinese firms choose the contract-based mode as their internationalization path? (2) What are the determinants of the process and path of contract-based internationalization?

10.2 Literature review

10.2.1 An overview of contract-based internationalization

Contract-based entry refers to an entry method in which a firm transfers one or a number of its intangible assets, without involving the firm's stock or property rights, to a foreign firm. The transferor of the asset(s) receives relevant fees and remuneration from the user. Instead of exporting products, a firm transfers intellectual property rights (including industrial property rights and copyrights) to foreign firms; its entry modes include licensing agreement, franchising, turn-key contract, and management contract, among others.

A licensing agreement is a legal document made by the licensee and the licensor concerning the transference of the rights to use patents, technologies, and trademarks, among others. A licensing agreement stipulates a series of restrictive conditions such as term of use, terms of payment of use fee, and so forth. It is a low-cost market entry path. Compared to the FDI mode, it reduces risks caused by uncertainties in the target market; compared to the exchange-based entry mode, it circumvents market barriers and overcomes cost barriers resulting from high exportation cost. Therefore, a licensing agreement is an ideal mode for small and medium-sized enterprises (SMEs) that possess technological expertise.

Franchising is a special form of licensing agreement. It is an operation model in which the franchiser provides a series of products and services, including technology, trademark, uniform business practices, and personnel training, to the franchisee in return for continuous commission and other forms of financial compensations. As an international market entry model, franchising can take advantage of management information systems to rapidly obtain international market information, enter the international market, acquire steady franchising benefits, effectively reduce management levels, guarantee organizational flattening and decentralization, and avoid institutional bureaucracy. The weakness of the franchising mode is that the franchiser has weak control over the franchisee and therefore may raise potential competitors.

Turnkey contract refers to an entry mode in which a multinational takes advantage of its expertise and experience in design, construction, and production and its prowess in completing engineering projects. The firm signs a contract with an equipment buyer from its target market. The firm helps the buyer complete a series of activities, such as researching feasibility, designing plans, purchasing equipment, building facilities, running tests, and official launching, and thus enters the target market. Common forms of turnkey contracts include build-operate-transfer (BOT), build-own-operate (BOO), and build-own-operate-transfer (BOOT). The turnkey contract mode may be exposed to political risks, market risks, technical risks, financing risks, and force majeure.

A management contract gives a firm the authority to manage the daily operation of firms in the target market by means of contracts. Such contracts do not authorize a firm to perform fundamental management or formulate policy that concerns such matters as new capital investment, dividend distribution, and change of ownership. The management is confined to daily operation only but does not involve a property rights arrangement. In the 1990s, new forms of management contract, conspicuously OEM and ODM, became widely adopted. On the one hand, this enables the parent firm to focus resources on core business and reduce the risks and costs of cross-national operation; on the other hand, many firms located in developing countries take advantage of management contracts to explore the international market.

10.2.2 Review of classic theories about firms' international market entry modes

1 Stage model

Since the mid-1970s, the Nordic School, represented by Johanson and Vahlne, proposed the stage model of internationalization. They point out that firm internationalization is a continuous and incremental process, as manifest in the following aspects. (1) Geographical sequence of firms' market expansion: from local market, to regional market, national market, neighboring country markets, and the global market. (2) Evolution of firms' cross-national operation: purely domestic operation, indirect export through middleman, direct export, establishment of overseas sales division, and overseas production. According to the stage model, firms tend to initially choose a psychically close market to export and then gradually expand into psychically more distant markets. Lu and Li (2003) conduct a survey on 112 private manufacturing firms in Wenzhou that operate overseas business and find that the internationalization of small and middle-sized firms in Wenzhou still follows the incremental internationalization mode.

Another type of incremental internationalization mode is the American innovation mode (Bilkey & Tesar, 1977; Cavusgil, 1980), which suggests that the internationalization of firms is a process in which firms keep carrying out behavioral innovations.

Malhotra *et al.* (2003) comprehensively examine the influences of market factors, global strategic factors, transaction-specific factors, and government-imposed factors on firms' overseas market entry modes. The authors discuss the possible entry mode arrangements for firms at different phases of their products and eventually construct an integrated theoretical analysis framework based on influential factors and phases of product development.

The research of Lamb and Liesch (2002) proposes that the relationship between the three constructs of firm internationalization (namely, market commitment, market knowledge, and market involvement) is unidirectional and problematic. Instead, these three constructs are interacted and bi-directional. Therefore, the internationalization of smaller firms is a dynamic process of growth and learning.

Bartlett and Ghoshal (1998) propose a cross-national operation model that integrates product innovation (including the transnational transference of product development), proximity to market (including localization strategy, product differentiation, and local adaptation, etc.), and cost reduction through competition (global production, standardization, and rationalization), enriching and advancing Vernon's product life cycle theory.

Johanson and Vahlne (1977, 1990) propose two identifiable internationalization models. First, in terms of entry mode, a firm goes from low resource commitment gradually to higher resource commitment, following such an establishment chain: no regular export, independent representative (agent), overseas sales subsidiary, and overseas production subsidiary. Second, in terms of target market selection, a firm shows the tendency of increasing psychic distance. It initially starts with neighboring countries, then gradually expands into other countries based on the degrees of cultural, economic, and political differences and geographical distance until eventually it reaches countries with the greatest differences. In the 1990s, firms faced a complicated and volatile international market environment. During this period, plenty of research in the field of international business used strategic management theory to study and explain the international behaviors of firms.

The behaviorism internationalization theory, which emerged in the mid-1970s, replaces the assumption of "economic man" with "rational man" and considers internationalization as a continuous evolution process, suggesting that firms' entry mode into specific markets and firms' overseas market selection follow some predictable paths. The behaviorism perspective stresses incremental development of the internationalization path and views internationalization as a dynamic learning and feedback process. Scholars advocating behaviorism propose that the greatest obstacle to overseas operation is firms' lack of relevant knowledge and experience and indicate that transaction may be the safest choice with the highest rate of success when the firms begin to conduct transnational business. International operation knowledge and experience that have been acquired in an incremental manner help firms gain insight on overseas markets, develop internationalization expertise and skills, and overcome the risks and disadvantages of being "foreign firms." As market knowledge increases, firms' international commitment would increase accordingly.

Leonidou and Katsikeas (1996) divide the export development process into three broad phases: pre-engagement, initial, and advanced. The pre-engagement phase includes firms that are active in the domestic market but not engaged in exporting activities. During the initial phase, firms are involved in sporadic export activity and consider various options. In the advanced phase, firms are regular exporters with extensive overseas experience and commit to international business. To sum up this theory, firms first gain the information, experience, and knowledge necessary for their market expansion by engaging in exporting activities continuously. As they build up experience and become more confident, they go in for broader exporting activities and achieve better internationalization performance. On the other hand, a failure experience may lead firms to reevaluate or reduce previous efforts. Internationalization process theory explains the region choice and international operation model choice in the process of firms' internationalization. This theory emphasizes the standard model of firm behavior. It is reviewed to be strongly deterministic, mechanical in its explanation of the internationalization development process without considering the effects of firm decision makers in the internationalization process.

2 The transaction cost theory

The second perspective originates from Coase's transaction cost theory. The basic assumption of this theory is that lower cost is the driver of firms' internalization activities. If other markets can provide cost advantages, firms will externalize their businesses. Representative research of transaction cost theory includes Anderson and Gatignon.

When categorizing selection mode, the theory views control as the most important factor affecting firms' risks and benefits in overseas markets. Based on the degrees of control over overseas firms, it divides market entry strategy modes intro three types: a high-control mode in which the firm owns a substantial proportion of stock rights, an intermediate-control mode that features balanced stock rights ownership, and a low-control mode with diffuse stock ownership. Factors affecting the degrees of control include transaction-specific assets, external uncertainty, internal uncertainty, and free-riding potential.[1] These four factors are positively related to degrees of control over overseas firms.

Anderson (1990) presents nine propositions regarding market entry mode choice:

1   Modes of entry offering greater control are more efficient for highly proprietary products or processes.
2   Entry modes offering higher degrees of control are more efficient for unstructured, poorly understood products and processes.
3   Entry modes offering higher degrees of control are more efficient for products customized to the user.
4   The more mature the product class, the less control firms should demand of a foreign business entity.
5   The greater the country risk and transaction specificity of assets, the higher the degree of control.
6   The degree of control of a foreign business entity should be positively related to the firm's cumulative international experience.
7   When sociocultural distance is great, the efficiency ranking (from high to low) is low-control, high-control, intermediate levels. High-control levels

are more efficient only when there is a substantial advantage to conducting business in the entrant's way.

8 Entrants' control level is negatively related to the size of the foreign business community in the host country.

9 Entry modes offering higher degrees of control are more efficient the higher the value of a brand name.

3 The eclectic paradigm of investment theory

The choice of entry mode is affected mainly by three factors: ownership paradigm, location attractions, and internalization advantages (Dunning, 2000). Location attractions include the national risks of the host country and the multinational's familiarity with the host country. Ownership paradigm and internalization advantages are more concerned with relevant variables of specific industries and specific firms.

When a firm only possesses ownership advantages, it would choose the licensing mode to explore the international market. When a firm possesses both ownership and internalization advantages, it would choose the export mode. Only when a firm possesses all the three types of advantages could it choose the foreign direct investment mode to enter the international market.

In recent years, building on the transaction cost theory, the eclectic paradigm, and internationalization theories, many western scholars have enriched the theoretical analysis of multinationals' international entry mode choice. Specifically, two kinds of factors/variables affecting multinationals' entry mode choice have been proposed: environmental factors and transactional factors. In 1990s, Kim and Hwang (1992) incorporated multinationals' global strategy as a variable in the theoretical analysis of entry mode choice and proposed a comprehensive analysis framework of entry mode choice.

10.2.3 Internationalization theories of late-mover countries

This stream mainly explains the advantages and features of the internationalization of private firms in late-mover countries, especially in developing countries. Such theories are extremely instructive. Representative theories include small-scale technology theory, technology localization theory, and comparative advantages theory.

1 Small-scale technology theory

American scholar Louis Wells proposed the small-scale technology theory, which proposes that the technological advantages of developing countries' firms are very special and reflect the market environment of the investment country. Three specific matters are noteworthy:

First are small-scale technological advantages. Market pressure forces developing country firms to modify imported technologies and make them more flexible to provide a greater variety of products to meet small-scale, diversified market demands, thus creating the features of small-scale technologies. Such modified, small-scale technologies become developing country firms' special advantages in making foreign direct investment.

Second are local purchasing and special product advantages. The FDI of developing country firms often shows distinct national characteristics and can provide special products with strong ethnic features that sometimes could become overwhelming operation advantages.

Third are the advantages of inexpensive and high-quality products. Compared to developed countries, labor cost and advertising expenditures in developing countries tend to be much lower.

2 Technology localization theory

The technology localization theory indicates that developing country firms can digest, improve, and innovate foreign technologies and make the products better suited to local economic conditions and demands. Such innovation is not simply a passive imitation of the technology but the regeneration of it. Such innovation activity injects new vitality into the imported technology, creates new competitive advantages for the firm that imports it, and gives the developing country firm competitive advantages in the local market and in neighboring country markets. Lall's (1983) technology localization theory is an important theory for analyzing the internalization motivations of developing country firms. According to the theory, technology localization is a unique innovation activity that helps promote developing country firms' international operation and hence creates competitive advantages.

3 Comparative advantages theory

Japanese scholar Kiyoshi Kojima proposed the "comparative advantage theory" (or marginal industry expansion theory) based on studying "Japanese-style" FDI. The logic of this theory is exhibited as follows. First, "marginal industries" refer to industries that have lost or are about to lose their comparative advantages in the home market but exhibit apparent or potential comparative advantages in overseas markets. Second, the smaller the technological differences between home and host country, the easier to secure overseas market share, especially in a developing country. The standard of FDI technological choice is not monopolistic advantage but comparative advantage. Third, the technological levels of SMEs with marginal efficiency are closer to the host country's levels than those of innovative large firms. These SMEs are better suited to local production conditions. They can create more job opportunities for the host country. Therefore, they would be more easily accepted by the host country. Fourth, neither the home country nor the host country needs a monopolistic market structure, so size is not important in FDI or cross-border operation. Compared to large firms, smaller firms can develop comparative advantages and become "marginal firms" more easily. Hence, smaller firms are easier to conduct foreign investments.

10.3 Analytical framework and methodology

10.3.1 Analysis structure

This chapter conducts case study from three dimensions: internationalization process, internationalization drivers, and internationalization performance.

1 Internationalization process

1 INCREMENTAL INTERNATIONALIZATION MODE

Johanson and Vahlne (1977, 1990) point out that in terms of entry mode, incremental internationalization progress from low resource commitment gradually increases to higher resource commitment. The development path is as follows: no regular export, export representative (agent), establishment of overseas sales subsidiary, and eventually the establishment of overseas production subsidiary. In addition, in terms of target market selection, incremental internationalization shows the tendency of increasing psychic distance. In specific, firms initially start with neighboring countries, then gradually expand into other countries based on the degrees of cultural, economic, and political differences and geographical distance until eventually they reach the most distant countries. Stage models have four assumptions: first, firms develop the domestic country before exporting; second, there are obstructions at the initial stage of foreign market involvement; third, firms start exporting activities first in psychically close countries; finally, the whole internationalization process is irreversible.

2 LEAP-FORWARD INTERNATIONALIZATION MODE

Bell (1995) studies small computer software firms and finds that the conventional stages theory cannot properly explain these firms' internationalization processes. Bell finds that client followership, market segmentation targeting, and industry-specific factors, rather than the psychic distance from the export destination, strongly influence these firms' processes and manners of internationalization. Bell also discovers that some firms have not even been established in the domestic market before they start exporting. In addition, Rennie (1993) finds that these firms generally compete on quality and value created through innovative technology and product design. Moreover, they are very close to their customers in international niche markets (such as scientific instruments or machine tools), flexible, and able to adapt their products to quickly changing demands. Jolly *et al.* (1992) point out that for small high-tech exporters, the potential effectiveness (volume, intensity of competition, etc.) of the market is the key factor affecting the choice of their initial export market and that psychic distance is largely irrelevant in export market selection. Chetty and Campbell-Hunt (2004) conduct in-depth cases study on four small and medium-sized international firms that follow the traditional stage model and six born-global firms, all from New Zealand. By comparing born-global firms and traditional-global firms, the authors identify 10 unique attributes of born-global firms. Regarding the specific indices and criteria of born-global firms, scholars have proposed different measurement standards due to differences of research purposes and research contexts. There are mainly two dimensions: first, the length of time between establishment and export; second, the percentage of overseas sales in total sales (Hu & Chen, 2007).

Besides the born-global model, there are also other international expansion models that are different from the traditional stage model, and we categorize them all as leap-forward internationalization models. For instance, some firms follow the overseas development model of establishing overseas subsidiaries at the initial stage of their internationalization. Table 10.1 summarizes the main drivers for firms' internationalization.

2 The dimensions of internationalization drivers

Scholars have extensively investigated the driving forces of internationalization. The categorization and analysis of Kojima (1978) and Dunning (1981) are widely accepted academically. In this chapter, we divide factors that drive firms to internationalize into two main groups: external drivers and internal drivers.

Table 10.1 Drivers of internationalization

External drivers	Internal drivers
Inadequate domestic market, excess capacity	Strategic goals
Comparative advantages	Market seeking, natural resource seeking, low cost seeking, and strategic asset seeking
Technological accumulation	Firm capabilities
Cost advantages	Leader qualities
Human resource advantages	Organizational form: knowledge management, etc.
Industrial advantages	
Technology standardization	Production technology
Exchange rate fluctuation	Source of funding
Convenience of science and communication technology	Talent advantages
Government policy support	Management standardization and adaptation, such as quality management system, service system, etc.
	Marketing tools and channels

EXTERNAL DRIVERS

In the traditional Uppsala model, insufficient domestic market and excess capacity are considered important drivers of internationalization. In specific, the Uppsala model includes the following aspects:

Industrial comparative advantages   Kojima proposes that when an industry possesses comparative advantages not domestically but internationally, this industry would be prone to conduct foreign trade. Moreover, when an industry faces market restraints and excess capacity in domestic market, it would seek exporting opportunities. When an industry does not possess comparative advantages internationally, however, it would be prone to make foreign direct investment. In developing countries, the ratios of capital to manpower and technology to manpower are rather low. Since it is very difficult to develop technology-intensive and capital-intensive industries, direct investment becomes a more desirable choice. Foreign direct investment is a subcategory of foreign trade. Therefore, developing countries would export businesses with comparative advantages and make foreign investments in comparatively disadvantageous businesses. Therefore, possession of comparative advantages is an external driver of firm internationalization.

Technology advantages   Based on the small-scale technology advantages theory, Cantwell and Tolentino (1990) propose that technological accumulation is a stimulus to economic development for any country. In addition, they find that technological innovation is a fundamental driving force for the development of a country's industries and enterprises. Different from firms from developed countries, the main advantage of developing-country firms is that they can take advantage of their unique learning experience and organizational capabilities to exploit existing technologies. Technological advantage drives the progress of firm internationalization.

Labor and quality advantages   Abundant human resource is an important comparative advantage for Chinese firms. According to Lewis's dual-economy theory, less developed countries would see the existence of the dual-sector model for a rather long period. The modern industrial sector absorbs rural surplus labor with a fixed wage rate and thereby continues to reinvest in the modern economic sector to increase its proportion. The process will continue until capital accumulation catches up with population growth so that rural labor surplus is exhausted and wage rises to above subsistence level. This point is known as the Lewis Turning Point. In other words, before the Lewis Turning Point, cheap labor cost represents an advantage. Some scholars suggest the Lewis Turning Point has two phases: the first phase is characterized as the wage level of the capital sector begins to rise. Salary rise can be caused by exogenous changes such as the increased opportunity cost of labor supply caused by a richer traditional sector. The second phase is caused by the endogenous change from labor surplus to labor shortage. Therefore, the second phase is also viewed as a supply-demand turning point, and it is a crucial one. At its current stage, China has not yet reached the Lewis Turning Point.

Technology standardization   As an important approach of promoting technology-economy synergy, participating in market competition, and expanding technological monopoly, technology standardization is gradually becoming a central issue among multinationals and international conglomerates. As international competition intensifies, developed-country firms are attaching more importance to the application of technological standard strategy. They use technological standard as an important tool for trade protection and as an approach to maintain the domestic market and explore foreign markets.

INTERNAL DRIVERS

Another important force for firm internationalization is internal resources, mainly including internationalization goals, entrepreneur characteristics, and firm capabilities.

Internationalization goals   Dunning (1998) suggests that natural resource seeking, market seeking, and production factors seeking are three major classes of drivers of firms' making foreign direct investments. The goals of Chinese firms' pursuing internationalization strategies include: market seeking, natural resources seeking, low cost seeking, and strategic assets seeking.

Entrepreneur characteristics   Different from the sequential internationalization process, as proposed by traditional internationalization theories, new internationalization theories stress the importance of management leaders in seizing international opportunities and taking proactive actions to carry out internationalization activities. Thanks to the development of information technology and the improvement of transportation efficiency, an increasing number of firm executives possess extensive prior international business experience before the inception of firms, enabling firms to skip certain stages of traditional internationalization. Entrepreneurial orientation refers to a firm's propensity to make innovations, take risks, act preemptively, take initiative, and forge ahead to achieve strategic goals. Innovation is the fundamental task of a firm that possesses entrepreneurial spirit and is the core of entrepreneurship. A firm with a strong entrepreneurial orientation often shows a risk-taking tendency, and its foresight and preemptive action give the firm a forward-looking perspective. Therefore, a firm with an entrepreneurial orientation would make active effort to learn new knowledge, new technologies, and new processes. It would embrace high risks that result from uncertainties. The entrepreneur's mental characteristics to seize opportunities, confront risks, and engage in innovation independently drive the firm to accelerate its internationalization process.

Firm capabilities Atuahene-Gima (2005) analyzes the relationships between the two dimensions of market orientation (namely customer orientation and competitor orientation) and firm viability. Moreover, under the transaction cost economics (TCE) framework, a firm's production function is composed of technological factors and organizational factors; technological factors reflect organizational capabilities, and capability heterogeneity inevitably exists among firms. Organizational factors include managerial factors and organizational structure, and technological factors include a firm's technological leadership and patents, and so on. Therefore, firm capabilities, including a firm's technology, human resources, and organizational factors, constitute the basic drivers of firm internationalization.

In terms of capabilities, the congruence between a firm's operation activities in an overseas market and its existing knowledge base is an important factor in cooperation decision-making. If a firm operates in a distant overseas market or is not familiar with the industry, it needs to acquire necessary supplementary knowledge due to the inadequacy of its current capabilities. Knowledge management is a form of firm capability. Because the cost to develop capability in a new field could be very high and the result might not be ideal, the alternative would be to "graft" others' knowledge onto the firm's resources and integrate it into the firm's knowledge base.

3 Internationalization performance

Many scholars (e.g., De Castro & Chrisman, 1995; Montgomery & Lieberman, 1998) have studied the relationship between international market entry mode and firm performance, and they find that international market entry strategy is related to performance. According to empirical research findings, firms that entered the host country first and survived enjoy satisfactory operation performance (Lilien & Yoon, 1990; Kerin, 1992). Luo and Park (2001) suggest that the timing of entry strategy has a crucial effect on international operation performance. In other words, the performance dimension and the internationalization process dimension are significantly related, and strategic timing is a very important factor. This chapter assumes that internal drivers drive strategic-timing choice and that powerful internal drivers would enable firms to choose the right strategic timing. We name these firms "the first firms to enter the host country." Through case study we find that the contract-based internationalization strategies of contracting and outsourcing are highly similar, but due to the differences of internal drivers and external drivers the resulting performances differ greatly. We will discuss this in detail in the following analysis.

10.3.2 Methodology

This chapter adopts a cross-case study method. In specific, we followed the literature to categorize firms according to three dimensions as "internal/

external drivers," "leap-forward/incremental internationalization," and "superior/inferior performance" and draw four-scenario tables for each pair. In addition, this chapter examines the differences of the sub-dimensions so as to observe the relationships between these three variables. In the following step, using the grounded theory method, we depict the basic characteristics of the cases and observe the interplay between different factors. In the matter of case selection, the chapter takes the following factors into consideration: (1) Firms' industrial characteristics (industry type, status, and technological features) influence the drivers, structural choice, and development trend of firms' R&D internationalization; (2) Firms' organizational characteristics (size and age) influence the drivers, structural choice, and development trend of firms' R&D internationalization. Based on the prior discussion, this chapter screens several case study objects and finally chooses a few representative contracting and outsourcing firms from the high-tech industry. In order to preserve the diversity of the cases, we chose large and outstanding firms as well as smaller and newly established firms; some of them internationalize in a leap-forward manner and some incrementally; some perform excellently while others perform not so well.

Eventually, we selected five representative firms. We conducted in-depth onsite investigations, interviewed senior executives, and compiled detailed case reports based on the interviews and audio recordings. We then analyzed interview materials to guarantee the reliability and validity of the material arrangement and analysis process. In order to improve construct validity, we collected data through numerous sources, including in-depth face-to-face interviews with founders or overseas business managers of these firms, company websites, internal documents provided by these companies, questionnaires completed by interviewees, product and company brochures, and other secondhand information. Because some of these firms are not publicly listed, performance information was obtained by inquiring of the decision makers and internal personnel of these firms, and the reference rights of such data have also been acquired.

At the stage of case establishment, we conducted interviews again in order to achieve construct validity, confirming key data as well as asking new questions. We used the grounded theory method to code and organize the cases and obtained similar storylines. In the following step, we organized five cases, which are of different types, according to the dimensions mentioned in the theory review, revealing the characteristics of each type of firm and the problems they face. In addition, we used the same research process, question framework, and method for each case to ensure reliability and finally established a relatively comprehensive research case library.

10.4 Cases study and analysis

Table 10.2 lists the basic information and characteristics of cases studied in this research.

Table 10.2 Basic information about the cases

Firm characteristics	CNBM Hefei Research and Design Institute	China Tianchen Engineering Corporation	Wuxi Pharma Tech Inc.	Fuman Limited	Joinn Laboratories Inc.
Year of establishment/ internationalization	Transformed into a private firm in 1984/2000	1953 (ownership transformed in 1992)/1990	2000/2000	2000/2002	1995/2008
Main business	R&D and manufacturing of cement production technology and equipment; cement plant (engineering design, technological service, complete set of equipment, turnkey projects, etc.); turnkey projects being the core of its development strategy	Petrochemicals, fine chemicals, organic chemicals, inorganic chemicals, coal chemicals, synthetic fiber, fertilizer, soda ash, chlor-alkali, calcium carbide, light industry, medicine, storage and transport projects, industrial and civil buildings, municipal engineering project planning, feasibility study, engineering planning, engineering, equipment and material procurement, construction management, engineering supervision	1. Lab services, including the whole process from drug discovery to development; testing of biological and medical devices, and toxicology services 2. Production services, medicine intermediates, API production, cell bank service, cryotherapy, and cGMP manufacturing	Export-purposed consumer products, daily necessities, and chemical products; beginning to switch to the Contract Research Organization (CRO) service industry after appreciation of exchange rate	The first private firm in China to engage in pharmacology and toxicology research of new drugs

(Continued)

Table 10.2 (Continued)

Firm characteristics	CNBM Hefei Research and Design Institute	China Tianchen Engineering Corporation	Wuxi Pharma Tech Inc.	Fuman Limited	Joinn Laboratories Inc.
Location	Hefei, Anhui Province	Headquartered in Beijing, with home office in Tianjin and subsidiaries in Shanghai and Heilongjiang	In China, two development bases in Shanghai and pharmacology test bases in Tianjin and Suzhou; in the US, acquired subsidiaries located in St. Paul, Minnesota; Atlanta, Georgia; Philadelphia, Pennsylvania	A small industrial park in downtown Shenyang	Headquartered in Beijing, with subsidiary in Washington State
Employee size	Regular employees: 700–800; among them 80 professor-level senior professionals, 210 senior professionals, and 430 intermediate-level professionals	1,350	2,100	70–80	193
Source of clients	Initially, foreign associates; at present, multiple channels, including bidding and embassy bidding	(1) Agent recommendation; (2) Previous proprietor recommendation; (3) Chinese government agencies and chambers of commerce abroad; (4) Sought by operation personnel		Mainly through word of mouth, mainly from Japan, Southeast Asia, the US, and Canada; initially founder's acquainted clients, later meeting new clients in Canton Fair	Foreign offices, hiring local workers, facilitating communication between local clients and company, therefore attracting new clients

Region of source of projects	Middle East sees the biggest operating revenue: Saudi Arabia, the United Arab Emirates, Yemen, Palestine, Sudan, Ethiopia, among others; in addition: South America, including Brazil; Central Asia, including Kazakhstan and Kirghizstan, Russia, etc.	Pakistan, Turkey, Thailand, Bangladesh, and Central Asian countries like Kazakhstan, Uzbekistan, Belarus, etc.	9 of the world's top 10 pharmaceutical companies are Wuxi PharmaTech's clients, with more than 80 clients in more than 20 countries worldwide	Japan, Europe and the US, etc.	Mainly Chinese clients; foreign clients mainly from the US and Japan
Shareholders or partners	Attached to China Building Materials Academy and China National Building Materials Group	The former No. 1 Design Institute of the Ministry of Chemical Industry; state owned	Funded by venture capital upon establishment; IPO in New York Stock Exchange on August 9, 2007	4, mainland Chinese	5–6, renowned pathologists
Percentage of international business in total sales	More than 50%	More than 40%	More than 99%	70% in 2008; declining since 2009 to only 10% in 2010	Less than 10%
Sales	Completing contract value of RMB 2,429.51 million; annual sales: RMB 3 billion	Completing contract value of RMB 4,210.78 million; annual sales: RMB 3 billion	US$270 million	Export: more than US$2 million	Operating income in 2010: RMB 40 million
Profit	More than 20%	16.6%; pretax income: RMB 500 million, with RMB 350 million in net profit	US$52,870,000; total profit rate: 38%	Not available	10%
Business growth	20% on average	Average annual growth rate in the past 5 years: 27%–28%	20% on average	Declining continuously	20% on average

10.4.1 CNBM Hefei Research and Design Institute

1 Company information

Hefei Cement Research and Design Institute is attached to China National Building Materials (CNBM) Group. It is a key scientific research institute in China's construction materials industry and a Grade-A design institute. Currently, it has 2,598 employees, among them 80 professor-level senior technicians, 210 senior technicians, and 420 intermediate-level technicians. It has 16 specialized subsidiaries. This firm is engaged mainly in the R&D and manufacturing of cement production technology and equipment, engineering design, technological service, whole-set equipment, and Energy Performance Contracting (EPC) contracting of cement plants.

In terms of R&D, Hefei Cement Research and Design Institute has developed and expanded scientific projects following the principles of energy conservation and emission reduction, environmental protection, and integrated utilization. It has completed the R&D of numerous integrated utilization-related projects, including carbide slag and low-temperature waste-heat power generation and waste incineration, helping it improve resource and energy use efficiency and reach the leading level of the industry. In terms of scientific industrialization, the institute has pursued a branding strategy and developed famous brands by taking advantage of its R&D strength and by absorbing and improving imported technologies. Its HFCG series of roller presses have been awarded "Renowned Chinese Brand," creating a precedent of winning the "Renowned Chinese Brand" for independently developed and manufactured products in China's building materials industry.

In recent years, in order to improve its core competence, Hefei Cement Research and Design Institute has formulated and implemented a development strategy centering on turnkey projects. This strategy has not only enhanced its existing advantages in engineering design and core equipment manufacturing but also promoted the rapid development of its turnkey business. It has obtained contracts to build 1,500–6,000 tons per day (t/d) cement clinker production lines in Saudi Arabia, Sudan, Russia, Vietnam, Pakistan, Ethiopia, Chile, and Indonesia. In September 2007, Saudi Arabia's NAJRAN 6,000 t/d clinker production line was officially put into production, marking the completion and launch of Hefei Cement Institute's, as well as CNBM's, first complete turnkey project.

By following a synergic development path that integrates scientific R&D, design, industrialization, and turnkey projects, Hefei Cement Research and Design Institute has been transformed from a scientific research institution into a high-tech firm with an annual output value of nearly 4 billion (RMB).

2 The internationalization process dimension

Now we will examine the internationalization process of Hefei Cement Research and Design Institute from the four assumptions in incremental internationalization. Table 10.3 summarizes the internationalization process of CNBM Hefei Research and Design Institute.

Sources of the firm's projects are diversified, and very often it is a subcontractor; 80% of its projects are turnkey projects (from plant building to turning over the key), and a smaller proportion of its projects are equipment

Table 10.3 Internationalization process, the serial internationalization dimension

Sub-dimensions	Relative to the case	Congruent
Domestic advantages of the export manufacturer	Ranking 13th among China's top 100 engineering prospecting and design firms, and ranking 1st among design institutes in the building materials industry; ranking among the top 3 in the top 20 firms of China's building materials machinery industry for five years in a row; named one of world's 225 largest international contractors in 2009; one of the first group of firms with AAA credit ratings in China's building materials industry; given the honor of "China's 100 Model Enterprises of Innovation"	Yes
Internationalization is a passive instead of active strategy (dimension: driven by internal drivers and external drivers)	Driven by external drivers	Yes
Export beginning with psychically close countries or regions(dimension: region and reason of project entry)	Geographic distribution of clients of CNBM Hefei Cement Research and Design Institute: Southeast Asia: Vietnam is the country with the largest number of the institute's clients; the country's industrial system is out of balance, with a large number of cement plants under construction. Other countries in this region include Laos and Pakistan. The Middle East sees the firm's biggest operating revenue: Saudi Arabia, the United Arab Emirates, Yemen, Pakistan, Sudan, and Ethiopia, among others. Additional projects contracted also in South America including Brazil and Central Asia including Kazakhstan and Kirghizstan, Russia, etc. However, the psychic distance from the host country is irrelevant here. International business is largely driven by the existence of potential markets. Nevertheless, the market entry of Hefei Cement Research and Design Institute still follows the rule of continuous learning and continuously entering new markets. When it entered Southeast Asia it didn't think it would be able to enter the Middle East market.	No
Internationalization is a serial process	From labor export initially to turnkey project now, commitment keeps increasing	Yes

procurement or commissioning. The Hefei Institute has a bigger proportion of commissioning and equipment procurement.

3 Motivations for internationalization

In order to expand its market, CNBM Hefei Cement Research and Design Institute pursues the traditional, passive following strategy. That is because the entire industry was forced to take part in internationalization passively after it became internationalized.

Firstly, external drivers are shown in Table 10.4

China's cement industry has benefited greatly from China's reform and opening up policy and has become one of the most important industries in the world. China's cement contracting industry, on the other hand, has gone through several development phases to achieve its huge comparative advantages, including labor export, technology import, technological breakthroughs, and turnkey projects development.

The grounded theory was used to analyze the interview, and the following storyline was obtained:

1 LABOR EXPORT

In the 1980s, China's cement equipment and contracting technology lagged greatly behind those in foreign countries. Back then, many teams exported labor to countries like Iraq, working for other cement contractors. Iraq and other Middle East countries had sufficient capital and technology to build plants, but they did not have enough manpower, so China exported a lot of labor. There is a scene in the book *Kerbela Take-off* where, in a cement plant in Kerbela, Iraq, all the workers are Chinese.

In the decade between 1980 and 1990, Chinese workers could be seen in projects in Vietnam, Myanmar, and Pakistan. Engineers had been trained and accumulated experience there. Those migrant workers came in contact with advanced technology, improved their capabilities, and expanded their horizons. That laid a talent foundation for the future of China's cement industry.

2 NATIONAL TECHNOLOGY IMPORT

In the 1990s, guided by government policy, whole production lines (from design to equipment parts) were imported, and a number of plants were built as models and leading enterprises of the industry. The three largest plants were exemplary. The first was in Lingbo, which later became China's largest cement company, Conch Cement. It imported the entire production line from Mitsubishi Heavy Industries. The second one was built in Jinzhong, Tangshan, also importing a whole production line. The third one was Huaihai Cement Plant in Xuzhou, which was the predecessor of Julong Group, importing a production line from Denmark. Through these efforts, the hardware of China's cement industry was significantly improved.

Table 10.4 External drivers

Sub-dimensions		*Relevant contents to the case*
Insufficient domestic market and excess capacity		In recent years, China's cement and building industries have been under state control. Market potentials become smaller, but production capacity keeps expanding. The result is that the domestic industry begins to shrink, the number of projects decrease, and capital and loans lessen.
		Therefore, in the context of increasing construction cost, province-level building contractors began to go abroad and carry out international business.
Comparative advantages	Technological accumulation	The government's technology import in the 1990s resulted in huge technological advancement in China's cement industry.
	Cost advantages	China always has cost advantages, and the flexibility and high efficiency of Chinese workers make the cost advantages of whole projects more apparent and improve core competence. China is capable of producing a wider variety of product equipment (higher technology); services provided by specialized foreign manufacturers may be of high quality, but too expensive.
	Human resource advantages	Labor export in earlier years lays the foundation for creating internationalized and high-tech human resource advantages.
	Industrial advantages	Total international contract volume of China's cement industry is now the biggest in the world. This has been driven by the development of the national economy. The development of the domestic cement industry and the improvement of its competence drive its internationalization.
		Industrial advantages have been created through four phases of accumulation.
	Government policy support	The Chinese government's support for scientific and technological research in the 1990s has been more efficient than any firm's scientific effort in the creation of China's cement industry's huge technological advantages over other countries.
	Convenience of science and communication technology	Not mentioned.

Thanks to scientific and technological research, China's cement industry became a world leader. During the 8th Five-Year Plan, the government led design institutes to tackle key technical problems of cement production and equipment. Supported by national power the technological level of China's cement industry saw considerable improvement. Meanwhile, at the end of the economic depression from the 1990s to 2000, the Chinese economy developed rapidly, and fundamental industries enjoyed enormous growth. Thanks to capital accumulation and industrial development, China's cement industry saw extensive growth, and supporting industries became more mature and advanced. In Zhejiang, capital, technology, and production lines were all in position. A 2,500-ton production line, from project initiation to commissioning, could be completed in one year, an efficiency that saw no rival in the world. Now most machines and equipment could be manufactured domestically. Although the quality may not be as high as those in Europe and America, the technology involved ranks among the best of the world.

3 TURNKEY PROJECTS

As the domestic market shrank and building cost went up, more and more cement companies began to seek growth overseas.

In the 1980s and 1990s, even until 2005, most projects have been located in Vietnam, Myanmar, and Pakistan (the worker who died in an accident in 2005 was an employee of Hefei Cement Research and Design Institute). After 2005, CNBM's Tianjin Institute, Nanjing Institute, and Hefei Institute entered Saudi Arabia and other Middle East countries. The projects there have higher standards and significantly higher requirements. Meanwhile, the number of projects from Africa increases. European and American cement contractors, such as Danish and German firms, follow rigid operating modes. Their efficiency is far lower than Chinese firms, and they often fail to complete projects in time and therefore could not meet clients' requirements.

From this analysis, we know that external drivers are strong for CNBM Hefei Cement Research and Design Institute. The interviewee mentioned on several occasions that they were "forced to internationalize."

From this analysis, we can infer that the first result of powerful external drivers is the internationalization of the entire cement industry, which nationalizes international competition. For instance, the interviewee mentioned that cement is a long-cycle industry. At one point there were so many projects in the Middle East that there were not enough contractors to undertake them. First-rate contractors pay attention to international business, and second-rate contractors are devoted only to the domestic market. When international competition becomes domestic, price wars are inevitable. The interviewee said that the Chinese style is that when one person takes the lead everyone will follow. All institutes ended up taking part in the competition, and each has its own advantages. For instance, when Hefei Cement Institute entered the market it snatched orders from Tianjin Institute using a price strategy.

Such price wars have two outcomes: first, with low price and high efficiency, contractors from other countries simply cannot compete. When many of them go out of business the competition becomes mainly among Chinese contractors; second, because of vicious price competition the profit of Chinese contractors also goes down.

The second result of powerful external drivers is that the negotiation power of China's cement industry would become greater. The interviewee said that as the degree of internationalization of the whole industry increases more contractors understand the working and rules of foreign contracts and therefore increase their negotiation power. Contracting builders also have access to turnkey projects and therefore reduce the power of channel monopolists, giving them more advantage in negotiation.

In the following step, we analyze the internal drivers of the firm's internationalization (as shown in Table 10.5).

We can see that internal factors do not represent the main driving force of the internationalization of CNBM Hefei Cement Institute. First of all, its strategic goal is mainly to seek market instead of non-strategic assets. This is the result of external drivers. The Hefei Cement Institute began to internationalize because channel operators sought it. Contracting projects internationally has become the prevalent trend in China's cement industry. All competent institutes and manufacturers have entered the international market. Hefei Cement Institute only pursues a following strategy.

The organizational capabilities of Hefei Institute have not been realigned because of its internationalization. First, its internal structure is not conducive to the communication of market knowledge, resulting in unsmooth information flow. Second, firm executives have plenty of domestic operation experience but do not have matching international experience.

In addition, it is funded by the government, which means that its internationalization performance is not a determinant of whether its international operation would continue. Apart from pricing, its marketing tools and channels do not represent advantages over its competitors, and compared to the CNBM group its talent pool does not represent an advantage either.

The result of strong external drivers and inadequate internal drivers is that when competing against foreign firms Hefei Cement Institute possesses significant advantages, but when competing against domestic firms it doesn't have any advantage. This leads to a third dimension: performance.

4 The internationalization performance dimension

The internationalization performance of Hefei Cement Institute did not meet expectations. It needs domestic business to make its international operation profitable.

However, performance did not cause Hefei Cement Institute to change its internationalization process. The interviewee said that firm executives believed it was a necessary cost to pay for its education so they could keep optimizing their ways of completing projects. They believed that the value of international projects and the size of the international market were much greater than those in China and that in time they would make profits out of those international projects.

In fact, the firm has indeed been learning international rules and norms. Conditions are improving, and losses are narrowing down. However, we find that the firm's internal drivers for its internationalization are inadequate. Its capabilities are not congruent with internationalization, which somewhat affects its internationalization capabilities, as reflected in the following aspects:

Table 10.5 Internal driving forces

Sub-dimensions	Relevant contents to the case
Strategic goals: Market seeking, natural resource seeking, low cost seeking, and strategic asset seeking	According to material, mainly market seeking. The volume of contracts in the international market is far greater than that in the domestic market; generally, if the average amount of a contract in China is RMB 200 million, the average amount internationally would be RMB 800 million.
Firm capabilities — Leader qualities	Guided by the thinking of increasing the size and improving the competences of their firms, executives are willing to explore the market, but overlook risk evaluation. International business profitability needs to be improved.
Organizational form: knowledge management, etc.	The organizational form of Hefei Cement Research and Design Institute is not suitable for internationalization and has not been adjusted. When it started its international operation the firm didn't have sufficient knowledge of the market. Risks and unexpected problems have occurred due to the firm's inadaptability to international engineering contracting rules and unfamiliarity to the procedure. Division of profit and communication within the organization was not smooth. The firm did not have turnkey projects five years earlier, so there was no conflict among these three factors. But now, in an international contracting project, the signing of contract, coordination, and execution would require different personnel, and many new conflicts have thus arisen. Similarly, communication between project members and proprietors has not been smooth either.
Production technology	As a science research institution, Hefei Cement Research and Design Institute possesses huge advantages in terms of equipment manufacturing technology.
Source of funding	As a state-owned enterprise, it has strong capital advantages.
Talent advantages	Compared to CNBM, the Hefei Cement Institute does not possess apparent advantages in terms of high-level researchers.
Management standardization and adaptation, such as quality management system, service system, etc.	Services: Japanese service is the best but too expensive. For Chinese workers, working extra hours is normal. The uncertainties of project contracting are very high, requiring many extra hours and commissioning. Chinese are more flexible than Europeans and Americans in this aspect. Punctuality: in terms of working hours, Chinese workers have the highest efficiency, but they may have difficulty complying with regulations.
Marketing tools and channels	Price strategy: when facing competition from a Chinese firm, it tends to pursue a low-price strategy.

First, the firm's knowledge management and organizational structure are not congruent with their international environment, and the result is that international knowledge cannot flow within the organization in the process of its internationalization. Moreover, due to inadequate knowledge of the international market, the firm's initial cost estimation often differs greatly from actual cost, thus greatly compromising project profitability. For instance, Hefei Cement Institute had a project in Saudi Arabia. Temperature in the desert in daytime could be as high as 40 degrees Celsius. Ordinary shoes could not work, and specially made iron-soled shoes were needed. The firm did not know that until too late and had to have special shoes made. The project was delayed, and extra cost was incurred. Another example is that the firm did not anticipate the inadequacy of the transport capacity of Dammam Port, and 8,000 tons of its equipment were held up in the port for three months. In Ethiopia, the delivery of a fluorimeter from the port to the construction site was delayed by three months because of the inefficiency of local workers.

Second, the degree of project management standardization is in urgent need of improvement and should be aligned with the international level. The procedure of an international project is different from that of a Chinese project. A consulting firm (from India or another country) is hired as the project supervisor whose job is to supervise the contractor on behalf of the proprietor, setting forth specifications, making a list of all necessary equipment, and so on.

Besides insufficient internationalization drivers, some unexpected risks in the international market have also made it difficult for the initial quotation to effectively reflect the budget and profit. Such risks include the following:

The first aspect is exchange rate. Since the exchange rate reform in 2006 exchange rate has become an unpredictable factor. For instance, in a Saudi Arabian project, RMB appreciated by 2% two weeks after the signing of the contract. The firm's quotation had been based on equipment and production cost in China, but the contract was signed in US dollars, so unanticipated losses were incurred.

Second involves political turmoil. As conspicuously pointed out in the case, the Libyan war had caused huge losses. According to the statistics of the State-owned Assets Supervision and Administration Commission, China's state-owned enterprises suffered losses of RMB 17 billion in the war, and contractors were hit the hardest. The main business model during the Iran-Iraq war was labor export. Workers were pulled back when the war broke out, but compensation still needed to be made when the war was over. Nonetheless, the war-related problems of labor export are completely different from those of contracting.

Contractors may suffer from problems like construction site destruction, equipment outage, and not being able to receive payment for delivered equipment. The contractor may go bankrupt because of the multiple roles in which it is involved, equipment provider being one of them. The Libyan war put China's cement industry in a predicament both domestically and internationally, dealing a huge impact on the industry. Workers also suffered psychological impacts, because those who saw and narrowly escaped death were prone to psychological problems, and that incurred very high cost, because the firm would need to pay a lot more to persuade technical and managerial personnel to go abroad under those circumstances. Moreover, such a major political crisis would inflict damage on the entire contracting industry chain.

10.4.2 China Tianchen Engineering Corporation

1 Firm information

The predecessor of the China Tianchen Engineering Corporation (TCC) was the No. 1 Design Institute of the Ministry of Chemical Industry, which was established in 1953 and the first state-level design institution in the chemical system. In 1992 the organization was renamed Tianchen Engineering Corporation, its business transformed from engineering design to turnkey projects. For years it has been on the Top 225 Global Contractors list published by Engineering News Record.

The main business of TCC is turnkey projects. The company has Grade-A qualifications in design and general contracting and operation permits in import and export. Businesses the company is certified to operate include: petrochemicals, fine chemicals, organic chemicals, inorganic chemicals, industrial and civil buildings, municipal engineering project planning, feasibility study, engineering planning, equipment and material procurement, construction management, and engineering supervision. The company attaches great importance to international standards. In 1994 it was the first company in China's prospecting and design industry to pass the ISO9001 quality system certification; in 2000, it was also one of the first companies to pass the 2000 version of ISO9001 quality system certification; in 2002, it passed the ISO14000/GBT28000 vocational health and safety and environment management system certification. In addition, the company upholds the tenet that "user satisfaction is the sole criterion of TCC's service." Through management control measures, the company guarantees that its project services comply with the laws and regulations of the host country/region and meet clients' requirements and environment safety requirements. Since inception, the company has completed more than 500 large-scale and medium-scale projects and turnkey contracts home and abroad; 120 of its projects have been given national and provincial awards for design and professional expertise. Table 10.6 summarizes the internationalization process of China Tianchen Engineering Corporation.

2 Internationalization process

TCC is congruent with the characteristics of incremental internationalization, but it does not fit the assumptions of incremental internationalization due to the particularity of turnkey projects contracting. A turnkey project includes not only features of trade and service export but also the contract-based entry mode of the stage model. It is not the advanced form of pure trade export,

Table 10.6 Internationalization process, the serial internationalization dimension

Sub-dimensions	Relative to the case	Congruent
Domestic advantages of the export manufacturer	The predecessor of TCC was the No.1 Design Institute of the Ministry of Chemical Industry, which was established in 1953 and the first state-level design institution in the chemical system. In 1992 the organization was renamed Tianchen Engineering Corporation, its business transformed from engineering design to turnkey projects. For years it has been on the Top 225 Global Contractors list published by Engineering News-Record (ENR).	Yes
Internationalization is a passive instead of active strategy (dimension: driven by internal drivers and external drivers)	Mainly driven by internal drivers	No
Export beginning with psychically close countries or regions (dimension: region and reason of project entry)	The internationalization of TCC started in the 1980s, when decision makers of the firm spotted opportunities in the international market and decided to take the initiative to internationalize. Then the firm began to undertake projects in Albania, Pakistan, Bangladesh, and Russia. Its international business concentrated in such fields as chemicals, oil refining, and power plants. The firm is currently watching the Iranian and the Qatari markets, accumulating market knowledge without getting involved. 40% of TCC's profit comes from its international business, and the profit rate of international business is higher than domestic business because competition in the international market is less intense than in the domestic market. Now the firm's clients cover Pakistan, Turkey, Thailand, Bangladesh, and some Central Asian countries like Kazakhstan, Uzbekistan, and Belarus, among others. The reason TCC chose to enter these countries is not that they are similar to China culturally or economically, but that they have large markets there. The differences between the more than 30 countries that TCC has a presence in are huge.	No
Internationalization is a serial process	TCC follows the incremental process of internationalization, from design service initially to turnkey projects export later. In the process of its turnkey contracting, all equipments are exported from China to the host country. In some civil engineering projects, TCC, whose core business is factory design, would subcontract the projects to some domestic construction companies.	Yes

but the overlap of trade export, trading, and direct investment. TCC's turnkey projects are not simply trading. They include export of services such as design, equipment supply, onsite installation, technological patent transfer, technical instruction, and training. These projects involve the export of equipment, labor, and technology.

For developed markets, TCC only provides services. For instance, TCC provides only design or feasibility reports to new projects in America, without exporting equipment or labor. Still, turnkey projects represent 90% of its export business.

TCC has subsidiaries in Thailand, Kazakhstan, and Gabon (Africa). In spite of that, TCC has a total number of less than 30 employees living abroad on a regular basis. Once an overseas project is confirmed, TCC hires many Chinese workers, generally for one to three years. Most design engineers and senior installation and welding technicians are Chinese, but locals do jobs like digging, moving things, and transportation. As a turnkey project contractor, TCC performs its core business, such as design, and outsources low-end and generic engineering work. It has comprehensive control over the brand, quality, and reputation of its subcontractors.

In China, project supervision is the responsibility of the government. However, in international project management, it is the proprietor's responsibility to supervise the subcontractors, and the bearer of the responsibility may be the proprietor themselves or a third party. Therefore, although TCC may be congruent with the characteristics of incremental internationalization, it does not fit the assumptions proposed by the incremental model. Table 10.7 summarizes the external drivers of China Tianchen Engineering Corporation's internationalization.

3 Internationalization drivers

We can see that the external driving forces of TCC's internationalization are not very strong, in spite of the fact that competition in the international market is not as fierce as in China. The comparative advantages of domestic industries are not apparent, and government support policy is not sufficient. Nonetheless, TCC's internal drivers for internationalization are very strong (see Table 10.8).

The goals of the firm's internationalization are not only to seek markets. Neither is its internationalization the helpless result of the shrinkage of the domestic market. Instead, it is a proactive action to seek strategic resources such as brands. Meanwhile, the firm can actively adapt its capabilities to internationalization. First, its executives have had internationalization experience and have developed long-term strategic goals. It has adjusted its organizational structure to suit international operation, improved knowledge management, increased knowledge of internationalization, guaranteed its ability to control internationalization-related risks, and therefore achieved better performance. In consequence, through investigation, planning, and strategy implementation TCC has managed to minimize risks and has entered countries with rather high operation risks. Meanwhile, the firm possesses apparent human resource

Table 10.7 External drivers

Sub-dimensions		Relevant contents to the case
Insufficient domestic market and excess capacity		Compared to the international market, the domestic market has fiercer competition, plenty of homogenized products, and too many brands. Currently, the international market is vast, with smaller competition pressure, more opportunities, and greater market potentials.
Comparative advantages	Technological accumulation	China possesses some technological advantages in certain individual technologies, such as undertaking the gasification design project for the US. Overall, China does not possess significant technological advantages.
	Cost advantages	For China's chemical contractors, sheer price reduction is not the main direction. Although they have price advantages over western competitors, they still need to maintain their technological level. Entering markets that competitors couldn't enter would create significant advantages.
	Human resource advantages	China trains a large number of professional technicians every year. The low cost of advanced technical talents is the source of firms' cost advantages.
	Industrial advantages	China's chemical industry does not enjoy such huge advantages in the world as China's cement industry does. Turnkey projects target mainly third-world countries, including Pakistan, Bangladesh, Central Asia, and Africa, where the degrees of infrastructure industrialization are still very low.
		However, Europe and the US's growth models are no longer dominated by the chemical industry but leaning more heavily on the service sector, in spite of the existence of time-tested chemical firms like Mobil, Shell, and BASF, among others. Now, however, they rely on the possession of resources and oil fields or some high-tech products. They do not build new factories domestically but overseas. They build new factories even in China (i.e., Shanghai and other development zones in South China).
	Government policy support	The government's policy support for internationalization is not sufficient. For instance, funding needs government support, but the procedure is lengthy and requires communication and coordination of many parties; if certain intermediate processes get stuck the whole project may be aborted.
		Banks and government do not provide sufficient support to firms, and their efficiency is hardly satisfactory.
Convenience of science and communication technology		Not mentioned.

Table 10.8 Internal drivers

Sub-dimensions		*Relevant contents to the case*
Strategic goals: market seeking, natural resource seeking, low cost seeking, and strategic asset seeking		The goals of TCC are market seeking and strategic asset seeking. Market seeking: decision makers attach equal importance to the domestic market and the international market. Currently, the international market is vast, with smaller competition pressure, more opportunities, and greater market potentials. TCC has clients all over the world. It is not restrained by cultural or economic factors. Any country could be its potential market, and countries with many project opportunities are its focal markets, such as Turkey, Pakistan, Central Asia, and Africa. Its internationalization and entry into a foreign market is driven by the potential of the market. In developing countries, all sectors of the economy need to be revived, so there would be more projects to be built. In Europe and the US, there are not many such projects. Strategic assets (brands): the driving effect is apparent for business-to-business (B2B) projects. One project can lead to the exploration of a national market and successful marketing in a region.
Firm capabilities	Leader qualities	All decision-making executive managers have project implementation experience abroad. In as early as the 1980s decision makers already saw that the domestic market was limited and that internationalization was the long-term strategy to pursue; 20 years later, internationalization has become one of the firm's strategic goals.
	Organizational form: knowledge management, etc.	TCC chooses active market entry strategies, so it conducts investigations in advance. Before it enters a country or a market, it collects market knowledge and information first. TCC's project information source holds a safe lead in the industry. This knowledge includes proprietor information including credit and financial standing, project information, project feasibility and fittingness of external conditions, the suitable location, and basic conditions for implementation; local market conditions, including supply of generic labor, supply of raw materials such as cement, steel, sand, etc.; local laws and regulations, taxation rules, and transport problems; local customs and manners, including hugging or handshaking. Besides onsite investigations, market knowledge can also be obtained through networks and personal connections.

(*Continued*)

Table 10.8 (Continued)

Sub-dimensions	Relevant contents to the case
	Because it pursues proactive strategies from the outset, TCC's procedure is very suitable for carrying out international projects.
	The organizational structures and operations of TCC's domestic business unit and international business unit are independent of each other.
Production technology	TCC possesses a large number of patents. Some of these patents are developed by TCC itself, such as caustic soda, soda ash, and PPC chemical apparatuses. Some of the technologies have been purchased from foreign firms like GE or East China University of Science, such as the gasification technologies of coal chemicals. For instance, the diesel fuel project in Pakistan used technologies that had been purchased from the US's Universal Oil Products Company (UOP).
Source of funding	The predecessor of TCC was the No. 1 Design Institute of the Ministry of Chemical Industry. It has sufficient funding, but funding for its internationalization projects still needs government support.
Talent advantages	All project managers have prior overseas project implementation experience. They have accumulated knowledge about overseas markets and projects. 72% of TCC's employees hold intermediate (and above) professional titles, a much higher percentage than other firms in the industry.
Management standardization and adaptation, such as quality management system, service system, etc.	TCC attaches great importance to service quality and communication in order to understand the needs of proprietors. It introduced the Early Vendor Involvement system long ago. Meanwhile, the improvement of managerial capability also represents an advantage of TCC. Therefore, it can attract clients.
Marketing tools and channels	TCC's overseas operation division is responsible for seeking overseas projects. Relational marketing, through the networks and association of firms' decision makers and employees, also plays a role, including recommendation by friends, agents, and other firms.
	It obtains export business through multiple channels, including: (1) agent recommendation; (2) recommendation by prior proprietors; (3) government agencies or chambers of commerce abroad; (4) sought by operation personnel.
	Its bidding modes include: invitation bidding (namely seeking out two to three companies), public bidding (extensive search, such as publishing information about the project on newspaper, TV, and websites), and single bidding (one to one, directly negotiating contract with a firm it has decided to work with).

advantages and technological advantages. Its requirements for technological standardization and service adaptability are all capabilities it has developed for internationalization.

A project manager is the brain of a project and has a huge influence on the project. Therefore, managers with excellent language and managerial skills are often assigned to foreign projects. The interviewee stressed that there are no fixed standards for managers' qualifications, but some skills are preferred. Of course, the overseas experience of decision makers has also played an important role. For instance, if the choice of a project manager or procedure is consistent with previously arranged standards but doesn't meet the proprietor's requirements and results in proprietor complaints or project delay or major schedule changes, then senior executives of the firm can adjust personnel structure and organizational structure in a timely manner.

It's fair to say that the drivers of TCC's internationalization are mainly internal.

4 Internationalization performance

The profit of TCC's international business is much higher than its domestic business. Since the firm's internationalization, a substantial part of its performance has depended on its international business. Aaby and Slater (1989) suggest that born-global firms' consideration for export is to seize the "first-mover" advantages and acquire international competitive advantages. For them exporting is self-motivated. They actively seek overseas target market segments and increase their involvements in overseas markets. Although TCC developed the domestic market first and improved its competence before internationalization, it also exhibits some born-global features because of its proactive internationalization strategies.

Currently, the firm has not yet established its brand. Turnkey projects are large in sums of money and small in number. A firm can establish its brand equity once it completes five to six projects in a country. TCC has built its brand in Bangladesh and Pakistan but not in other countries, as it has done only one or two projects in other countries.

There are still some unforeseeable risks in firm performance. Although TCC manages to reduce risks to certain extent thanks to its proactive strategies and advantages in information collection and its flexible organizational structure and personnel structure, its export performance would nonetheless be subject to the influence of unpredictable risks.

10.4.3 Wuxi Pharma Tech

1 Company information

Wuxi Pharma Tech is the largest CRO firm in the world. It went public on the New York Stock Exchange (NYSE) in 2007. With more than 80 clients from more than 20 countries worldwide, the firm has permanent establishments only in the US and China. In 2008, the firm established its American subsidiary and acquired the US's AppTec Laboratory Services Inc. The acquisition enabled the firm to gain biologics production capacity and expertise, to get hold of important American business, and to expand its client base and market volume. The merging of Pharma Tech's and AppTec's Chinese and American businesses enabled Wuxi Pharma Tech to provide whole-package chemical and biological outsourcing services to pharmaceutical, biologics, and medical instrument clients worldwide.

2 Internationalization process

Wuxi Pharma Tech follows a typical leap-forward internationalization mode. It is an exemplary born global; 99% of its revenue comes from its international business, and most of its clients are from developed countries, particularly European countries and the US. This is because of the nature of the medical research outsourcing market. In addition, in the choice of client the firm merged with an American medicine plant directly without considering psychic distance, exhibiting its born-global nature. Table 10.9 summarizes the external drivers of Wuxi Pharma Tech's internationalization.

3 Internationalization drivers

External drivers have promoted the establishment and growth of Wuxi Pharma Tech. In the meantime, the R&D outsourcing of the drug industry in the international market has also been growing.

Wuxi Pharma Tech is a pioneer of the pharmaceutical R&D service outsourcing industry. In its early years, China's pharmaceutical R&D outsourcing industry has not yet taken shape. Quxi Pharma Tech's internationalization has indeed been driven by HR cost advantage, which is an external factor. However, as a born global, it has been driven more by internal factors, especially by the capabilities of its leaders (see Table 10.10).

We can see that internal factors drive the internationalization of Wuxi Pharma Tech and its rapid growth as an international innovative firm. Among these factors, leader qualities play a vital part.

4 Internationalization performance

Since its establishment, Wuxi Pharma Tech's contract value has been growing at an annual rate of 100% every year. Back in 2005, its profit was already 100 times its initial profit. According to its annual report, the firm's net operating income in 2009 increased by 7% year on year, to US$270 million. As it grows in size the firm is also attempting to construct integrated services. In 2003 Pharma Tech began to provide process research services and has since added service capabilities including chemical analysis, biological analysis, formulation, pharmacology, and toxicology, among many others.

Table 10.9 External drivers

Sub-dimensions		Relevant contents to the case
Insufficient domestic market and excess capacity		The reason Wuxi Pharma Tech doesn't enter the Chinese market has also been determined by environment. China's pharmaceutical industry is a typical dualistic market structure. After the state-owned enterprise reform and China's accession to the WTO, thousands of pharmaceutical factories in China rely on price competition, manufacturing, and sales of generic drugs with not much branding effort, whereas more than 20 foreign firms maintain control of the high-end drug market by rapidly introducing new drugs after China's WTO membership. These foreign firms are beginning to move the whole process of new drugs R&D to China. China's pharmaceutical firms do not possess adequate motive power for new drug R&D. According to statistics, the R&D investment of largest Chinese pharmaceutical firm accounts for less than 2% of their total revenues. Most of them are engaged in the production of generic drugs or at best acquire some research achievements from universities or scientific research institutes. Large pharmaceutical firms have their own R&D divisions, but smaller firms can't afford to outsource. Up until now the only relationship between China's pharmaceutical industry and Wuxi Pharma Tech is that Chinese firms sometimes use the firm's equipment to do some data testing or separate the chemical composition of some Chinese medicines. China's CRO outsourcing industry started with Wuxi Pharma Tech. The industry didn't exist before Wuxi Pharma Tech.
Comparative advantages	Technological accumulation	When Wuxi Pharma Tech was established, the medical R&D market in China was still at an early stage and didn't have much technological accumulation.
	Cost advantages	R&D cost in China is 40%–50% lower than that in the US.
	Human resource advantages	When properly trained the large number of chemical graduates in China every year can become excellent talents. In pharmaceutical R&D HR cost accounts for a significant proportion. Wages in China are only one-tenth of those in America. However, there is a scarcity of comprehensive talents in China, such as middle-level and more senior managers, even though Chinese universities provide a huge number of graduates of relevant disciplines. Very often these graduates do not possess sufficient integrated capabilities and need a lot of continuous training. In recent years, the growth of the Chinese economy has also attracted more and more top talents to return to China.

(*Continued*)

Table 10.9 (Continued)

Sub-dimensions	Relevant contents to the case
Industrial advantages	When Wuxi Pharma Tech was established, China's medicine industry did not possess any industrial advantage. For many years, to the embarrassment of China's pharmaceutical industry, few truly new drugs had been created. Not until the 21st century did a number of Chinese firms begin to emerge on the front end of the industrial chain, taking the industrial form of CRO and appearing in the chemical compound synthesis link. They become integrated in the global new drug R&D chain by providing outsourcing services.
Government policy support	Not mentioned.
Convenience of science and communication technology	Not mentioned.

It is fair to say that Pharma Tech has achieved desirable performance in its internationalization. The firm's excellent capabilities and ability to catch opportunities by the forelock make it the leader of the industry.

10.4.4 Liaoning Fuman Limited

1 Firm information

The firm is a relatively small born-global firm founded by four people who had previously been managers in foreign firms. At the beginning of its establishment, the firm was engaged mainly in the export of consumer goods such as daily necessities and chemical products. However, its business was heavily impacted as its cost advantages were negated by exchange rate changes and the influence of the economic crisis. The firm switched to CRO service and looked for opportunities.

2 Internationalization process

Fuman followed a typical leap-forward internationalization mode. It was established in 2000 and got involved in international business in the next year, with export accounting for up to 40% of revenue. The company has very high technological standards, and its products are sold mainly to Japan. Although it is a born-global firm, its decision makers said that when choosing the country to export to the firm was influenced by psychic distance. The Japanese culture is similar to the Chinese culture in many aspects. Japan is the biggest customer of Fuman; other markets include Spain, Australia, and Italy, among others. Sales are not impressive in these other countries, and their requirements for quality are not as high as the company's existing standard.

Table 10.10 Internal driving forces

Sub-dimension	Relative to the case
Strategic goals: market seeking, natural resource seeking, low cost seeking, and strategic asset seeking	Market seeking: in the past 15 years, CRO services have been extended to all aspects of drug development process. As of 2009, cooperative R&D outsourcing accounted for up to 50% of total pharmaceutical R&D cost, whereas it was 5% in the early 1990s. Currently the CRO market is growing at 20% to 25% annually and is estimated to reach US$36 billion in 2010. Strategic asset seeking: as one of the earliest CRO service companies in China, Wuxi Pharma Tech possesses client resources and brand equity. Before its IPO in 2007, its clientele already included all the top 20 global multinational pharmaceutical companies. It is the first CRO service firm to be listed on NYSE.
Firm capabilities — Leader qualities	Before Wuxi Pharma Tech, the firm's founder, Li Ge, had founded another company that went public on NASDAQ. He possesses marketing and technological experience of new drugs development. After realizing the vast scientific talent pool and the absence of business model in China, he returned to China and founded Wuxi Pharma Tech, a CRO firm. Thanks to his overseas experience and keen sense of business, the founder chose the drug discovery outsourcing export model: providing advanced intermediates, lab R&D, and Application Programming Interface (API) development and manufacturing services based on customer needs. The firm uses synthetic chemistry technologies to synthesize a large variety of chemical compounds for pharmaceutical and biotech companies at high quality and low price and helps pharmaceutical firms screen, discover, and optimize products so as to improve the efficiency of the new drug discovery process. All decision makers of the company, including the founder, have previously worked in foreign pharmaceutical firms or similar firms. They have extensive knowledge about this industry in the international context and have access to some channel resources.
Organizational form: knowledge management, etc.	The firm's decision makers maintain an enterprising spirit and keep improving the procedure. They are constantly looking for ways to reduce costs. They insist on following international standards and technology from the outset. These are all reasons why Pharma Tech has been able to maintain its lead in the industry.
Production technology	The interviewee said that Pharma Tech had built a powerful R&D team. In fact, technical monopoly is one of its advantages but not the overarching advantage. Instead, efficiency resulting from innovative management is the most important organizational capability.

(*Continued*)

Table 10.10 (Continued)

Sub-dimension	Relative to the case
Source of funding	Initially Pharma Tech was funded by venture capital and the founders. On August 9, 2009, it went public on NYSE, raising nearly US$185 million at a stock price of US$14/share.
Talent advantages	Because of its apparent HR advantages and its management team's possession of core technologies and knowledge of international standards, Pharma Tech became the first choice of outsourcing partner in China for multinational corporations. More than 80% of its employees hold a bachelor's or higher degree. The firm has more than 60 overseas returnees and a large number of young, vigorous, and imaginative research talents. This powerful R&D team provides a strong support to the firm's success. New employees do not need to be trained in the US. If need be they can be trained for specific projects by clients (pharmaceutical companies). They do not need extensive, systematic training.
Management standardization and adaptation, such as quality management system, service system, etc.	Operational innovation results in lower price and higher efficiency. Pharma Tech's R&D efficiency is higher than that of foreign counterparts. The low cost of Chinese talents makes it possible to perform innovative research in an industrialized manner, therefore creating economies of scale. Meanwhile, the firm reduces cost by means of operational innovations, such as industrialization and mass production. It achieves better customer satisfaction and efficiency by improving production model and customer attention. Such systemic advantages increase its operation efficiency. The most important thing about pharmaceutical synthesis is to achieve "customized innovation" guaranteeing timely delivery and quality.
Marketing tools and channels	As the largest CRO company in the world and working with the world's most powerful pharmaceutical companies, Pharma Tech has established its own brand and enjoys advantages like brand premium.

However, since the exchange rate reform and appreciation of the RMB in 2006 the firm's original business was heavily hit. Before 2008 export accounted for about 80% of the firm's total operating income. The percentage decreased gradually after 2009, to merely around 10% in 2010. Before entering the international R&D outsourcing market, Fuman investigated the domestic and the international markets, objectively analyzed foreign and domestic competitors, and looked for entry points based on its own advantages. Main decision makers of the firm do not have overseas studying or work experience. Most of the technical personnel of the new CRO business have studied or worked abroad before, which is related to the characteristics of the industry. At present CRO is developing rapidly in China. Many major American and European firms commission China's CRO firms to do the new product R&D work for them. Therefore, the firm chooses to cooperate mainly with developed countries.

3 Internationalization drivers

With its small size and short history and with more than 400 CRO firms already in China, Fuman's decision to explore international markets has been driven by external factors.

The change of exchange rate negates the firm's cost advantage and the industrial advantage of the manufacturing industry, causing Fuman to lose clients and business and the proportion of its international business to go down every year. Before 2008 export accounted for about 80% of the firm's total operating income. The percentage decreased gradually after 2009, to merely around 10% in 2010. Foreign political situations, China's policy, and the RMB exchange rate all have significant influences on the export processing industry, and profit has been squeezed out bit by bit. Therefore, Fuman plans to call off its export processing business and switch to technology outsourcing services that are of higher technological content and added value. China's labor cost is rather low. Hence, the prices of labor-intensive products are lower than international standards. Moreover, regulations on such aspects as animal testing and environmental protection are more lenient. In addition, in terms of CRO workers, the Chinese's qualities, technology, and efficiency are better than their Indian counterparts. In the past, the CRO industry concentrated in India. As more and more overseas returnees and researchers join the industry, China now possesses international comparative advantages in this industry.

In summary, Fuman's switching to outsourcing as its mode of internationalization is driven by external factors instead of international factors. In this field, profit in the international market is significantly better than in the domestic market. Large international firms invest a lot more in R&D than Chinese firms do. Still, the firm has not yet completely built up its brand. Table 10.11 summarizes the internal drivers of Fuman's internationalization.

From Table 10.11 we can see that Fuman does not have sufficient internal drivers to support its CRO-based internationalization. Its involvement in internationalization has mainly been driven by external factors.

4 Internationalization performance

It is still too early to judge Fuman's performance in CRO projects as the firm started the business not long ago, but judging from its previous product export venture its performance has not been satisfactory, mainly because of the continuous appreciation of exchange rate that canceled its cost advantages. Although it possesses some advantages in terms of technology and quality and even service, such advantages are of little use for the OEM in consumer goods. This is

Table 10.11 Internal drivers

Sub-dimensions		Relevant contents to the case
Strategic goals: market seeking, natural resource seeking, low cost seeking, and strategic asset seeking		Market seeking: Fuman did not enter the international market because of its high profit but because of large demand, high quality requirements, and guaranteed payment (full payment could be received soon after all the necessary documents are ready).
Firm capabilities	Leader qualities	Main decision makers of the firm do not have overseas studying or work experience. Most of the technical personnel of the new CRO business have studied or worked abroad before, which is related to the characteristics of the industry. At present CRO is developing rapidly in China. Many major American and European firms commission China's CRO firms to do the new product R&D work for them.
	Organizational form: knowledge management, etc.	To take part in cooperation in the international market, the firm needs to meet requirements of the international market and follow its rules. Therefore, it needs to understand the rules of the international market, improve service awareness, and meet client demands in a way even better than they expect. They meet these demands by continuously improving technological competence and building capabilities. Another difficulty is how to explore the market. This requires increased investment.
	Production technology	Fuman's technological advantages are improving; it can quickly respond to client requests and possesses quality advantages.
	Source of funding	Funded by the four partners.
	Talent advantages	Compared to product export, in which it possessed market resources, Fuman has hardly any R&D outsourcing resources. Now it hires professionals in relevant fields in the US to help the firm develop its business, penetrating the market by gradually improving its popularity.
	Management standardization and adaptation, such as quality management system, service system, etc.	The firm has adapted its personnel structure, quality management system, production technology, and marketing tools to international market conditions and rules. Market order in the international market is much better than in the domestic market, so it would be easier for the firm to gain higher profit after the adjustment.
Marketing tools and channels		Not mentioned.

also the reason why it has switched from the low-end OEM mode to CRO services export.

10.4.5 Joinn Laboratories Inc.

1 Firm information

Joinn Laboratories Inc. is the first private firm in China to be engaged in new drug pharmacology and toxicology research. It is a comprehensive drug evaluation services provider. Founded in August 1995, the firm now has a technical team of more than 200 professionals and is one of the largest preclinical evaluation services providers in China. In July 2005, the firm passed the Good Laboratory Practice (GLP) inspection. In January 2008, a subsidiary was established in Washington State, in the US, and in June the same year the firm passed the Association for Assessment and Accreditation of Laboratory Animal Care (AAALAC) inspection and received the certification in October. In July 2009 the firm accepted the Food and Drug Administration (FDA)'s onsite audit and received an outstanding evaluation. The firm operates in: safety evaluation, animal care and use, efficacy study, ADME (absorption, distribution, metabolism, and excretion) studies and biopharmaceuticals analysis, central lab services, Phase I to IV clinical trials, among others. The firm has always been committed to international development. It has built experiment facilities and technical specifications that comply with international standards. For more than 10 years it has accumulated extensive international service experience. It has worked with and carried out technical exchange with foreign firms in countries like the US and Japan. Joinn has established subsidiaries in the US, and its American staff includes legal experts familiar with FDA rules and evaluation criteria and technical experts on pharmacology and toxicology, guiding and supporting the operation of international business in China.

2 Internationalization process

Joinn's internationalization process is an unusual but representative one. It fits most assumptions of incremental internationalization, but it follows the leap-forward internationalization path (see Table 10.12).

Its decision to set up an overseas subsidiary and make direct investment even preceded its decision to internationalize. This kind of leap-forward internationalization is driven primarily by internal factors. The firm internationalizes so as to seek more resources and establish an organizational structure that is suitable for international outsourcing services. Table 10.13 summarizes external drivers of Joinn's internationalization.

3 Internationalization drivers

There are several external drivers for Joinn Laboratories' internationalization. Joinn had focused attentively on the domestic market, but a favorable

Table 10.12 Internationalization process, the serial internationalization dimension

Sub-dimensions	Relative to the case	Congruent
Domestic advantages of the export manufacturer	The first private firm in China to engage in pharmacology and toxicology research of new drugs and currently one of the largest preclinical evaluation services providers in China.	Yes
Internationalization is a passive instead of active strategy (dimension: driven by internal drivers and external drivers)	Mainly driven by internal factors.	Yes
Export beginning with psychically close countries or regions (dimension: region and reason of project entry)	For more than 10 years, it has accumulated extensive international service experience. It has worked with and carried out technical exchange with foreign firms in countries like the US and Japan.	Yes
Internationalization is a serial process	Joinn is not congruent with this condition. It adopts the leap-forward internationalization mode. It established a subsidiary in the US before its operation and hires local employees to facilitate communication between local clients and the firm.	No

industrial environment has urged it to internationalize. However, the driving force of its internationalization has mainly been provided by internal factors (see Table 10.14).

This shows that Joinn Laboratories possesses both external and internal drivers, but internal drivers are more powerful. Hence, its internationalization appears to be more self-motivated. The direct result is that it follows a leap-forward internationalization mode, establishing subsidiary first, making direct investment, collecting information, and then carrying out transactions.

4 Internationalization performance

The interviewee said that completing an international contract requires a substantial amount of effort on such aspects as language and experiment quality management, so as to ensure a long-term business relationship with the client. In addition, in order to maintain cost advantage over foreign competitors, the contract profit rate of international business is only a little bit higher. There is no point of taking the order if the profit is not even a little bit higher. The average profit of Joinn Laboratories is about 20%, and international profit is slightly higher, an excellent performance compared to other firms in the same trade.

Table 10.13 External drivers

Sub-dimension		Relevant contents to the case
Insufficient domestic market and excess capacity		Not found this problem.
Comparative advantages	Technological accumulation	A substantial amount of CRO firms have up to 10 years' development history. They have some technological accumulations, and the patent strength of relevant firms has been improved.
	Cost advantage	Cost advantage is diminishing but will exist for a long time. The cost advantage is no longer the key advantage. After all, the high-tech service sector relies on quality and efficiency instead of low cost.
	HR advantage	Similar to Wuxi Pharma Tech, the large number of chemical graduates in China every year, when properly trained, can become excellent talents. In pharmaceutical R&D HR cost accounts for a significant proportion. Wages in China are only one-tenth of those in America
	Industrial advantages	The industrial environment is conducive to the development of pharmaceutical CRO. Affected by the economic crisis, many overseas bio-medical firms choose to work with Chinese and Indian CRO firms in order to reduce R&D cost; some overseas CRO firms have also come to China, representing healthy competition that urges firms to improve their service quality.
	Government policy support	Currently official policy environment is very good. The bio-medical industry is listed as a key industry in the 12th Five-Year Plan. The government's support to major new drugs development platform construction and to candidates' R&D has boosted the growth of CRO because the act of supporting drug R&D itself boosts pharmaceutical firms' needs for CRO.
Convenience of science and communication technology		Not mentioned.

Table 10.14 Internal factors

Sub-dimensions		Relative to the case
Strategic goals: market seeking, natural resource seeking, low cost seeking, and strategic asset seeking		Market seeking Strategic asset seeking (building industrial chain and brands)
Firm capabilities	Leader qualities	The firm's founders include some of China's best-known pathologists and a medical association chairperson. They are visionary and highly professional. Some of the founders are foreign experts.

(*Continued*)

Table 10.14 (Continued)

Sub-dimensions		Relative to the case
	Organizational form: knowledge management, etc.	The firm has established an international division specifically for the international market. It has hired foreign experts to work in its own labs. The firm has conducted numerous surveys and investigations, not merely to learn about foreign markets but also to learn the operation management and software and hardware configuration of international labs from firms in the same industry.
	Production technology	The firm's technology has been recognized by China's CFDA and the US's FDA. High technological standards give it more confidence in developing the international market. The firm conducted its first specialized research project in 1996 and had performed more than 1,000 specialized trials on 220 new drugs from 1995–2008. It is one of the organizations in the industry in China that have performed the greatest number of trials and type-1 medicine evaluations.
	Source of funding	Most other firms in the industry in China are government-backed laboratories. They are under no competition pressure. As a private firm, however, the firm may not survive if clients are not satisfied. Therefore, the firm has always attached great importance to service quality and client evaluation and keeps improving its technology to guarantee service quality and efficiency.
	HR advantage	The firm's business is technology and knowledge process outsourcing. Its employees are well educated, with more than 25% of its staff holding master's or higher degrees and 10% doctors (PhD) and overseas returnees. It attracts talents with relevant overseas work experience to work for it and give play to their advantages.
	Management standardization and adaptation, such as quality management system, service system, etc.	The firm's key comparative advantage lies in that it can meet the requirements of new drug registration in both China and the US at the same time. This is partly attributed to the firm's international development in recent years, which has not only opened the firm to the world but also attracted more overseas pharmaceutical firms that are intending to enter the Chinese market. Now the firm's technology has been recognized by both China's SFDA and the US's FDA. A high technology level gives the firm more confidence in developing the international market.

(*Continued*)

Table 10.14 (Continued)

Sub-dimensions		Relative to the case
	Marketing tools and channels	Doing its best to provide better services to foreign clients and build a good reputation. Hoping to become more widely known through word of mouth. Establishing offices abroad and hiring local workers to facilitate communication with clients.

10.5 Conclusions

Knight and Cavusgil (1996) and Rasmussen *et al.* (2000) suggest that to be considered as born-global, a firm should simultaneously meet the following two requirements: (1) start to sell products to the international market within three years of establishment; and (2) at least 25% of sales come from overseas markets.

According to these two criteria, CNBM Hefei Cement Research and Design Institute and Joinn Laboratories are traditional-global firms and TCC and Wuxi Pharma Tech are born-global firms. Chetty and Colin (2004) point out that traditional firms follow the stage model, usually developing the domestic first before expanding gradually into new overseas markets. The driving force of export is usually insufficient domestic demand due to market saturation. Firms internationalize in order to seek greater markets. Moreover, Hu and Chen (2007) suggest that one of the driving forces for the formation of born-global firms is leaders' characteristics. Research shows that leaders affect the formation of born-global firms at least in the following aspects: relationship networks, risk appetite, global mindset, manager experience, and industrial experience.

First, founders and managers of born-global firms tend to have relevant overseas work experience and international visions. They have comprehensive knowledge of overseas market risk or possess more channel resources (previous clients or partners upstream or downstream of the value chain). For instance, Chen Ge, founder of Wuxi Pharma Tech, used to be the founder of a NAS-DAQ-listed company, which became the first client of Wuxi Pharma Tech.

Second, prior to inception managers of born-global firms generally have extensive experience that enables their firms to enter the international market at an early stage and acquire international competitive advantages. Chetty and Campbell-Hunt (2004) suggest that managers of born-global firms possess more prior knowledge and work experience that could reduce the psychic distance to specific markets and minimize risk and uncertainty. TCC's decision makers all had international project management and execution experience before they joined the firm and, therefore, had more knowledge about market potentials and project operation risks. In these cases, compared to Hefei Cement Research and Design Institute, TCC would often conduct deep investigations before starting a new project. TCC often searches for such information as: the client's financial standing and credit, project feasibility, and suitability of external conditions; whether basic conditions in the location are suitable for implementation, such as the supply of simple labor in the local market and availability and price of raw materials; local laws and regulations, taxations, and transport problems; and even customers and manners in the host country, such as hugging or handshaking.

Third, managers of born-global firms are global oriented and better at spotting market opportunities that others frequently ignore. Aaby and Slater (1989) suggest that born-global firms' consideration for export is to seize "first-mover" advantages. For instance, at the beginning of Wuxi Pharma Tech's establishment there were not many CRO firms in the Chinese market; in the global market, drug development cost rocketed, major pharmaceutical companies were coming up with few new drugs, and new drug R&D cost rose from US$138 million in 1975 to US$802 million in 2001. At this time, the founder discovered that China's chemical and pharmaceutical talent reserve and their specialized knowledge are similar to those in the international market, but the cost is only one-tenth of that in the US. Therefore, he spotted the opportunity and founded Pharma Tech in 2002. Seizing the first-mover advantages and relying on China's huge human resources, the firm grew to be the largest CRO in China. By comparison, although leaders of Joinn Laboratories, which did not enter the international market until 2008 following the traditional international mode, are pharmacologists in China, they didn't see the international opportunities at an early stage and confined the firm's market to China. All these cases follow a similar pattern, indicating that firm leaders are an important driver of firms' internationalization.

The export of born-global firms is self-motivated. They actively explore overseas market segments and increase involvement in the international market. Their overseas market involvement decision-making is quick, and they internationalize in an accelerated manner. The expansion mode of born-global firms is to develop the domestic market and the international market at the same time, or even develop the latter first. Their choice of overseas market is determined by factors like networks and associations. In these cases, both Pharma Tech and TCC exhibit such attributes. According to TCC's "10 billion" strategy the firm intends to achieve more than 50% of its revenue from international sales, and the growth of international business would be faster than that of domestic business. The target market of Pharma Tech, on the other hand, has been the international market from inception. If we use industry as a controlling factor, we find that both TCC and Hefei Cement Institute belong to the contracting industry while Pharma Tech and Joinn Laboratories are both R&D outsourcing firms, with even their time of establishment being much alike, but the difference of leaders results in one firm being a born-global firm while the other being a traditional one.

The overseas project operation experience and international vision of firm leaders (not necessarily the experience of the founders) are important determinants. Such firms have greater congenital learning and experimental learning capabilities, are better as using the latest technology, and can reduce risks in international operation, enabling them to accelerate their international business shortly after establishment. These are also the most important determinants of the formation of born-global firms.

Madsen and Servais (1997) indicate that due to inherent scarcity of resources, born-global firms need to seek and maintain partnership with a large number of external network organizations. In our investigation, however, few interviewees attached much importance to the role of networks. For the contracting and outsourcing industry, except for firms that are not of small or medium size in our study, networks can't provide specialized and diversified information concerning international standards and the huge risks of construction in a strange land. Joinn Laboratories approached this problem by hiring technical experts in the host country. They hired American technical experts the moment they decided to internationalize. Pharma Tech relied on the extensive personal connections and relevant project experience of its founder. TCC would conduct onsite investigation before launching every project. In other words, network resources are of some use, but in our study they are not vital for the formation of born-global firms.

Chetty and Campbell-Hunt (2004) and Knight *et al.* (2001) suggest that the domestic market of a born-global firm tends to be small, therefore forcing the firm to internationalize in order to survive and develop. Research concerning born-global firms in Northern Europe indicates that firms in small domestic markets are more likely to pursue internationalization than ones in large domestic markets.

In our cases, TCC's domestic market is big enough, and its consideration for the international market is mainly its potentials. Hefei Cement Institute and CNBM both belong to the cement industry. Years back Hefei Cement Institute used to possess large market potential in the domestic market. In recent years, the cement industry began to become saturated and to shrink under government control. Consequently, it adopted the incremental internationalization mode. In the field of pharmaceutical CRO, there is not much funding for pharmaceutical R&D in China, so the new drug synthesis business, which is Pharma Tech's main business, does not have a large market in China, but the global CRO market is huge. On the contrary, the pathological research market that Joinn Laboratories is devoted to is relatively bigger, which is one of the reasons the firm failed to spot opportunities in the international market. Therefore, firms with small domestic market potentials or a large international market are more likely to follow a born-global internationalization process.

For traditional-global firms psychic distance is an important criterion in their choice of a target market. When expanding into overseas markets, they tend to choose a psychically close market first before gradually choosing psychically more distant markets, so as to avoid potential risks and uncertainties. In the case of Hefei Cement Research and Design Institute we can see a typical stages-model internationalization path. Its clients started with developing countries in Central Asia and Eastern Asia; as the firm gained more knowledge about international standards and established its brand, channels into the Middle East began to seek it out, and thus it entered the Middle East market. TCC, however, didn't choose its markets according to psychic distance; instead, its selection criterion is the size of the market. There are more opportunities of chemical factory construction in developing countries. In the relatively short period of time of TCC's internationalization it managed to enter more than 30 countries that differ greatly from one another, thanks largely to information acquired from onsite investigations. Similarly, Joinn Laboratories established an office in the US first. The reason it conducts business in the US and Japan is that 13 of the world's top 20 pharmaceutical firms are either American or Japanese.

Relevant research indicates that born-global firms tend to launch their operation in the domestic market and the international market at the same time, or even in the latter first, and that their overseas market selection is largely irrelevant to psychic distance. For example, in the case of Pharma Tech, its targets have always been the world's largest drug makers since its inception. It has now entered more than 20 countries and established working relationships with more than 80 corporate clients. Fuman, on the other hand, follows a market entry sequence in accordance with psychic distance. Because Japan is similar to China in terms of economy, culture, and consumption habits, and geographically close, the firm started its international business with Japan first and gradually expanded to Australia and Southern Europe.

In the internationalization process of foreign-oriented contracting and outsourcing firms (regardless of whether they are born-global firms or traditional-global firms), their entry modes and processes are not much relevant to psychic distance but related to international markets' size and growth potentials.

Note

1 Transaction-specific assets refer to special investments tailored to the special needs of one or a few clients. Such assets do not have an existing exchange market due to the limitedness of the market. External uncertainty refers to the uncertainty of the changes of firms' external environment. Firms with higher uncertainty are more likely to adopt a low-control entry mode. Internal uncertainty refers to operational risks caused by a firm's internal factors. Free-riding is the possibility of one party of a transaction using the efforts of another to acquire benefit.

References

Aaby N E, Slater S F. (1989). Management influences on export performance, a review of the empirical literature 1978–1988. *International Marketing Review*, 6(4), 7–26.

Aaker D A. (1991). *Managing Brand Equity*. The Free Press, New York.

Aaker D. (1996). Measuring brand equity across products and markets. *California Management Review*, 28(3), 102–120.

Aaker D A, Joachimsthaler E. (1999). *Brand Leadership*. The Free Press, New York.

Ahmed S A, d'Astous A, Eljabri J. (2002). The impact of technological complexity on consumers' perceptions of products made in highly and newly industrialised countries. *International Marketing Review*, 19(4), 387–407.

Ahmed Z U, Johnson J P, Yang X, Kheng Fatt C, Sack Teng H, Chee Boon L. (2004). Does country of origin matter for low-involvement products? *International Marketing Review*, 21(1), 102–120.

Alashban A A, Hayes L A, Zinkhan G M, Balazs A L. (2002). International brand-name standardization/adaptation, antecedents and consequences. *Journal of International Marketing*, 10(3), 22–48.

Alden D L, Steenkamp Jan-Benedict E M, Batra R. (1999). Brand positioning through advertising in Asia, North America, and Europe, the role of global consumer culture. *Journal of Marketing*, 63(1), 75–87.

Alden D L, Steenkamp Jan-Benedict E M, Batrac R. (2006). Consumer attitudes toward marketplace globalization, structure, antecedents and consequences. *International Journal of Research in Marketing*, 23(3), 227–239.

Anderson J C, Gerbing D W. (1988). Structural equations modeling in practice, a review and recommended two-step approach. *Psychological Bulletin*, 103(3), 411–423.

Andersen O. (1993). On the internationalization process of firms, a critical analysis. *Journal of International Business Studies*, 24(2), 209–231.

Anderson R. (1990). *Calliope's Sisters*. Englewood Cliffs, NJ, Prentice Hall.

Arnold D J, Quelch J A. (1998). New strategies in emerging markets. *Sloan Management Review*, 40(1), 7–20.

Aspelund A, Moen Ø. (2001). A generation perspective on small firms' internationalization, from traditional exporters and flexible specialists to born globals, in Axinn, Catherine N, Matthyssens, Paul, Eds., *Reassessing the Internationalization of the Firm* (Advances in International Marketing, 11). JAI/Elsevier Inc., Amsterdam, pp. 197–225.

Atuahene-Gima, K. (2005). Resolving the capability—rigidity paradox in new product innovation. *Journal of Marketing*, 69(4), 61–83.

Aulakh P S, Kotabe M, Teegen H. (2000). Export strategies and performance of firms from emerging economies, evidence from Brazil, Chile, and Mexico. *Academy of Management Journal*, 43(3), 342–361.

Bagozzi R P, Yi Y. (1988). On the evaluation of structural equation models. *Journal of the Academy of Marketing Science*, 16(1), 74–94.

Balabanis G, Diamantopoulos A. (2008). Brand origin identification by consumers, a classification perspective. *Journal of International Marketing*, 16(1), 39–71.

Barela M J. (2003). Executive insights, united colors of Benetton, from sweaters to success, an examination of the triumphs and controversies of a multinational clothing company. *Journal of International Marketing*, 11(4), 113–128.

Barney J. (1991). Firm resources and sustained competitive advantage. *Journal of Management*, 17(1), 99–120.

Bartlett C A, Ghoshal S. (1989). *The Transnational Solution*. Harvard Business School Press, Boston.

Bartlett C A, Ghoshal S. (1998). Beyond strategic planning to organization learning, lifeblood of the individualized corporation. *Strategy & Leadership*, January/February, 34–39.

Batra R, Ramaswamy V, Alden D L, Steenkamp J-B E M, Ramachander S. (2000). Effects of brand local/nonlocal origin on consumer attitudes in developing countries. *Journal of Consumer Psychology*, 9(2), 83–95.

Bell J. (1995). The internationalization of small computer software firms, a further challenge to stage theories. *European Journal of Marketing*, 29(8), 60–75.

Bello D C, Gilliland D I. (1997). The effect of output controls, process controls, and flexibility on export channel performance. *Journal of Marketing*, 61(1), 22–38.

Bentler P M. (1990). Comparative fit indexes in structural models. *Psychological Bulletin*, 107(2), 238–246.

Bilkey W J. (1978). An attempted integration of the literature on the export behavior of firms. *Journal of International Business Studies*, 9(1), 33–46.

Bilkey W J, Tesar G. (1977). The export behavior of smaller-sized Wisconsin manufacturing firms. *Journal of International Business Studies*, 8(1), 93–98.

Birnik A, Bowman C. (2007). Marketing mix standardization in multinational corporations: A review of the evidence. *International Journal of Management Reviews*, 9(4), 303–324.

Brouthers L E, Xu K F. (2002). Product stereotypes, strategy and performance satisfaction, the case of Chinese exporters. *Journal of International Business Studies*, 33(4), 657–677.

Brush C G. (1992). *Factors Motivating Small Companies to Internationalize: The Effect of Firm Age*. School of Management, Boston University, Boston.

Burgel O, Murray G C. (2000). The international market entry choices of start-up companies in high-technology. *Journal of International Marketing*, 8(2), 30–41.

Burgmann I, Kitchen P J, Williams R. (2006). Does culture matter on the web? *Marketing Intelligence and Planning*, 24(1), 62–76.

Buzzell R. (1968). Can you standardize multinational marketing? *Harvard Business Review*, 46(6), 102–113.

Buzzell R, Quelch J A, Bartlett C. (1995). *Global Marketing Management: Cases and Readings*, 3rd edition. Addison-Wesley, Boston.

Cantwell J, Tolentino P E E. (1990). *Technological Accumulation and Third World Multinationals*. University of Reading, Department of Economics, Reading, UK.

Carmines E G, Mclver J P. (1981). *Analysing Models with Unobserved Variables, Analysis of Covariance Structures, in Social Measurement, Current Issues*. Sage, Beverly Hills, CA.

Cavusgil S T. (1980). On the internationalization process of firms. *European Research*, 8(November), 273–281.

Cavusgil S T, Chan K, Zhang C. (2003). Strategic orientations in export pricing: A clustering approach to create firm taxonomies. *Journal of International Marketing*, 11(1), 47–72.

Cavusgil S T, Zou S. (1994). Marketing strategy-performance relationship, an investigation of the empirical link in export market ventures. *Journal of Marketing*, 58(1), 1–21.

Cavusgil S T, Zou S, Naidu G M. (1993). Product and promotion adaptation in export ventures: An empirical investigation. *Journal of International Business Studies*, 24(3), 479–506.

Cayla J, Arnould E J. (2008). A cultural approach to branding in the global marketplace. *Journal of International Marketing*, 16(4), 86–112.

Chaudhuri A, Holbrook M B. (2001). The chain of effects from brand trust and brand affect to brand performance: The role of brand loyalty. *Journal of Marketing*, 65(2), 81–93.

Chen Honghui, Luo Xing (2008). Is OEM an obsolete strategy?—Evidence from manufacturing firms in Guangdong province. *China Industrial Economics*, 1, 96–104.

Chen Xi, Hu Zuo-hao, Zhao Ping. (2008). Price leadership or branding? A study on the relationship between marketing strategy and market performance by Chinese exporters in the manufacturing industry. *Journal of Marketing Science*, 4, 58–67.

Cheng J M S, Blankson C, Wu P C S, Chen S S M. (2005). A stage model of international brand development, the perspectives of manufactures from two newly industrialized economies-South Korea and Taiwan. *Industrial Marketing Management*, 34(5), 504–514.

Chetty S. (1996). The case study method for research in small-and medium-sized firms. *International Small Business Journal*, 15(1), 73–86.

Chetty S, Campbell-Hunt C. (2004). A strategic approach to internationalization, a traditional versus born global approach. *Journal of International Marketing*, 12(1), 57–81.

Chetty S K, Hamilton R T. (1993). Firm-level determinants of export performance, a meta-analysis. *International Marketing Review*, 10(3), 26–34.

Chhabra S S. (1996). Marketing adaptations by American multinational corporations in South America. *Journal of Global Marketing*, 9(4), 57–74.

Chung H F L. (2002). An empirical investigation of marketing programme and process elements in the home–host scenario. *Journal of Global Marketing*, 16(1/2), 141–186.

Colton D A, Roth M S, Bearden W O. (2010). Drivers of international e-tail performance: The complexities of orientations and resources. *Journal of International Marketing*, 18(1), 1–22.

Cordell V V. (1993). Interaction effects of country-of-origin with branding, price and perceived performance risk. *Journal of International Consumer Marketing*, 5(2), 5–20.

Covin J G, Slevin D P. (1989). Strategic management of small firms in hostile and benign environments. *Strategic Management Journal*, 10(1), 75–87.

Craig C S, Douglas S P. (2000). *International Marketing Research, 2nd edition*. John Wiley & Sons, Chichester.

De Castro J O, Chrisman J J. (1995). Order of market entry, competitive strategy, and financial performance. *Journal of Business Research*, 33, 165–177.

Dimofte C V, Johansson J K, Ronkainen I A. (2008). Cognitive and affective reactions of US consumers to global brands. *Journal of International Marketing*, 16(4), 113–135.

Doherty G, Ennew C T. (1995). The marketing of pharmaceuticals, standardization or customization? *Journal of Marketing Practice, Applied Marketing Science*, 1(3), 39–50.

Dominguez L V, Sequeira C G. (1993). Determinants of LDC exporters' performance, a cross-national study. *Journal of International Business Studies*, 24(1), 19–40.

Donnelly J H, Ryans J K Jr. (1969). Standardized global advertising: A call yet unanswered. *Journal of Marketing*, 33(2), 57–64.

Douglas S P, Craig C S. (1989). Evolution of global marketing strategy, scale, scope, and synergy. *Columbia Journal of World Business*, 24(Fall), 47–59.

Douglas S P, Craig C S, Nijssen E J. (2001). Integrating branding strategy across markets, building international brand architecture. *Journal of International Marketing*, 9(2), 97–114.

Douglas S P, Wind Y. (1987). The myth of globalization. *Columbia Journal of World Business*, 22(4), 19–29.

Dow D, Larimo J. (2009). Challenging the conceptualization and measurement of distance and international experience in entry mode choice research. *Journal of International Marketing*, 17(2), 74–98.

Dunning J H. (1998). Location and the multinational enterprise: A neglected factor? *Journal of International Business Studies*, 29(1), 45–66.

Dunning J H. (2000). The eclectic paradigm as an envelope for economic and business theories of MNE activity. *International Business Review*, 9(2), 163–190.

Dunning J H. (1981). *International Production and the Multinational Enterprise*. Allen and Unwin, London.

Eckhardt G M. (2005). Local branding in a foreign product category in an emerging market. *Journal of International Marketing*, 13(4), 57–79.

Eisenhardt K M. (1989). Building theories from case study research. *Academy of Management Review*, 14(4), 532–550.

Eisenhardt K M. (1991). Better stories and better constructs: The case for rigor and comparative logic. *Academy of Management Review*, 16(3), 620–627.

Eisingerich A B, Rubera G. (2010). Drivers of brand commitment: A cross-national investigation. *Journal of International Marketing*, 18(2), 64–79.

Elinder E. (1961). How international can advertising be? *International Advertiser*, (December), 12–16.

Ettenson R. (1993). Brand name and country of origin effects in the emerging market economies of Russia, Poland and Hungary. *International Marketing Review*, 10(5), 14–36.

Evans J, Mavondo F T, Bridson K. (2008). Psychic distance, antecedents, retail strategy implications, and performance outcomes. *Journal of International Marketing*, 16(2), 32–63.

Farr A, Hollis N. (1997). What do you want your brand to be when it grows up: Big and strong? *Journal of Advertising Research*, 37, 23–36.

Fina E, Rugman A M. (1996). A test of internationalization theory and international theory: The Upjohn Company. *Management International Review*, 36(3), 199–213.

Fisher A B. (1984). The AD biz gloms onto global. *Fortune*, 12(November), 77–80.

Fornell C, Larcker D F. (1981). Evaluating structural equation models with unobservable variables and measurement error. *Journal of Marketing Research*, 18(1), 39–50.

Fornell C, Cha J. (1994). Partial least squares, in Bagozzi R P, Ed., *Advanced Methods of Marketing Research*. Blackwell Publishers, Cambridge, MA, pp. 52–78.

Foster R N. (1986). *The Attacker's Advantage*. McKinsey & Company, Inc., New York.

Gabrielsson M. (2005). Branding strategies of born globals. *Journal of International Entrepreneurship*, 3(3), 199–222.

Ganitsky J. (1989). Strategies for innate and adoptive exporters: Lessons from Israel's case. *International Marketing Review*, 6(5), 50–65.

Glaser B G, Strauss A L. (1967). *The Discovery of Grounded Theory: Strategies of Qualitative Research*. Wiedenfeld and Nicholson, London.

Grant R M. (1991). The resource-based theory of competitive advantage, implications for strategy implementation. *California Management Review*, 33(3), 114–135.

Grassl W. (1999). The reality of brand: Towards an ontology of marketing. *American Journal of Economics and Sociology*, 58(2), 313–359.

Green R T, Cunningham W H. (1975). The determinants of US foreign investment: An empirical examination. *Management International Review*, 15(2/3), 113–120.

Griffith D A, Hu M Y, Ryans J K. (2000). Process standardization across intra- and intercultural relationships. *Journal of International Business Studies*, 31(2), 303–324.

Guzmán F, Paswan A K. (2009). Cultural brands from emerging markets, brand image across host and home countries. *Journal of International Marketing*, 17(3), 71–86.

Hair J F, Anderson J R E, Tatham R L, Black W C. (1998). *Multivariate Data Analysis with Readings, 5th edition.* Prentice Hall, Englewood Cliffs, NJ.

Han C M, Terpstra V. (1988). Country-of-origin effects for uni-national and bi-national products. *Journal of International Business Studies*, 19(2), 235–255.

Harris K R. (1985). Conceptual, methodological, and clinical issues in cognitive-behavioral assessment. *Journal of Abnormal Child Psychology*, 13, 373–390.

Hassan S S, Craft S, Kortam W. (2003). Understanding the new bases for global market segmentation. *Journal of Consumer Marketing*, 20(5), 446–462.

Hassan S S, Katsanis L P. (1991). Identification of global consumer segments, a behavioural framework. *Journal of International Consumer Marketing*, 3(2), 11–29.

Häubl G. (1996). A cross-national investigation of the effects of country of origin and brand name on the evaluation of a new car. *International Marketing Review*, 13(5), 76–97.

Hedlund G, Kverneland A. (1985). Are strategies for foreign markets changing? The case of Swedish investment in Japan. *International Studies of Management and Organization*, 15(2), 41–59.

Heide J B. (1994). Interorganizational governance in marketing channels. *Journal of Marketing*, 58(1), 71–85.

Heide J B, John G. (1992). Do norms matter in marketing relationships? *Journal of Marketing*, 56(2), 32-44.

Heslop L A, Papadopoulos N. (1993). But who knows where and when, reflections on the images of countries and their products, in Papadopoulos N, Heslop L A, Eds., *Product–Country Images, Impact and Role in International Marketing.* International Business Press, New York, pp. 39–76.

Hewett K, Bearden W O. (2001). Dependence, trust, and relational behavior on the part of foreign subsidiary marketing operations: Implications for managing global marketing operations. *Journal of Marketing*, 65(4), 51–66.

Hill J S, Kwon U. (1992). Product mixes in U.S. multinationals: An empirical study. *Journal of Global Marketing*, 6(3), 55–74.

Hofstede G. (1993). Cultural constraints in management theories. *The Executive*, 7(1), 81–94.

Hofstede G. (2001). *Culture's Consequences, 2nd edition, Comparing Values, Behaviors, Institutions and Organizations Across Nations.* Sage, Thousand Oaks CA.

Holt D B, Quelch J A, Taylor E L. (2004). How global brands compete. *Harvard Business Review*, 68(9), 68–75.

Hsieh M H. (2002). Identifying brand image dimensionality and measuring the degree of brand globalization: A cross-national study. *Journal of International Marketing*, 10(2), 46–67.

Hsu C W, Chen H, Jen L. (2008). Resource linkages and capability development. *Industrial Marketing Management*, 37(6), 677–685.

Hu L, Bentler P M. (1998). Fit indices in covariance structure modeling, sensitivity to under parameterized model misspecification. *Psychological Methods*, 3(4), 424–453.

Hu Zuo-hao. (2002a). The controversy about standardization versus adaptation in international marketing. *Nankai Business Review*, 5(5), 29–35.

Hu Zuo-hao. (2002b). Global operation and domestic marketing. *China Business and Market*, 16(2), 57–60.

Hu Zuo-hao, Chen Xi. (2007). Born globals: Review and perceptions. *China Soft Science (Special Issue)*, 112–117.

Hu Zuo-hao, Chen Xi, Zhao Ping. (2007). The effect of channel control on manufacturer's export performance, an investigation of indigenous Chinese exporters. *Journal of Industrial Engineering, Engineering Management*, 21(3), 4–8.

Hu Zuo-hao, Koyo Shion. (2006). International marketing strategies of Chinese multinationals. *General Geographical Research*, 33(2), 43–60.

Hu Zuohao, Kondo F (2002). *The Marketing Innovations in Japanese Appliance Companies.* Tsinghua University Press, Beijing.

Hu Zuo-hao, Wang G. (2005). Analysis on the international marketing strategies of Chinese enterprises, an example from consumer electronics manufacturing enterprises. *Business Research Movement* (China Business Research Center of Tsinghua University), 91, 1–16.

Hu Zuo-hao, Wang Gao. (2009). International marketing strategies of Chinese multinationals, the experience of Bird, Haier, and TCL, Chinese multinationals, in Larcon, Jean-Paul, Ed., *Chinese Multinationals.* World Scientific Publishing, Singapore, pp. 99–126.

Hu Zuo-hao, Yi Fan, Han Shun-ping, Chen Xi. (2009). Antecedents and consequences of distribution adaptation and price adaption, a study of Chinese firms. *Journal of Industrial Engineering, Engineering Management,* 23(3), 45–50.

Huber G P. (1996). Organizational learning, the contributing processes and the literature, in Cohen M, Sproull L, Eds., *Organizational Learning.* Sage, London, pp. 88–115.

Hulland J, Todiño Jr H S, Lecraw D J. (1996). Country-of-origin effects on sellers' price premiums in competitive Philippine markets. *Journal of International Marketing,* 4(1), 57–79.

Hultman M, Robson M J, Katsikeas C S. (2009). Export product strategy fit and performance: An empirical investigation. *Journal of International Marketing,* 17(4), 1–23.

Jain S C. (1989). Standardization of international marketing strategy, some research hypotheses. *Journal of Marketing,* 53(1), 70–79.

Jaworski B J, Stathakopoulos V, Krishnan H S. (1993). Control combinations in marketing, conceptual framework and empirical evidence. *Journal of Marketing,* 57(1), 57–69.

Jing Ming-hua. (2004). From OEM to creating international brand. *Academic Exchange,* 6, 83–86.

Johanson J, Vahlne J-E. (1977). The internationalization process of the firm-a model of knowledge development and increasing foreign market commitments. *Journal of International Business Studies,* 8(1), 23–32.

Johanson J, Vahlne J-E. (1990). The mechanism of internationalization. *International Marketing Review,* 7(4), 11–24.

Johanson J, Wiedersheim-Paul F. (1975). The internationalization of the firm-four Swedish cases. *Journal of Management Studies,* 12(3), 305–323.

Johansson J K. (1993). Missing a strategic opportunity: Managers' denial of country-of-origin effects, in Papadopoulos N, Heslop L A, Eds., *Product–Country Images, Impact and Role in International Marketing.* International Business Press, New York, pp. 77–86.

Johansson J K, Ronkainen I A. (2005). The esteem of global brands. *Journal of Brand Management,* 12(1), 339–354.

Jolly V K, Alahuhta M, Jeannet J-P. (1992). Challenging the incumbents, how high technology start-ups compete globally. *Journal of Strategic Change,* 1(2), 71–82.

Joreskog K G, Sorbom D. (1989). *LISREL 7, A Guide to the Program and Applications,* 2nd edition. SPSS, Chicago.

Kadomatsu M, Oishi Y. (1996). *International Marketing.* Mineruva Publishing House, Kyoto

Kapferer J-N. (2005). The post-global brand. *The Journal of Brand Management,* 12(5), 319–324.

Katsikeas C S, Samiee S, Theodosiou M. (2006). Strategy fit and performance consequences of international marketing standardization. *Strategic Management Journal,* 27(9), 867–890.

Kaynak E, Kuan W K. (1993). Environment, strategy, structure, and performance in the context of export activity, an empirical study of Taiwanese manufacturing firms. *Journal of Business Research,* 27(1), 33–49.

Keegan W J. (1995). *Global Marketing Management.* Prentice-Hall, New York.

Keegan W. (1999). *Global Marketing Management*, 6th ed. Prentice-Hall, Upper Saddle River, NJ.

Keller K L. (1993). Conceptualizing, measuring, and managing customer-based brand equity. *Journal of Marketing*, 57(1), 1–22.

Keller K L. (1998). *Strategic brand management: Building, measuring, and managing brand equity.* Prentice Hall, Upper Saddle River, NJ.

Keller K L. (2008). *Strategic Brand Management*. Prentice-Hall, Upper Saddle River, NJ.

Kerin R A. (1992). Marketing's contribution to the strategy dialogue revisited. *Journal of the Academy of Marketing Science*, 20(4), 331–334.

Killough J. (1978). Improved payoffs from transnational advertising. *Harvard Business Review*, 56(4), 102–110.

Kim C, Park J H. (2010). The global research-and-development network and its effect on innovation. *Journal of International Marketing*, 18(4), 43–57.

Kim W C, Hwang P. (1992). Global strategy and multinationals' entry mode choice. *Journal of International Business Studies*, 23(1), 29–53.

Knight G A, Cavusgil S T. (1996). The born global firm, a challenge to traditional internationalization theory. *Advances in International marketing*, 8, 11–26.

Knight G A, Cavusgil S T. (2004). Innovation, organizational capabilities, and the born-global firm. *Journal of International Business Studies*, 35(2), 124–141.

Knight J, Bell J, McNaughton R. (2001). Born globals: Old wine in new bottles. *ANZMAC: Bridging Marketing Theory and Practice. Massey University, Palmerston North, CD ROM*, 1.

Knight J, Bell J, McNaughton R B. (2003). Satisfaction with paying for government export assistance, in Greaves, I, Wheeler, C, Eds., *Advances in International Business*, Palgrave Publishers, Hant, UK, pp. 223–240.

Kojima K. (1978). Direct Foreign Investment: A Japanese Model of Multinational Business Operations. Croom Helm, London.

Kondo F. (1995). International marketing of household appliance, a case of Sony, international marketing by Japanese companies, in Kakumatsu M, Ed., Otsuki Publishing House, Tokyo, pp. 193–209.

Kotabe M. (1990). Corporate product policy and innovative behavior of European and Japanese multinationals, an empirical investigation. *Journal of Marketing*, 54(2), 19–33.

Kotler P. (1986). Global standardization-courting danger. *Journal of Consumer Marketing*, 3(2), 13–15.

Kotler P. (2003). *Marketing Management, 11th edition.* Prentice-Hall, Upper Saddle River, NJ.

Kreutzer R T. (1988). Marketing-mix standardization: An integrated approach to global marketing. *European Journal of Marketing*, 22(10), 19–30.

Lall S. (1983). Determinants of R&D in an LDC: The Indian engineering industry. *Economics Letters*, 13(4), 379–383.

Lamb P W, Liesch P W. (2002). The internationalization process of the smaller firm, reframing the relationships between market commitment, knowledge and involvement. *Management International Review*, 42(1), 7–26.

Leclerc F, Schmitt B H, Dubé L. (1994). Foreign branding and its effects on product perceptions and attitudes. *Journal of Marketing Research*, 31(2), 263–270.

Lenormand J M. (1964). Is Europe ripe for the integration of advertising? *The International Advertiser*, 5(March), 14.

Leonidou L C, Katsikeas C S. (1996). The export development process, an integrative review of empirical models. *Journal of International Business Studies*, 27(3), 517–551.

Levinthal D A, March J G. (1993). The myopia of learning. *Strategic Management Journal*, 14(2), 95–112.

Levitt T. (1983). The globalization of markets. *Harvard Business Review*, 61(3), 92–102.

Lilien G L, Yoon E. (1990). The timing of competitive market entry, an exploratory study of new industrial products. *Management Science*, 36(5), 568–585.

Lord M D, Ranft A L. (2000). Organizational learning about new international markets, exploring the internal transfer of local market knowledge. *Journal of International Business Studies*, 31(4), 573–589.

Lu Tong, Li Chao-Ming. (2003). Internationalization of Wenzhou enterprises in China. *World Economy*, 5, 1–10.

Luo Y. (2007). A coopetition perspective of global competition. *Journal of World Business*, 42(2), 129–144.

Luo Y, Park S H. (2001). Strategic alignment and performance of market-seeking MNCs in China. *Strategic Management Journal*, 22(2), 141–155.

Luostarinen R, Mika G. (2004). Finnish perspectives of international entrepreneurship. *Handbook of Research on International Entrepreneurship*, 2, 383–403.

Lutze L. (1985). From Bharata to Bombay: Change and continuity in Hindi film aesthetics, in Pfleiderer B, Lutze L, Eds., *The Hindi Film: Agent and Re-Agent of Cultural Change*. New Delhi, Manohar, pp. 3–15.

Madsen T K. (1989). Successful export marketing management, some empirical evidence. *International Marketing Review*, 6(4), 41–57.

Madsen T K, Rasmussen E, Servais P. (2000). Differences and Similarities Between Born Globals and Other Types of Exporters, in Yaprak, Attila, Tutek, Hulya, Eds., *Globalization, the Multinational Firm, and Emerging Economies* (Advances in International Marketing, 10), Emerald Group Publishing Limited, West Yorkshire, pp. 247–265.

Madsen T K, Servais P. (1997). The internationalization of born globals, an evolutionary process. *International Business Review*, 6(6), 561–583.

Malhotra Y, Galletta D F. (2003). Role of commitment and motivation in knowledge management systems implementation, theory, conceptualization, and measurement of antecedents of success. *Proceedings of the Hawaii International Conference on Systems Sciences (HICSS 36)*, available at, www.brint.org/KMSuccess.pdf.

Manchanda P, Dubé J P, Goh K Y, Chintagunta P K. (2006). The effect of banner advertising on internet purchasing. *Journal of Marketing Research*, 43(1), 98–108.

Marquardt R, Makens J, Larzelere H. (1965). Measuring the utility added by branding and grading. *Journal of Marketing Research*, 2(1), 45–50.

Martenson R. (1987). Is standardization of marketing feasible in culture-bound industries? A European case study. *International Marketing Review*, 4(3), 7–17.

Matthyssens P, Pauwels P. (1996). Assessing export performance measurement, in Cavusgil S T, Madsen T K, Eds., *Advances in International Marketing*, Jai Press, Greenwich, CT.

Maxwell J A. (1996). *Qualitative Research Design: An Interactive Approach*. Sage, Thousand Oaks.

McDougall P P, Shane S, Oviatt B M. (1994). Explaining the formation of international new ventures, the limits of theories from international business research. *Journal of Business Venturing*, 9(6), 469–487.

McKinsey & Co. (2003). *Emerging Exporters. Australia's High Value-Added Manufacturing Exporters*. McKinsey & Company and the Australian Manufacturing Council, Melbourne.

Melewar T C, Badal E, Small J. (2006). Danone branding strategy in China. *Journal of Brand Management*, 13(6), 407–417.

Melewar T C, Pickton D, Gupta S, Chigovanyika T. (2009). MNE executive insights into international advertising programme standardisation. *Journal of Marketing Communications*, 15(5), 345–365.

Menon A, Bharadwaj S G, Adidam P T, Edison S W. (1999). Antecedents and consequences of marketing strategy making, a model and a test. *Journal of Marketing*, 63(2), 18–40.

Menon A, Varadarajan P R. (1992). A model of marketing knowledge use within firms. *Journal of Marketing*, 56(4), 53–71.

Miller D. (1988). Relating Porter's business strategies to environment and structure: Analysis and performance implications. *Academy of Management Journal*, 31(2), 280–308.

Moen Øystein, Servais P. (2002). Born global or gradual global? Examining the export behavior of small and medium-sized enterprises. *Journal of International Marketing*, 10(3), 49–72.

Montgomery D B, Lieberman M L. (1998). First-mover (dis) advantages: Retrospective and link with the resource-based view. *Strategic Management Journal*, 19(12), 1111.

Möller J, Martin E. (2010). A global investigation into the cultural and individual antecedents of banner advertising effectiveness. *Journal of International Marketing*, 18(2), 80–98.

Morgan N A, Kaleka A, Katsikeas C S. (2004). Antecedents of export venture performance, a theoretical model and empirical assessment. *Journal of Marketing*, 68(1), 90–108.

Neilson L C, Chadha M. (2008). International marketing strategy in the retail banking industry: The case of ICICI Bank in Canada. *Journal of Financial Services Marketing*, 13, 204–220.

Nevin J R. (1995). Relationship marketing and distribution channels: Exploring fundamental issues. *Journal of the Academy of Marketing Science*, 23(4), 327–334.

Nie Xiu-dong, Wang Zhi-gang. (2006). The empirical research on Chinese export brand construction. *Commercial Research*, 18, 16–20.

Nijssen E J, Douglas S P. (2008). Consumer world-mindedness, social-mindedness, and store image. *Journal of International Marketing*, 16(3), 84–107.

Nijssen E J, Herk H. (2009). Conjoining international marketing and relationship marketing, exploring consumers' cross-border service relationships. *Journal of International Marketing*, 17(1), 91–115.

Ohmae K. (1985). *Triad Power, the Coming Shape of Global Competition*. The Free Press, New York.

Ojala A. (2009). Is globalization reducing distances between countries? Some empirical evidence from foreign software firms operating in Japan. *Journal of Japan Academy for Asian Market Economies*, 12(1), 95–101.

Onkvisit S, Shaw J J. (1988). The international dimension of branding, strategic considerations and decisions. *International Marketing Review*, 6(3), 22–34.

Oviatt B M, McDougall P P. (1994). Toward a theory of international new ventures. *Journal of International Business Studies*, 25(1), 45–64.

Oviatt B, McDougall P. (1995). Global start-ups, entrepreneurs on a worldwide stage. *Academy of Management Executive*, 9(2), 30–44.

Oviatt B M, McDougall P P. (2005). Defining international entrepreneurship and modeling the speed of internationalization. *Entrepreneurship Theory and Practice*, 29(5), 537–554.

Özsomer A, Prussia G E. (2000). Competing perspectives in international marketing strategy, contingency and process models. *Journal of International Marketing*, 8(1), 27–50.

Özsomer A, Simonin B L. (2004). Marketing program standardization, a cross-country exploration. *International Journal of Research in Marketing*, 21(4), 397–419.

Palmer I, Hardy C. (2000). *Thinking About Management: Implications of Organizational Debates for Practice*. Sage, London.

Perlmutter H V. (1969). The tortuous evolution of the multinational corporation. *Columbia Journal of World Business*, 4(1), 9–18.

Pine II B J. (1993). Mass customizing products and services. *Strategy & Leadership*, 21(4), 6–55.

Porter M E. (1980). *Competitive Strategies.* The Free Press, New York.

Porter M E. (1985). *Competitive Advantage.* The Free Press, New York.

Porter M E. (1991). Towards a dynamic theory of strategy. *Strategic Management Journal,* 12(S2), 95–117.

Prahalad C K, Hamel G. (1990). The core competence of the corporation. *Harvard Business Review,* 68(3), 79–91.

Quelch J A, Hoff E J. (1986). Customizing global marketing. *Harvard Business Review,* 64(May–June), 59–68.

Rafee H, Kreutzer R T. (1989). Organizational dimensions of global marketing. *European Journal of Marketing,* 23(5), 43–57.

Rasmussen E S, Madsen T K, Evangelista F. (2001). The founding of the born global company in Denmark and Australia: Sense making and networking. *Asia Pacific Journal of Marketing and Logistics,* 13(3), 75–107.

Reid S. (1983). Firm internationalization, transaction costs and strategy choice. *International Marketing Review,* 1(2), 44–56.

Rennie M W. (1993). Born global. *The McKinsey Quarterly,* 4(4), 45–52.

Rialp A, Rialp J, Knight G A. (2005). The phenomenon of early internationalizing firms, what do we know after a decade (1993–2003) of scientific inquiry? *International Business Review,* 14(2), 147–166.

Rocha D A, Christensen C. (1994). The export experience of a developing country, a review of empirical studies of export behavior and the performance of Brazilian firms. *Advances in International Marketing,* 6, 42–111.

Roostal I. (1963). Standardization of advertising for Western Europe. *Journal of Marketing,* 27(4), 15–20.

Rosen B N, Boddewyn J J, Louis E A. (1989). US brands abroad, an empirical study of global branding. *International Marketing Review,* 6(1), 7–19.

Rosenbloom B, Larsena T, Mehta R. (1997). Global marketing channels and the standardization controversy. *Journal of Global Marketing,* 11(1), 49–64.

Rundh B. (2003). Rethinking the international marketing strategy, new dimensions in a competitive market. *Marketing Intelligence & Planning,* 21(4), 249–257.

Samiee S, Roth K. (1992). The influence of global marketing standardization on performance. *Journal of Marketing,* 56(2), 1–17.

Samiee S, Shimp T A, Sharma S. (2005). Brand origin recognition accuracy: Its antecedents and consumers' cognitive limitations. *Journal of International Business Studies,* 36(4), 379–397.

Sanders P. (1982). Phenomenology, a new way of viewing organizational research. *Academy of Management Review,* 7(3), 353–360.

Sandler D M, Shani D. (1992). Brand globally but advertise locally? An empirical investigation. *International Marketing Review,* 9(4), 18–31.

Scherer, Ross D R. (1990). *Industrial Market Structure and Economic Performance.* Rand-McNally, New York.

Schlegelmilch B B, Ross A G. (1987). The influence of managerial characteristics on different measures of export success. *Journal of Marketing Management,* 3(2), 145–158.

Schuiling I, Kapferer J-N. (2004). Real differences between local and international brands, strategic implications for international marketers. *Journal of International Marketing,* 12(4) 97–112.

Schuiling I, Lambin J-J. (2003). Do global brands benefit from a unique worldwide image? Symphonya, *Emerging Issues in Management,* available at, www.unimib.it/symphonya.

Shanks D C. (1985). Strategic planning for global competition. *Journal of Business Strategy,* 5(3), 80–89.

Sharma D D, Blomstermo A. (2003). The internationalization process of born globals: A network view. *International Business Review*, 12(6), 739–753.

Sheth J. (1986). Global markets or global competition? *Journal of Consumer Marketing*, 3(2), 9–11.

Shocker A D, Srivastava R K, Ruekert R W. (1994). Challenges and opportunities facing brand management: An introduction to the special issue. *Journal of Marketing Research*, 31(2), 149–158.

Shoham A. (1996). Global marketing standardization. *Journal of Global Marketing*, 9(1–2), 91–120.

Shoham A, Albaum G. (1994). The effect of transfer of marketing methods on export performance: An empirical examination. *International Business Review*, 3(3), 219–241.

Shoham A, Brencic M M, Virant V, Ruvio A. (2008). International standardization of channel management and its behavioral and performance outcomes. *Journal of International Marketing*, 16(2), 120–151.

Sorenson R Z, Wiechmann U E. (1975). How multinationals view marketing standardization. *Harvard Business Review*, 53(3), 38–167.

Stalk G, Evans P, Shulman L E. (1992). Competing on capabilities, the new rules of corporate strategy. *Harvard Business Review*, 70(2), 57–69.

Steenkamp J-B E, Batra R, Alden D L. (2003). How perceived brand globalness creates brand value. *Journal of International Business Studies*, 34(1), 53–65.

Stern L W, El-Ansary A I. (1992). *Marketing Channels*. Prentice Hall, Upper Saddle River, NJ.

Still R R, Hill J S. (1984). Adapting consumer products to lesser-developed markets. *Journal of Business Research*, 12(1), 51–61.

Sudhaman A. (2004). Samsung style or daewoo dull? *Media Asia*, 6(4), 24–24.

Takeuchi H, Porter M E. (1986). Three roles of international marketing in global strategy, in Porter M E, Eds., *Competition in Global Industries*. Harvard Business Press, Cambridge, MA, pp. 111–146.

Tao Feng, Li Shi-tian. (2008). Knowledge spillovers and learning effects in global value-chain OEM/OBM. *Management World*, 1, 115–122.

Tasoluk, B. (2006). *A Contingency Framework for Global Branding: A Multi-Level Interaction Model*. Doctoral dissertation, Department of Marketing and Supply Chain Management, Michigan State University.

Thakor M V, Lavack A M. (2003). Effect of perceived brand origin associations on consumer perceptions of quality. *Journal of Product and Brand Management*, 12(6), 394–407.

Tse D K, Gorn G J. (1993). An experiment on the salience of country-of-origin in the era of global brands. *Journal of International Marketing*, 1(1), 57–76.

Tse D K, Lee W N. (1993). Removing negative country images: Effects of decomposition, branding, and product experience. *Journal of International Marketing*, 1(4), 25–48.

Turnbull P W. (1987a). A challenge to the stages theory of the internationalization process, in Rosson P J, Reid S D, Eds., *Managing Export Entry and Expansion-Concepts and Practice*. Praeger, New York, pp. 21–40.

Turnbull P W. (1987b). *Managing Export Entry and Expansion*. Praeger, New York.

Venkatraman N, Prescott J E. (1990). Environment-strategy coalignment: An empirical test of its performance implications. *Strategic Management Journal*, 11(1), 1–23.

Vida I. (2000). An empirical inquiry into international expansion of us retailers. *International Marketing Review*, 17(4/5), 454–475.

Vorhies D W, Morgan N A. (2003). A configuration theory assessment of marketing organization fit with business strategy and its relationship with marketing performance. *Journal of Marketing*, 67(1), 100–115.

Voss K E, Tansuhaj P. (1999). A consumer perspective on foreign market entry: Building brands through brand alliances. *Journal of International Consumer Marketing*, 11(2), 39–58.

Walters C J. (1986). *Adaptive Management of Renewable Resources*. Macmillan, New York.

Walters P G P, Samiee S. (1990). A model for assessing performance in small U.S. exporting firms. *Entrepreneurship, Theory and Practice*, 15(2), 33–50.

Wang Zhile (2004). *Chinese Multinational Companies: How to go to International Markets*. China Business Publishing House, Beijing.

Wernerfelt B. (1984). A resource-based view of the firm. *Strategic Management Journal*, 5(2), 171–180.

Whitelock J, Fastoso F. (2007). Understanding international branding, defining the domain and reviewing the literature. *International Marketing Review*, 24(3), 252–270.

Whitelock J, Pimblett C. (1997). The standardization debate in international marketing. *Journal of Global Marketing*, 10(3), 45–66.

Wind Y, Douglas S P, Perlmutter H V. (1973). Guidelines for developing international marketing strategies. *Journal of Marketing*, 37(2), 14–23.

Wong H Y, Merrilees B. (2007). Multiple roles for branding in international marketing. *International Marketing Review*, 24(4), 384–408.

Wooldridge B, Floyd S W. (1989). Strategic process effects on consensus. *Strategic Management Journal*, 10(3), 295–302.

Wu Shui-long, Lu Tai-hong, Hu Zuo-hao. (2010). An empirical study on the effects of corporate brand on product evaluations, the moderating role of consumer company identification. *Journal of Marketing Science*, 6(3), 92–107.

Wu Xiao-yun, Deng Zhu-jing. (2007a). Empirical research on global marketing strategy of China multinational enterprises based on CGMS model from 97 China multinational enterprises. *Journal of Marketing Science*, 3(1), 67–80.

Wu Xiao-yun, Deng Zhu-jing. (2007b). Literature review of global marketing theories, research stage, topics and key points. *Journal of Marketing Science*, 3(2), 100–120.

Wu Xiao-yun, Yuan Lei. (2003). On global marketing strategy and integrating global marketing strategy model – Implications for Chinese enterprises to develop mutinational strategy. *Nankai Business Review*, 6(6), 57–62.

Xu Hui. (2003). A study on the international market development of Chinese enterprises, entry mode decision and tactics based on the empirical analysis of Chinese enterprises in the Netherlands. *Nankai Business Review*, 6(1), 26–30.

Yalcinkaya G, Calantone R J, Griffith D A. (2007). An examination of exploration and exploitation capabilities: Implications for product innovation and market performance. *Journal of International Marketing*, 15(4), 63–93.

Yin R K. (1989). *Case Study Research-Design and Methods*. Sage, Beverly Hills, CA.

Yin R K. (1998). The abridged version of case study research, in Bickman L and Rog D J Eds., *Handbook of Applied Social Research Methods*, Sage Publications, Thousand Oaks, pp. 229–259.

Yip G S. (1989). Global strategy . . . In a world of nations?. *Sloan Management Review*, 31(1), 29–41.

Yip, G S. (1995). *Total Global Strategy*. Prentice-Hall, Upper Saddle River, NJ.

Zahra S A, Ireland R D, Hitt M A. (2000). International expansion by new venture firms, international diversity, mode of market entry, technological learning, and performance. *Academy of Management Journal*, 43(5), 925–950.

Zhang C, Hu Zuohao, Gu F F. (2008). Intra- and Interfirm coordination of export manufacturers, a cluster analysis of indigenous Chinese exporters. *Journal of International Marketing*, 16(3), 108–135.

Zhao H, Zou S. (2002). The impact of industry concentration and firm location on export propensity and intensity: An empirical analysis of Chinese manufacturing firms. *Journal of International Marketing*, 10(1), 52–71.

Zhao P, Mo Y. (2002). Determinants of consumer complaint behavior. The case of durable goods in China. *Journal of Tsinghua University (Philosophy and Social Science)*, 2(17), 32–38.

Zou S, Cavusgil S T. (1996). Global strategy: A review and an integrated conceptual framework. *European Journal of Marketing*, 30(1), 52–69.

Zou S, Cavusgil S T. (2002). The GMS, a broad conceptualization of global marketing strategy and its effect on firm performance. *Journal of Marketing*, 66(4), 40–56.

Zou S, Fang E, Zhao S. (2003). The effects of export marketing capabilities on export performance: An investigation of Chinese exporters. *Journal of International Marketing*, 11(4), 32–55.

Index

Note: Numbers in italics indicate figures or tables.

For Product Safety Concerns and Information please contact our EU
representative GPSR@taylorandfrancis.com
Taylor & Francis Verlag GmbH, Kaufingerstraße 24, 80331 München, Germany